ACQUIRING THE FUTURE

AMERICA'S SURVIVAL AND SUCCESS
IN THE GLOBAL ECONOMY

This book is dedicated to
Barbara, Matthew, and Catherine

ACQUIRING THE FUTURE

AMERICA'S SURVIVAL AND SUCCESS IN THE GLOBAL ECONOMY

Joseph E. Pattison

Dow Jones-Irwin
Homewood, Illinois 60430

© RICHARD D. IRWIN, INC., 1990
Dow Jones-Irwin is a trademark of Dow Jones & Company, Inc.

This publication is designed to provide accurate and
authoritative information in regard to the subject matter
covered. It is sold with the understanding that the
publisher is not engaged in rendering legal, accounting, or
other professional service. If legal advice or other expert
assistance is required, the services of a competent
professional person should be sought.

*From a Declaration of Principles jointly adopted by a Committee
of the American Bar Association and a Committee of Publishers.*
Sponsoring editor: Jim Childs
Project editor: Lynne Basler
Production manager: Ann Cassady
Jacket design: Tim Kaage
Compositor: Eastern Graphics Typographers
Typeface $11/13$ Times Roman
Printer: Arcata Graphics/Kingsport

Library of Congress Cataloging-in-Publication Data

Pattison, Joseph E.
    Acquiring the future : America's survival and success in the
global economy / Joseph E. Pattison.
        p.   cm.
    ISBN 1-55623-184-9
    1. United States—Foreign economic relations.   2. United States—
Commercial policy   3. Competition, International.   I. Title.
HF1455.P33   1990
337.73—dc20   89–17071
                                                        CIP

Printed in the United States of America
1 2 3 4 5 6 7 8 9 0 K 6 5 4 3 2 1 0 9

PREFACE

America's bookshelves are overflowing with quick-fix advice for the nation's economic woes. For years political and economic soothsayers have published volumes filled with zealous prescriptions for industrial restructuring, trade adjustment, technology infrastructure, "greening" of our economy, tax reform, and countless other vague but ambitious scenarios for a "new" America. Many of their proponents would have us believe that with a stroke of the legislative pen or the exercise of a few simple regulatory or management techniques, a vigorous new economy will emerge, as though we had but to crack the shell of some mystical egg to release the creature that will transport us to a glorious new prosperity.

Like most quick fixes, the panaceas offered by these overconfident gurus may treat a few symptoms, but never the underlying ills that caused them. As a practical matter, they are as useful and meaningful to most American businesses as theories about religion in ancient Abyssinia. Such "industrial policy" approaches do not lubricate machinery, enlighten managers, instill badly needed skills, or bring profits to the bottom line. These prescriptions, however, do share a common element that must be of compelling importance to anyone seriously interested in a new America. Conspicuously figuring in all such advice, whether by reference to comparative economics, export balances, competitiveness, reciprocity, or cross-border adjustment, is the global economy.

Implicit in this global focus has been a slow awakening to the fact that, as an international economic participant, the United States does not meet the full measure. This is the only common denominator that this book shares with those prior volumes. But where they reflect only an embryonic recognition of global realities, this book squarely confronts those realities in their hands-on practical aspects. Never in the history of our republic has such a fundamental aspect of our existence been so blatantly ignored by so many. The failure of American business to recognize, accept, and adapt to its global context has reached alarming dimensions.

The economy may be inescapably international, but Americans, including most managers and business leaders, typically don't treat it as such. The world in which they function, in which they make economic decisions and direct capital, in which they divest and invest and buy and sell, lies between the Atlantic and Pacific oceans. Despite the undeniable evidence to the contrary, the vast majority of Americans have defined their economic universe as the United States or North America and have shuttered off the rest of the planet. They may enjoy the amenities of visits to Europe and Asia, and many even enjoy profits on shipments overseas, but, still, the vast majority of American businesses, including many large "multinational" companies, have not begun to acknowledge the global forces shaping their destinies. Only after such recognition and acceptance can they learn to leverage those forces to their advantage. Until they are able to pull their heads out of the sand, they will remain victims of those forces.

This book examines the fundamental challenge of "being global" and the dismal record of America and American enterprises in meeting that challenge. Being global may start with the simple act of looking at the world in a fresh light, but even that effort has been obscured by myths, illusions, false pretenses, and decades of conflicting habit. But once that new perspective is gained, the real work can begin: attaining and exercising the global skills, instincts, leverage points, and other elements discussed here that combine to create the global winner.

The future has arrived already for many enterprises outside the United States that have been able to correctly balance transnational strengths and weaknesses to forge the truly global enterprises that our world now demands. They have acquired the viewpoints and strengths necessary to succeed in the global economy. They have acquired the future. Whether American enterprises will join them is in the hands of those enterprises themselves.

Joseph E. Pattison

CONTENTS

CHAPTER 1

AMERICA: THE FLAT EARTH MANAGERS

The lives of a nation and its people are shaped to a large degree by confrontations with the future. Reactions, or the lack thereof, to the introduction of new resources and materials, new business structures, new political alliances, new technology, and myriad other changes in their environments have determined the destinies of countless enterprises and even the future of entire generations. The Industrial Revolution, the discovery of electricity, the emergence of corporate centers of wealth through mass production, the world wars, to mention but a few of these forces, were dramatically infused into the lives of the planet's population, bringing with them irresistible, irrevocable change.

Today a force of equally compelling dimensions has entered our lives. Its reach is inescapable. Its effects may be as subtle as a pawn's gambit, such as the filing of a patent. They may also be as blatant as a hurtling locomotive, such as the hostile takeover by some industrial juggernaut. But in all its varying guises, no task can be more important today than understanding that force. It is the global economy.

After more than a generation of life with jet aircraft and transoceanic broadcasts, clichés about the planet becoming smaller, or the "global village" we inhabit have become commonplace to most Americans and other members of the industrial world. Yet, ironically indeed for a nation that is the planet's great melting pot, one fact is becoming painfully clear: Americans and American business are emphatically nonglobal.

In an earlier age, when even the most urgent travel to other continents was measured in days or even weeks, the limited world perspective of the American business community was not only palatable but natural, and cost the American economy relatively little. Today the American business community still wears blinders but those blinders have become an atavistic handicap that wreaks a profound economic penalty.

Explanations for this isolation of American business vary widely. International business is an arena best directed by the government say many highly respected economists and politicians; they would have us believe that American business cannot succeed offshore without a massive involvement on the part of the government, under the mantle of "industrial policy." Others have convinced themselves that overseas business is best assigned to experts or consultants in international trading companies or specialized departments; if pursued at all, it must be by segregated experts, just as lawsuits, tax returns, and waste removal must be handled by specialists. Many others insist that international business can only be profitably conducted by deep-pocket multinational conglomerates; the vast majority of America's small and midsized businesses have written off international efforts as too difficult.

When Arthur Vining Davis spun off Alcoa's foreign operations to separate ownership in the 1920s, he justified it by saying that U.S. managers "naturally preferred to sell in large quantities in the United States rather than bother, as they considered it, with smaller quantities abroad." Although Alcoa nonetheless later became a strong international player, the attitude reflected in Davis's comments still grips a sizable portion of American business. This perspective of international business as a "distraction" reflects the most common of the apologies for "noninternational" America: the American domestic economy is so large that we don't need to worry about the economy outside U.S. borders.

As revealed in these pages, all of the apologies described above are gravely mistaken.

Ultimately, the inescapable conclusion is that an alarming number of American enterprises evidence a gross disregard for the international milieu in which they exist. In the broadest sense this is the premise of this volume: American business has failed to meaningfully accept the global context of its existence and therefore has failed to successfully adapt to that context. Until it does so, no amount of industrial policy, restructuring, investment, new technology, or innovative management is going to meaningfully improve its relative position in the world economy. The same observation holds true for individual enterprises: new investment, management, or technology will not bring long-term success to most businesses unless they are developed and implemented with a global perspective.

THE DIMENSIONS OF OUR GLOBAL FAILURE

In May 1914, at the inaugural meeting of the U.S. National Foreign
Trade Council, James Farrell, president of what was then the largest
American corporation, U.S Steel, praised that new body's goal of expanding the international focus of U.S. business. "No issue is of more
vital importance" to the country, Farrell underscored. Unfortunately,
even though it had over 75 years to accept this seemingly obvious premise, the American business community largely seems to have ignored it.

The evidence of America's international failure can be found
throughout our economy, on a macro and microeconomic scale, in our
personal and our professional lives, in entire industries, and in individual
businesses ranging from the smallest to the very largest. This failure can
be measured statistically, as reviewed in this and later chapters, and it can
be measured by the records of individual enterprises, many of which are
reviewed throughout this volume.

It also can be gauged by the opinions of business and government
leaders. When the 21 public and private industry leaders of the Cuomo
Commission on U.S. competitiveness released its findings in 1988, its
most fundamental conclusion was that "America has failed to adjust to the
new reality of a global economy." Perhaps America's global crisis is best
revealed when Americans simply ask other Americans at large: a *Wall
Street Journal*/NBC News nationwide poll in 1988 revealed that 67 percent of Americans believe that "the U.S. has grown weaker relative to
other countries," and 65 percent were convinced that "America's industries aren't geared to keeping up with the changes taking place in the
world economy."[1]

For many open-minded managers in entities that have squarely faced
their world competition, *any* review of the evidence of America's global
shortcomings is superfluous: after sitting across the negotiation table in
overseas capitals, or in many cases watching their U.S. market shares
crumble under competitive pressure from abroad, they know intuitively
that they are not doing enough from the global perspective, that they are
not equipped to effectively respond to the complex dynamics of transnational competition. Nearly 80 percent of the executives polled in a recent
national survey confessed to lacking the proper skills for international

[1]*The Wall Street Journal*, May 16, 1988.

business. When Carnegie Mellon University recently surveyed senior and midlevel managers to identify the key issues of the 1990s, one out of four stated that the single most difficult issue for the remainder of the century will be "competing effectively on a global basis."[2] Yet even those managers may be shocked at the dimensions of our global shortcomings.

Compiling the Global Score

There is no single index that describes the degree of "globalism" in an economy, industry, or enterprise, or defines the ability to thrust and parry successfully amid global competitors. From the quantitative perspective—although quantitative analysis inevitably falls far short of capturing the full scope of the problem—myriad numbers must be sifted, balanced, and compared.

If asked to assess America's international economic performance, however, most Americans would reflexively turn to their country's trade account balances. To the extent that most Americans give any thought at all to gauging their country's performance in the international economy, it is indeed with respect to the much publicized reports of our trade accounts. "Trade account" itself seems an alien term for many contemporary Americans; a large number of commentators, investment analysts, and other observers have developed a revealing habit of referring instead to the "trade deficit" figures. Merchandise trade deficits of $152 billion in 1986, $158 billion in 1987, $129 billion in 1988, and a cumulative $675 billion deficit for the five years ending 1988 have monopolized many headlines and speeches in recent years as America tries to come to grips with the fact that international business is no longer an American success story. Current account figures, which include U.S. service exports, have paralleled those merchandise trade deficits.

Those figures are only part of a much broader and even more disturbing trend, one masked for many years by nominal trade surpluses. America's share of world exports generally has plummeted more than 35 percent since the late 1950s. Since 1950 the country's share of world trade overall has dropped by 50 percent.

Grading our performance in the international economy by the trade account figures alone, however, is rather like evaluating a thoroughbred

---

[2]*The Wall Street Journal*, November 15, 1988.

horse solely by its weight. As further discussed in Chapter 4, use of trade account figures can be a superficial technique more apt to mislead than to inform. Our global crisis was developing long before America's trade surpluses began to disappear. The true issues we must face are vastly more complex than whether we have more widgets stacked in boats embarking from our ports than stacked in the holds of vessels arriving in our ports. Likewise, for individual companies "being global" involves issues far wider than import/export transactions and company "balance of payment" figures.

A more realistic measure of a company's global integration is its use of subsidiaries, production facilities, and distribution structures offshore, as reflected in offshore investment. Calculating such data may be problematic due to the complexities of valuing overseas assets, but no matter which of many economic methods is used, it is clear that U.S. firms are not nearly as well integrated internationally as their foreign competitors. What's more, their investment overseas is sharply declining relative to the overall U.S. domestic economy.

The United Nations Center for Transnational Corporations has calculated that in 1970, 60 percent of all foreign direct investment derived from U.S. sources. By 1984 that figure had plunged to 12 percent.[3] Other studies show a drop only slightly less precipitous, on the order of a 30 to 40 percent decline during the same period. The share of U.S. foreign direct investment relative to U.S. gross domestic product dropped by 22 percent from 1980 to 1985 alone.

When the focus is shifted to a more detailed look at the use of specific corporate assets, it is found that *foreign investment by U.S. corporations as a percentage of their total assets peaked 20 years ago* at 3.2 percent. At last report, that figure was at the level *prevailing in 1950*. Meanwhile, European firms continue to expand their foreign direct investment at sharply increasing rates. West Germany's foreign investment activity currently represents at least 7.2 percent of total corporate assets. In Great Britain the figure is over 31 percent.[4] Meanwhile, the Department of Commerce reports that the amount of foreign assets in the United States surpassed those of U.S. companies overseas in 1984.

---

[3]United Nations Center for Transnational Corporations, *Transnational Corporations in World Development* (1988).

[4]Ibid.

The role of foreign sales relative to overall corporate activity provides another eye-opening benchmark. When 218 international companies with sales in excess of $1 billion were examined for this purpose, it was discovered that the ratio of non–home country sales to total sales is increasing everywhere *but* in the United States.

After analyzing such data, the United Nations Center for Transnational Corporations concluded in 1988 that *"the transnationalization of United States firms peaked somewhere between 1965 and 1975."*

On the once almost exclusively-U.S. list of the world's 30 largest enterprises, the United States accounts for only 12 today, and the number continues to erode. When the Conference Board analyzed corporations involved in manufacturing on an international basis, it reported in February 1989 that the number of U.S.-owned multinational manufacturers had dropped sharply since the late 1970s. In 1987, mounting concern over European market unification was being expressed by many American managers, prompting much talk about the need to acquire European operating bases. Did American firms "put their money where their mouth was?" They spent a meager $2.4 billion to acquire European companies. Europeans spent $37.1 billion to acquire U.S. firms that same year.

Which country today can claim the largest company in the world? When ranked by market value, Japan.[5] Ranked by sales, General Motors comes out on top, but only two other U.S. firms appear in the top 10 largest international firms. The combined revenues of the 500 largest non-U.S. companies are 61 percent higher than the combined revenues of the 500 largest U.S. companies.

Where is the world's largest bank? Not in the United States. Indeed, how many of the 30 largest (based on deposits) banks in the world are based in the United States or run by U.S. executives? One—Citicorp. Where is the U.S. world market share for manufactured goods headed? Sharply downward, dropping 10 percent from 1976 to 1986. Which country has the world's largest stock market? No longer the United States. Where does the United States stand in its share of world market capitalization? A strong 60.8 percent in 1977, a disturbing 36.1 percent in 1987. What portion of U.S. manufactured goods is exported? Approximately 10 percent, compared to 50 percent for Germany. What is the level of U.S. jobs devoted to exporting? Such jobs fell 25 percent from 1980 to 1984.

What of our vaunted stronghold, high technology? In 1980 sales in

---

[5]As ranked in 1987 on a market value basis by Morgan Stanley Capital.

the high technology sector provided a $27 billion surplus for our trade account. Currently we are suffering a $2 billion-plus deficit in our high technology account. In just three years preceding 1989, the U.S. share of the world electronics market plummeted from 50 to 40 percent. When *The Times* of London studied the electronics industry in 1988, it reported that many foreign producers believed that "in most areas of electronics, with the exception of computers and other very advanced equipment, the United States is no longer a significant factor." In the important indicator sector of biotechnology, perhaps the most widely agreed-upon "industry of the future," the Federal Republic of Germany exports far more than the United States.

Such high technology losses, further discussed in Chapter 3, will continue to depress our job content deficit, another important indicator. At last report from the International Trade Commission, 8.1 million jobs were calculated to be generated by imports into the United States, while exports accounted for 5.5 million U.S. jobs, for a deficit of 2.6 million jobs. The rejoinder that this deficit is caused by "low quality" positions in developing countries may be tempting but it would be inaccurate. Well over half—1.4 million—of these jobs funded by U.S. purchasers are in the high-wage industrialized countries of the Organization for Economic Cooperation and Development (OECD). While our showing in the complex cost-factor businesses involving highly skilled workers and high technology should be our strength, our export share in these businesses is declining.

The Impotent Giant

Although the figures are often distorted, and may distract from more important issues, much of America's international trade debate continues to be focused on import/export figures. It is therefore useful to return to those figures to place them in a realistic international context. U.S. export sales totaled $308 billion in 1988, a number larger than the gross domestic product for many individual nations. Indeed, our gross domestic product of $4.4 trillion eclipses that of any nation on earth. Evidence enough, apologists will assert, that we are the leading power in the world economy. Consequently, isn't it little more than a truism to conclude that we are the most successful player in the world economy? And even if that success has been clouded by trade deficits in recent years, isn't it true that once we eliminate those deficits we no longer will have any problem in the world economy? The answer on both counts is absolutely, unequivo-cally, no.

One would have thought that the U.S. business community long ago recognized that being the biggest is by no means equivalent to being the best or even being successful. Were the same James Farrell alive today who spoke to the National Foreign Trade Council in 1914, he would find sobering evidence of this in the history of his once omnipotent U.S. Steel. Largely by virtue of an inability to cope with the global economy, the U.S. steel industry incurred billions in losses, lost two thirds of its jobs, and slipped from top steel producer in the world to third place. Sobering evidence can also be found in the recent histories of other American in-dustries to support the fact that size alone never guarantees success; in the automotive sector, the United States has moved from an export surplus as late as 1967 to an import deficit of $60 billion today. Likewise, having a large export account by no means establishes that the United States is successful in the global economy.

What do our trade figures really signify about our economy? What do they say about the degree to which our production base is oriented toward global markets? What do the numbers communicate about the degree to which U.S. business takes advantage of overseas opportunities? It may be helpful to place them in a broader context.

First of all, the widely held assumption that the United States enjoys the largest export account in the world is a false one. Beginning in 1986, the United States was toppled from its post as the world's largest exporter of goods by a country with one fourth the population and less than one fifth the U.S. gross domestic product. The Federal Republic of Germany (FRG) exported $242 billion of hard goods in 1986, compared to the U.S. total of $217 billion; in 1987 the FRG exported $50 billion more in goods than the United States. Only by adding the much softer figures for export of services and other "invisibles," which have far less of a job-multiplier or positive ripple effect in the economy, is the United States able to claim a total export figure higher than that for Germany. And even those "invis-ibles" that are used to pad the U.S. export account are slipping drastically in the face of increased global services competition, reaching a multi-billion dollar deficit for the first time in 1988.

In relation to GDP in Germany, exports account for approximately 30 percent of that country's GDP. Thus one third of that nation's eco-nomic activity is directly oriented to foreign markets, not to mention a large portion of related economic activity among component suppliers, service companies, and other companies supporting German exporters.

Exports of neighboring Canada represent over 26 percent of her GDP. Great Britain exports 24 percent of her GDP, Belgium over 70 percent, France 20 percent, Sweden 28 percent, Switzerland 27 percent, and the Netherlands over 55 percent. All of these figures reflect the strong level of international integration present in those economies.[6]

What is the comparable figure for the United States? Obviously these countries have a greater incentive to export due to the smaller size of their home economies. But, surely the U.S. figure is at least 14 percent, the figure for Yugoslavia, Turkey, or Greece. No. At last report, the mighty United States sold only *5.2 percent* of its GDP in goods overseas. Expressed on a per capita basis, the United States exports less than $1,000 in goods per person. The comparable figure in Germany is over $3,000, and in many other industrial nations the number exceeds $2,000 per person.

Politicians and economists might well fantasize over the export performance of a Germany or Japan. Were the United States to generate the same level of proportionate economic activity as Germany does in its exports, it would be exporting $1.14 trillion worth of goods at the current GDP. The multiplier effect of exports would, of course, inflate the overall GDP considerably, creating a still higher, though not precisely predictable, export value. By one conservative estimate, if the United States had simply maintained the same share of export markets it enjoyed as late as 1980, U.S. domestic output would be at least 8 percent higher, meaning at least an additional $330 billion in GDP. U.S. government economists have stated, moreover, that for every $1 billion in added exports, $2 billion is added to the GDP, and $400 million is added to federal and state revenues.[7] In a U.S. economy in which even half the country's true export potential were realized, budget deficits, capacity underutilization, and a multitude of other perennial problems would certainly assume a more palatable dimension, if not disappear altogether. If, as the U.S. Department of Commerce has asserted, every $1 billion increase in exports creates 40,000 new jobs, a rise from $217 billion to over $1 trillion would obviously eliminate unemployment as a significant social and political issue.

---

[6]Export data based on Economic Surveys of the Organization for Economic Cooperation and Development for 1986, the latest year for which a comprehensive base of comparative data is available.

[7]International Trade Administration, U.S. Department of Commerce, *A Basic Guide to Exporting* (September 1986).

The Export Island

Based on current export levels, and Department of Commerce "state domestic product" figures, the entire U.S. export effort is equivalent to
channeling the domestic output of one large state, such as Illinois, into
overseas markets:[8] The remaining 49 states might as well then be sealed
inside a vast wall behind which they simply traded with themselves. From
another perspective, *the entire export output of the United States could be
matched by less than 41 percent of the state domestic product of California.* In other words, the output of a few counties in California matches the
entire export sales of the "international powerhouse" known as the United
States of America.

The country, in effect, has an "export island" of economic activity
focused overseas, while the remainder of the nation remains oblivious to
events outside its borders. This island may not exist physically, but as an
economic reality it is a fact of American life. A disturbing analogy can be
drawn to Imperial China, which for many years in the 19th Century conducted trade only through a handful of "treaty" ports, such as Canton and
Amoy, thinking it could successfully survive without intercourse with the
remainder of the planet. The result: a society propped up on false
strengths that ultimately crumbled into spoils grabbed by the rest of the
world.

The trend of these export figures is also highly revealing of the
United States's "global character." Success or failure in the international
economy is not created overnight. While exports by no means establish
that a country or an individual company is "global," exports do at least
indicate the orientation to overseas markets that is one vital element of
"being global." Successful participation in the global economy has
brought individual countries continuing years of export growth. Over the
last five years, for example, Germany has enjoyed an average 6.7 percent
growth in exports, Japan 6.8 percent, Canada 4.2 percent, and France 3.3
percent. Exports have soared to an 11.7 percent growth rate in Portugal,
10 percent in Ireland, 9.3 percent in Turkey, and 7.3 percent in Austria,
during the same period in which the soft dollar was "guaranteed" by many
U.S. economists and policymakers to help U.S. producers by stemming
the tide of exports from Europe and Asia.

---

[8]Department of Commerce, *Survey of Current Business* 30 (May 1988). Based on 1986 figures,
the last year for which state domestic product figures were compiled.

What is the comparable trend in the United States? After all, perhaps a low absolute level should be forgiven in the light of a healthy growth rate. Certainly, as world export markets continue to grow, the United States should at least be able to keep its share of those markets. Expressed as an average for the five years ending in 1987, U.S. exports declined at an average rate of *−1.4 percent*. From 1981 to 1985 alone, U.S. exports dropped a total of 9 percent. Except for the chronically struggling economy of Yugoslavia, no other industrial nation on earth posts a negative figure for the trend in its export accounts.

Concomitantly pointing to the overall positive growth in general consumption of goods as offsetting evidence to this trend is hollow comfort: well over 25 percent of the growth in U.S. consumption of goods is attributable to imports, or in other words, to success by foreign producers in penetrating U.S. markets. This international economic failure is not a short-term anomaly in an otherwise long record of success. This failure has been a fact of America's existence, and is only getting worse.

One might find some encouragement amid this gloom if our problem were simply that the export machinery across the nation was in downturn, that we simply needed to pump up export capacity that existed but was temporarily underutilized. Unfortunately this is not the case.

The American economy has cogently demonstrated that production capacity by no means equates with export capacity. A factory may have the capacity to turn out a million electronic widgets, but for the typical American company, use of capacity is a function of domestic pricing pressures, domestic costs, and domestic marketing. Capacity is a matter of capital equipment, materials, and skilled operators in the straightforward world of production engineers.

Export capacity, by contrast, consists of hardware, materials, and operators combined with the international perspective, sensitivities, and skills that are described in this book. In essence, production capacity must be combined with export capability, and ultimately export ability, to create even the potential for becoming a global competitor. In this age of modems, telecopiers, satellites, and endless "how to export" seminars, aren't the skills to turn production capacity into exports widely disbursed? A look at the U.S. export profile answers this question with a forceful no.

The Export Committee

The existence of the "Export Island" that accounts for U.S. shipments into overseas markets is sharply underscored by the fact that America's international business is heavily concentrated in the hands of a few enterprises. Year after year, *one fourth to one third of all U.S. export sales are made by only 50 companies.* As the Department of Commerce reported in 1987, another 60 percent of our exports are accounted for by 200 more firms. In sum, *at least 85 percent of U.S. export sales are made by only 250 companies.*[9] Despite the vast population and resources of the United States, only 250 companies constitute the primary population of America's Export Island.

The Department of Commerce has estimated that there exist approximately 300,000 manufacturing enterprises in the country. Thus, based on this total, less than one tenth of one percent of American manufacturers account for the overwhelming majority of U.S. shipments overseas. It is as though we had decided to delegate the responsibility for exporting, and international business as a whole, to a handful of enterprises, an "export committee."

The Small World Myth

But, some may say, American international economic performance in the past proves that we are the world's leading economic performer. In the early part of this century, international business *was* American business, and German, British, French, and other foreign firms were less involved in worldwide transactions and investment. Fifty years ago, essentially all the automobiles in Japan were made by U.S. producers. The international telecommunications market once was almost the exclusive preserve of one American company, International Telephone and Telegraph Corporation, that started overseas by merging two telephone companies in Cuba and Puerto Rico in 1920. Times have changed.

The world was a very different place 30 and more years ago. The global economy that so profoundly affects our lives did not exist. The planet was still operating in many respects on a colonial basis, with resources flowing from what today are better known as lesser developed or newly industrializing countries. The industrialized countries, of which in the post–World War II years the U.S. was almost by default the leader, simply produced, and the rest of the world had little choice but to buy.

---

[9]International Trade Administration, Department of Commerce, *The Export Trading Company Guidebook* (August 1987).

Since that era the world may have grown smaller for airline pilots, delivery services, and network news reporters. It has grown much larger and more complex for the rest of us. For economic, social, and even to a large extent political purposes, the world for the vast majority of the population in that era ended at a city limits sign, a state regional border, or certainly at the 48-state national perimeter. Today, inescapably, whether we admit it or not, that is not the case. As detailed in Chapter 2, the global economy defines the context in which we live. The idea that the world is getting smaller is at best a transient perception for pilots of transoceanic airliners and their passengers. Otherwise that cliché is a myth. A world with scores of markets, thousands of significant regulatory bodies, ever changing financial and production resources, and a seeming infinity of other factors to be assessed and balanced is vastly more complex than the homogenous one in which more narrowly focused businesses functioned a generation ago.

International business is no longer a matter of simple import/export transactions. The global economy has become a dynamo of financial, market, production, and regulatory change. The techniques of international trade, such as they existed, that were practiced when America was the undisputed leader among a fragmented array of national and regional economies are largely obsolete today.

So we see, at least in part, how the United States has weathered the years during which widely disparate economic forces congealed into a global economy. Judging from most economic data, one might reach two conclusions. For Japan, Germany, and a host of other successful international participants, when the going got tough, the tough got going. With respect to our own country, when the going got tough, the United States apparently dropped out.

THE GLOBAL RESPONSE

Rank upon rank of learned and not-so-learned observers have lined up to announce the reason why America's international performance has been so unsatisfactory. Readers' eyes have begun to glaze over from continually reading newspaper and magazine headlines asking, in more or less the same words, "Can America compete?"

The formulas prescribed by such observers have become so highly publicized as to become cliché. Entire mountainsides of forests have been leveled for paper to explain, under the imprimatur of such diverse institutions as Harvard University, the Business Roundtable, the Institute for International Economics, the International Trade Commission, the Joint Economic Committee, the Federal Reserve, and other venerable entities, that the United States suffers from poor relative productivity, high wages, unfavorable exchange rates, disproportionately low capital formation, inadequate research and development, poor raw materials balance, and similar macroeconomic maladies. This is what we have heard about America's international shortcomings for many years.

As a result, many Americans already have a generalized notion that we are indeed not competitive. They have equally nebulous notions that the solution for any disparity between the United States and other nations can be redressed through vague combinations of new technology, higher investment rates, improved productivity, and a softer dollar, all of which seem out of their personal control—issues most easily left to academia and government institutions to debate and ponder.

Two fundamental faults, however, undermine these perceptions. First, in recent years the United States has seen marked improvement with respect to nearly all of these aspects. The comparative cost position of the United States is today favorable relative to its major industrial competitors. Second, macroeconomic, quantitative approaches, although the most tempting to those looking for quick answers and quick fixes, ignore the critical qualitative aspects of being global, the more personalized strategic and tactical aspects that are the focus of this book and that are the keys to success for any enterprise in the global economy. It is, after all, not countries that ultimately succeed in the global economy, but enterprises and the people who constitute such enterprises. Those nations that can create a milieu for the international success of its enterprises joins in their success; nations who do not, share in the consequences of their failure.

Careful review of current economic data will demonstrate that, indeed, many of the long-bemoaned economic indicators today favor the United States. The Federal Reserve has achieved the soft dollar that was supposed to catapult U.S. exports over those of Asia and Europe. U.S. wages compare favorably to those in any other industrial country. Productivity is significantly up, as is investment. Certainly such news is good for America's relative performance in the global economy—and certainly export performance has improved over the short term. But experience shows that improvement in these aspects, however costly, will never guarantee success in the international economy. The consequence of focusing upon these factors to the exclusion of all else is the same as that for the enterprise that obsessively drives its employees constantly to prepare business plans and analyze and account for the smallest details of its operations. Without knowing how to put such plans into action, no strategic value can be derived from those details.

Cost effective use of capital, productivity, and innovation do indeed constitute some of the most important tools needed for global competitiveness. But like most tools, unless they are used skillfully and in synergy with others, their utility is greatly diminished or even lost. Our country's focus on them to the exclusion of the characteristics that define being global is inescapably self-defeating and only underscores America's preoccupation with cash and numbers: spend enough money, whether on automation, research, or capital equipment, and global success cannot be far away, many self-proclaimed mentors would have us believe. We might, with equal effect, give a precision racing car to someone who has never driven an automobile, or a priceless thoroughbred to someone who has never mounted a horse, and then expect them to begin winning races. In today's economy becoming truly competitive is impossible for many companies without first becoming global.

Having global skills, in fact, can overcome major disadvantages in other respects. For example, today's German producers suffer significant cost disadvantages as well as severe operational strictures imposed by unions, yet they are still able to outpace the combined economic force of American companies in exporting merchandise and making foreign investment. When Japan began a concerted effort to open its import markets in the late 1980s—primarily due to political jawboning from Washington—European firms expanded their exports to Japan at a growth rate that was double that of U.S. firms.

The great strides this country has made with respect to productivity, investment, technology, and exchange rates will be of little long-term benefit if America and American enterprises do not learn to be global players. The aspiring jockey is not going to win by knowing theories of equine aerodynamics or horse racing "industrial policy"; he needs to acquire the personal skills necessary to coax a trot, canter, or gallop. The potential Grand Prix driver must master the subtle interplay between brake and clutch or be condemned to inevitable failure. But while they only stand to lose a race, our continued failure to adapt to the global economy will have vastly more serious ramifications for the nation, its business enterprises, and ultimately its people. At stake is the greatest asset a person, an enterprise, or a country can have: *the future*.

The Flat Earth Managers

Are American businesspeople and American enterprises adept global players? For the vast majority, the answer is no. Judging by their actions, the world may as well end with precipitous dropoffs on the Atlantic and Pacific continental shelves. To them the globe is a geographic abstraction; their reality consists of a flat world in which the complexities of the global economy are conveniently ignored. To all too many, international business is a curiosity they read about with third-party detachment in business newspapers and journals. An international firm, to these typical managers, is a firm that is able to send goods offshore. While the international mettle of American managers is discussed at length later in these pages, *The Wall Street Journal* captured its essence when it profiled the "typical U.S. CEO" in February 1989. That CEO has little or no international experience or focus, the *Journal* emphasized, and "The first time he traveled overseas on business was as chief executive." Such managers may have a vague notion that important opportunities are to be found in overseas markets. This bears the same relationship to true global perspective as saying a recognition of where one's home town sits on a local map constitutes fluency in world geography.

The Atari Syndrome

America's international trade skills and sensitivity were cogently displayed in a short chapter from the not-too-distant past taken from the consumers electronics industry. When the Atari Corporation introduced its well-known televideo games less than 10 years ago, the products could not be produced fast enough. The high-visibility, hot-selling gadgets that converted television screens to arcade games were hailed as evidence of the U.S. private sector at its best: a company utilizing America's high technology supremacy to respond to a lucrative niche in the consumer marketplace. America became so enamored of the machines that some politicians proudly began to label themselves "Atari Democrats," to underscore their belief that American high technology and innovation would continue to maintain American leadership in the world.

Reality quickly overtook this symbol. The "high" technology was a matter of a few unprotected components that could be easily produced overseas. A large U.S. production facility for the product was built without regard to the fact that any number of Asian facilities could produce essentially the same components for a fraction of the cost. Commitments were made to U.S. workers, substantial capital invested, and huge sums spent on advertising the U.S.-built product without serious consideration being given to the fact, obvious from the global perspective, that the enterprise was totally vulnerable to lower-cost but high-quality production in Asia. Atari's confrontation with the future came quickly. Its U.S. promoters perhaps failed to appreciate that the word *Atari* was widely known to players of the chess-like Asian game *Go* as the term used to warn an opponent that he is about to be surrounded and engulfed by his opponents.

Inevitably, that encircling Asian competition surfaced within months. Hundreds of U.S. workers were soon out of work as Atari struggled to keep its products afloat by shifting its production, too late, to Taiwan. In an ironic twist of fate, Atari's products did indeed become a symbol of American economic performance: not that of a successful business but of the false assumptions regarding U.S. technology, innovation, and international business acumen that plague our nation.

Politicians around the country dropped their self-proclaimed titles like hot potatoes and, if they bothered to respond to these events at all, did so by attacking the "unfair" production in Asia rather than the series of false premises that had led to embarrassment—false premises that in broader fashion continue to handicap the American economy.

The Atari story is, of course, not limited to Atari or its industry—although the consumer electronics sector does provide some of the most glaring examples of this type. Nor is "flat earth" behavior confined to U.S. managers.

In 1972 a British company then known as EMI developed a major technological breakthrough with the first commercial CAT scanner, a product that has since provided a cornerstone for the multibillion dollar medical electronics industry. Hospitals and clinics around the world couldn't buy enough of these wonder machines. Soon scanners accounted for 20 percent of the company's earnings and with the firm's dominant market share and technological edge, the sky was the limit. The scanner market was virtually exploding. EMI was the darling of the British corporate community, the symbol of a bright high technology future for Great Britain.

In seven short years, however, the EMI CAT scanner business was in ruins. The company was forced into a merger, surrendering its scanner product line to a much more internationally adept competitor, General Electric. The reason was, in final analysis, a failure of global management. The company declined to enter into low-cost foreign sourcing of components, treated the world of vastly different customers with divergent product needs as if it were a homogenous market that would consume any scanner with the EMI label, ignored technical and marketing innovations introduced by overseas competitors, and insisted on a management structure that chilled any viable global strategic response.

Being competitive and being only national in focus may have become contradictions.

The Emperor Has No Clothes

The remainder of this volume is dedicated to understanding the global problems plaguing the American business community and exploring the means—emphatically rooted in individual, private sector initiative and innovation, not government action—for curing those problems. It does this by underscoring the global context of economic life in America, then examining how misunderstandings of key aspects of the global economy have blinded many to the mentality and skills needed to become global winners. A major myth is examined in Chapter 6: the supposed omnipotence of Japan in international business; this myth has long distorted efforts to move U.S. firms onto the global stage. The last half of the book examines the nature of the global enterprise and the elements that make it successful.

The symptoms of America's problem are as complex and varied as the global economy itself. The most compelling ones have little to do with the statistical data reviewed above. Rather it is in the marketplace, at the negotiation table, in the board room, and on the playing field with international competitors, where America's international mettle is best revealed.

In 1988 a Dutch manager of an international electronics business took an American visitor to a luncheon meeting of an international business association in Amsterdam. After a meal characterized by a number of embarrassing silences, the Dutch host explained a bit sheepishly to his old friend, "I'm very sorry. You know, halfway through the meal I realized that probably the most frequent topic of conversation at our lunches is stories of faux pas made by Americans when they come to do business in Europe."

Many more specific tales of the American commercial experience overseas are recounted in these pages. Some are entertaining. Some are almost tragic. But all of them should be quite sobering to any enterprise or manager committed to becoming a global winner.

American businessmen overseas all too often are viewed as "tourist-managers." They seem constantly on the defensive in global markets, reacting to the decisions of foreign competitors instead of causing their competition to react. Americans are notorious for flying into a foreign capital the night before key negotiations commence. Wearing "blinders" and not attempting to understand local rules of conduct, they constantly check airline schedules at the negotiation table, then fly out two days later, while complaining of the lack of commitment on the other side of the table. Many foreign executives are amazed at the sense of security, often completely false, that U.S. companies seem to have because they are strong in the U.S. market. Others are puzzled by what to them seems like an American obsession with organization and reorganization. "If my American competition ever decided to do something other than either study their own organization chart or hire consultants to study their organization charts," commented a Swedish telecommunications executive during a 1987 industry seminar, "they might even become a global threat to us."

Again and again, experienced executives who have successfully managed domestic enterprises for years behave like sophomore business students when confronted with an international business decision. Chapter 8 discusses the phenomenon of the "water factor," that causes seasoned managers to lose all sense of judgment whenever they fly over an ocean. Most telling of all have been the global efforts of many of America's largest companies. In the minds of many, affixing the label *multinational* to these companies seems to distinguish them as international experts. Yet the overseas records of many of these standard bearers for America's global business bear testimony to the fact that merely because a company conducts sales or production overseas does not mean that it is a global success.

Again and again, U.S. companies have been caught napping by Asian and European competitors with a better grasp of global strategy and better skills for implementing that strategy. A classic example of a global failure is America's abdication in the vitally important and highly lucrative global consumer electronics industry. Typical of the mentality that has handicapped America internationally was the rush to fight early imports of video cassette recorders, not with engineers and innovation, but with lawyers and politicians. Giant General Motors stumbled so badly overseas in the early 1980s that it suffered a staggering $2.2 billion in offshore losses. Businesses as diverse as Sears Roebuck, ITT, Lionel Trains, AT&T, General Motors, and many others discussed in these pages provide international tales of sometimes disturbing dimensions but they provide valuable lessons for enterprises aiming at the ranks of global winners.

Many stories of international failure can be traced to reflexively searching for off-the-shelf solutions to global shortcomings, such as forming an export trading company, organizing a joint venture, using robots or quality circles, seeking government assistance, or using high-priced consultants, without having the broader strategic self-identity that characterizes the global winner. Again and again, companies tend to compartmentalize international functions, in essence guaranteeing that international perspectives will not be sufficiently integrated into sales, planning, financial, manufacturing, or research functions, as though international skills could be reduced to a "boutique" type specialty. Global skills and perspectives cannot be viewed as a specialty or segment of business today; they must be an integral part of an enterprise, totally integrated throughout all operations. That such integration has not been accomplished is reflected in a simple review of the boards of directors of America's largest "international" companies. The majority of such firms—despite the fact that 40 to 50 percent or more of their sales and profits originate offshore—do not have any non-U.S. members on their boards.

Ultimately, little evidence can be found for the popular perception that all of our multinational corporations are draped in the fine raiment of global business wisdom. Many of these corporations may reign sovereign over the Fortune 500 list, and be popularly revered for international prowess. But when they are cast in the harsh light of global reality, it can be seen that perhaps many of these "emperors" have no clothes.

GLOBAL THOUGHT, GLOBAL ACTION

One does not become global by virtue of a diploma, a language skill, a foreign bank account, a flight over the Pacific, losing money in a London-based mutual fund, or exchanging telexes with Zurich. Nor does one become international simply by being an exporter. Just as a passport does not make the holder an internationalist, shipping goods with foreign address labels by no means guarantees that a firm is global. Exporting may often be the first step in becoming international—and ultimately global—but a firm may be global in many respects without having shipped a single product offshore.

The global view recognizes that in today's economy business is the function of myriad production, market, financial, legal, and political factors that stretch far beyond national borders. As mentioned above, the typical contemporary American businessman, if he addresses international business at all, compartmentalizes international business in offices manned with specialists who are not genuinely integrated into corporate decision making. Individuals and firms share the penalty of that common syndrome: global thinking and global approaches are not integrated into operations and decision making as a whole.

The global manager recognizes that not only does the global economy define his or her business, but that it is never stagnant. The delicate balance of factors that define the global economy is forever changing, and success requires a constant flow of reliable and sophisticated information about those changes. No global firm is ever in only one business. At the least, it is always not only in its own product line but in the information exchange business as well. To receive, understand, and properly respond to that information, most American businesses must cast off their blinders and discover the planet. They must rethink the world.

Rethinking the World

It may be easy to speak of the global perspective that is required to leverage transnational advantages into a successful global enterprise; almost as easy as it is to recite a mathematical formula. But as simple as a formula such as Einstein's $e = mc^2$ may be to recite, a true grasp of the reasoning and phenomena implicit in the formula is profoundly difficult to achieve, and is a task that frequently may require discarding prior concepts and prior learning.

Attaining the proper level of global thinking, indeed, may be as challenging as understanding the theory of relativity. Understanding must begin with small steps, with analysis of the underlying elements, the many individual but interrelated factors that, when comprehended individually, will join to create a new plateau of understanding.

The most basic aspect of global thinking is the recognition that the context in which we function economically is inescapably a global one. As detailed in Chapter 2, the globalization of our economic life has become a fundamental reality that profoundly affects every American. This irrefutable fact is essentially without regard to geography, industry, or even type of job. The Wall Street lawyer working for a Brazilian aircraft company or the Boston executive working for an English advertising agency are but the conspicuous tip of the iceberg. The grain farmer in eastern Montana, the textile worker in South Carolina, the computer salesman in New Mexico, and the machine tool worker in Ohio are just as heavily involved in and affected by the global economy. And the car salesman in Florida or the steel worker in Pennsylvania certainly need no reminder of the non-U.S. factors affecting their lives.

VICTIMS OF THE FUTURE

It is readily apparent that a world in which one nation holds undisputed economic leadership exists only in the history books. The role played by the United States for so many years is not one likely to be repeated by any nation. That dominant U.S. role, moreover, was clearly not won by astute international business practice so much as by the sheer strength of U.S. economic resources, just as Britain's decline since her colonial days has proven that her prior success was a matter of power, not shrewdness or skill. As the world's economies began to conjoin and international success began to be a function of skills and sensitivities, the U.S. position began to steadily erode.

The United States's continued decline as an international performer has reached crisis proportions. Correction of that course is imperative, but will be difficult. The American business community is up to the challenge, but only if it squarely faces the new world that is defining its existence.

That new world in which knowledge, capital, and goods move with relative ease across continents and oceans is markedly different from the world that existed a generation ago but that still defines the perceptions of a large segment of the American business community. Some enterprises and governmental entities have adapted well to those changes; most have not. Government units around the world are only beginning to realize that they can no longer structure international trade and investment by decree; instead, in the global economy governments must react and adapt to new international economic forces. In the words of Professor Richard McKenzie of the Center for the Study of American Business, in the global economy, "politics . . . is having to yield to economics."

The greatest challenge, however, is in the private sector. Many revered multinationals, which established themselves internationally in the postwar years, have changed only cosmetically in the intervening period, thereby suffering from obsolete views and structures that will assure their demise if they are not altered. Other enterprises, including many small ones, have turned away from the international sector in the mistaken belief that they actually have a choice whether or not to participate in the international economy. Whether or not they like it, and whether or not they are prepared for it, they are global participants. If they do not acknowledge that fact and adapt their conduct accordingly they will not be winners, nor even participants in the global economy. Instead, they will be victims of the global economy and the future it defines.

CHAPTER 2

CONFRONTING OUR GLOBAL FUTURE

The prospect of the global age has not been unfamiliar to recent generations. For most of the business and political community, it has always loomed just over the horizon, a likely but nebulous event akin to interplanetary travel. For the past two decades we have been instructed regularly by professors, business leaders, legislators, economists, and even occasionally clergy to prepare for the global age. Many of these have zealously prophesied of an age of global consumers in which the flow of goods and services and other economic channels become intertwined across the planet.

The problem with such expectations is that they are wrong, and action, or inaction, based on them is also wrong and dangerously misleading. To paraphrase Samuel Clemens, predictions of the birth of the global age have been grossly exaggerated—it is already alive and healthy. It has been among us for many years. Those who continue to believe that the global economy is only a scenario of the future will suffer the same fate as those 14th century barons who scoffed at predictions that tiny grains of a black powder from China would annihilate their fortresses.

In reality, without any of the Flash Gordon glamor that many expected to accompany it, America has been swept by the global revolution. It has been a campaign lasting many years, reaching to every corner of the continent, in which nearly all Americans, knowing or unknowing, have been participants. The weapons of that revolution have ranged from banks, grains, and computers to automobiles, DNA, and machine tools. It has been waged in factories, on the high seas, in research labs, in supermarkets, and in jumbo jets at 40,000 feet. But ultimately that revolution has been irresistible—the global future is now.

U.S. Business Is International Business

The globalization of our economic life profoundly affects all Americans. In almost every sector, U.S. business, either directly or indirectly, is international business. Inside and outside the workplace, the American people live in what is very much a global society. Whether they reside in towns, villages, or large metropolitan areas, in the South, Midwest, or on the East or West coasts, the quality of their lives is inextricably interwoven with international products, markets, manufacturing, investments, financial transactions, and economic decisions made in all corners of the globe.

Continued failure to acknowledge this fact places Americans and their enterprises in an increasingly disadvantaged position. And until those enterprises truly integrate that recognition into their conduct no amount of investment, legislation, or industrial restructuring is going to do more than merely temporarily stimulate them. The most basic task for most Americans in this "rethinking their world" is that of grasping their own global economic context.

The issue is simple enough. The patient who doesn't know he is ill will never seek a cure. He may feel comfortable enough, and may be so busy with day-to-day affairs that he doesn't notice that those about him are a little stronger, a little healthier, and performing a little better. A degree of self-scrutiny, and looking about to study those who surround you, may be necessary before diagnosis can even be attempted. The company that does not *see* global will never *be* global.

THE GLOBAL AMERICAN CONSUMER

Although it is only the tip of the iceberg, the most obvious evidence of the role of the global economy in our lives lies in the goods we rely on everyday. It would be a challenge indeed—and probably impossible—to find an American household that did not heavily depend on products that have entered their homes as a result of the global economy.

American shopping carts overflow with foreign products. Over 70 percent of the goods sold in the United States compete with imports.[1]

---

[1] U.S. Department of Commerce, *United States Trade: Performance in 1987* 6 (1988).

Eighty-eight percent of all U.S. manufacturers utilize foreign components or materials in their U.S. manufacturing operations.[2] Imports account for 25 percent of all U.S. demand for goods. This demand never ceases to grow; from 1982 to 1986 U.S. imports increased by 80 percent. Even the most avid Buy-American proponent couldn't get through an average day without reliance upon imports.

To many consumers the import label has a certain high profile with irresistible cachet. The Mercedes, the Rolex, the bottle of Chanel or Perrier have an attraction that is inextricably linked to its being foreign. But such products represent a tiny fraction of our total import consumption. In most instances, we buy imports not because they are imports but because they are cost effective. Simply put, in the marketplace where purchasers make their choices, they are winners.

The fact that we are usually unaware of the foreign connections behind our goods only attests to how interwoven those connections have become with the fabric of our lives. A tour of the typical American household may help to underscore that fundamental point.

THE GLOBAL HOUSEHOLD

If we begin our tour in the kitchen, we will find kitchen cabinets and refrigerators that abound with imported goods. Twenty percent of all the fruits and vegetables we eat are grown in foreign orchards and fields. The vast majority of the seafood we consume is imported, including 72 percent of our shellfish and 82 percent of all fresh fish.[3] Despite the many vineyards dotting our countryside, 22 percent of our table grapes come from Chile. Ready for breakfast? In much of the country, our morning table is spread with bread, donuts, and milk supplied by Canadian-owned firms such as Johanna Farms (Labatt Ltd.) or Stroehmann Bakeries (George Weston Ltd.). In Philadelphia, 85 percent of the dairy market is controlled by Canadian interests, as is 20 percent in New York and 50 percent in New Jersey.

Our orange juice is almost invariably made from juice shipped from

---

[2]Based on a 1988 survey by the Association of Purchasing Managers.

[3]Import figures for food items provided by the Office of Industries, United States International Trade Commission.

Brazil in specially constructed juice tanker ships. That reference to Florida on the label often refers only to the processing facility. And if the label says Tropicana, it is being supplied by another Canadian-owned firm (Seagrams). Our coffee, of course, is imported (99.9 percent), and many of us drink popular brands such as Nescafé, Hills Brothers, or Taster's Choice, that are owned by offshore, global companies. The same is true for our tea (e.g., Lipton, owned by Unilever Plc. of the United Kingdom) as well as our hot chocolate (imported cocoa beans) and several of its major brands (e.g., Carnation and Nestle, both owned by Nestle of Switzerland).

Breakfast may be rounded out by American-made cereal, produced by companies that rely heavily for their success on foreign operations, and eggs produced by American chickens. But the bananas we slice on our cereal are not grown in America, the bacon or sausage we eat may be from a foreign-owned processor (e.g., Colonial Beef, half-owned by an Osaka firm), and the bowl and pans used to hold and cook our food are frequently of foreign origin. A list of the manufacturers' marks on the back of the spoons with which you and your neighbors eat their cornflakes could fill in a map of Asia.

This litany could easily continue for the rest of our meals and snacks. That most American of drinks, Coca-Cola, may hold a surprise for those who drink it in New England—the product many of them are drinking has been produced by Kirin Brewery of Japan, a major Coke bottler in the Northeast. The popular Yoo-Hoo chocolate beverage is produced by Pernod of France. Even if a particular food item isn't imported or produced by a U.S. company reliant on foreign operations, for many Americans the chances are that it was purchased in one of the many supermarkets owned in whole or part by a foreign enterprise. Included on this list are A&P, Bi-Lo, Giant, Food Lion, National Tea, and Carrefour.

Looking elsewhere in the kitchen, we would find that over 75 percent of our low-priced microwave ovens are produced outside the United States. Indeed, a close look at the cartons for our toasters, coffeemakers, mixers, blenders, food processors, electric can openers, electric frying pans, and the other modern conveniences that have become seeming necessities in our kitchens would reveal that the vast majority are of overseas origin.

On the wine rack one might quickly point to the many California labels that are competing successfully with foreign wines. But look closely—perhaps it is one of the many Almaden labels owned by Grandmet Holdings Plc. of the United Kingdom, a Zinfandel produced in the

Cupertino vineyard owned by Otsuka Pharmaceutical Company of Japan, a Pinot Noir from the Alexander Valley vineyard owned by A. Rake of West Germany, or one of the Beringer vintages produced in California by Nestlé of Switzerland.

The Foreign-Sourced Garage

It takes little imagination or investigation to confirm the same result in the typical American garage. Cars produced in Japan, Sweden, Germany, France, Italy, Great Britain, South Korea, and Yugoslavia have become the vehicles of choice for tens of millions of Americans. Of course, the foreign emblem on the body of a car is only half the story. An increasing number of the General Motors, Ford, and Chrysler vehicles sold in the United States are coming from foreign factories—400,000 in 1986 alone. Those "made in the U.S.A." usually depend heavily on parts made overseas; most U.S.-produced cars contain between 20 to 40 percent foreign content in the form of imported parts and components. Bicycles? From the costly Motobecanes of France to the economy models, foreign sourcing is heavy. Three out of every four Schwinn bicycles, for example, are manufactured abroad. Some key bicycle components, like derailleurs, are not made anywhere in the United States

The Electrical Connection

Back in the American home, down the hall and in the living room and bedroom, the critical role of globally supplied goods continues, particularly with respect to the high-value items of consumer electronics and clothing. The role of foreign, globally-oriented producers of televisions, radios, video cassette recorders, stereos, tape recorders, and other home entertainment items hardly needs to be elaborated to most Americans. No radios, except a few for automobiles, are made in the United States. U.S. producers of televisions all but surrendered to pressures from global producers years ago. The millions of televisions we buy every year are largely produced in Asia or in the factories of foreign firms who wisely decided to domesticate production in the vast U.S. market. Only one U.S.-owned company, Zenith, currently produces televisions in the United States—and at last report it hadn't made a profit since 1984.

Our stereos, likewise, are primarily of foreign origin. The albums we play on them are increasingly supplied by foreign-owned firms with such familiar names as CBS Records (Sony), RCA Records (Bertelsmann AG of West Germany), Capitol Records (Thorn EMI of the United Kingdom), or Arista Records (Bertelsmann AG).

What of the giant market for video cassette recorders (VCRs), the single biggest new consumer electronics product since television was introduced? There is no such thing as a U.S. company producing VCRs. Those with American labels are made in foreign factories either by the foreign owners of those labels or under contract with their U.S. distributors. Indeed, most of the likely U.S. candidates gave up without seriously trying. History is repeating itself with the emergence of the compact disc player. Like the VCR, it is based on U.S.-developed technology; and like the VCR, it has been only globally adept consumer electronic companies, none of which have been U.S. firms, that are successfully exploiting that technology.

Of course, sometimes many of us may seek a more tranquil environment by shutting off the electronic stimulation and picking up a good book. Publishing has traditionally been a domestically oriented business due to the aspects of language, national culture, and freight rates. The global economy has brought an end to that tradition. Non-U.S. companies, who became global long before their U.S. counterparts, looked offshore and now own a list of publishers with names familiar in any bookstore: Addison-Wesley, Atheneum, Delacore, Bantam, Doubleday, Dell, E.P. Dutton, Harper & Row, Henry Holt, MacMillan, New American Library, Salem House, Charles Scribner's Sons, and Viking are all owned by non-U.S. interests.

How many phone calls would be made without imports? The Department of Commerce estimates that over 90 percent of the telephones sold in the United States are made in Asia. What about those solid American names Radio Shack and AT&T? Turn over the unit and you'll likely see that it's made in Taiwan or Singapore. And photographs—we may use either American or Japanese film, but the camera we use it in is almost invariably made in the Far East—90 percent of all 35 mm. cameras are imported.

Everyone's Cosmopolitan Wardrobe

A large portion of the clothes in our closets and dressers have traveled halfway around the planet to get there. Their labels span the globe from Thailand to Portugal to Honduras. Over 40 countries supply the United

States with clothing. Those offshore items often fill every slot in our closets and drawers, from socks and pajamas to playsuits and sweaters. In 1987 alone, as reported by the U.S. International Trade Commission,[4] the needs of U.S. consumers were met by the importation of 64,524,000 handkerchiefs; 281,124,000 knitshirts for men and boys; 462,456,000 knitshirts for women and girls; 105,468,000 skirts; 209,232,000 sweaters; 258,960,000 trousers for men and boys; and 196,188,000 brassieres. For our beds we imported 154,560,000 pillowcases and 151,632,000 sheets in that same year. What about that stuffed panda on the pillow? Ninety percent of all dolls and stuffed toys are imported.[5]

Without purchases of offshore products most of us would also be barefoot. Ninety-seven percent of our athletic shoes are produced overseas. If our dress shoes have U.S. content, it's often only the leather, which is tanned, cut, sewn, and otherwise crafted overseas.

Our clothing imports have little to do with the consumer who must have Italian shoes or English woolens at whatever the cost. When the consumers buy shirts, shoes, blouses, ties, and other clothing items, they are buying on the basis of competitive quality, price, and style. It is companies that have learned the advantage of global operations that are satisfying those demands.

It is not only the producers of those goods that are foreign-based global concerns. Many of the retail outlets that distribute those goods, especially in the upper end of the market, are also in this category. Familiar names owned by foreign enterprises include Saks Fifth Avenue (BAT Industries Plc. of the United Kingdom), Jordan Marsh (Campeau Corporation of Canada), Marshall Field & Co. (BAT Industries Plc.), and Bonwit Teller, B.Altman, and Sakowitz (all owned by the same Australian firm, Hooker Corporation).

If we were suddenly to be deprived of the goods supplied by overseas sources, that is the goods that arrive in our homes as part of the global economy, we would be a country of nearly naked people living in barren houses with empty kitchens, no electronic entertainment, often empty garages, and no way to communicate with each other over our

---

[4]U.S. International Trade Commission, *U.S. Imports of Textiles and Apparel under the Multifiber Arrangement through 1987*, USITC Publication no. 2075 (March 1988).

[5]Import figures for toys and sporting goods provided by the Office of Industries, Miscellaneous Manufactures Branch, U.S. International Trade Commission.

electronic infrastructure. Small consolation might be obtained in knowing we wouldn't have to be totally disrobed—most of our brand name underwear is still made in the United States.

BEYOND IMPORTS

The more protectionist and naive segments of our population might argue that this reliance on imports could easily be ended—and properly so, they would add—by slamming the U.S. door. It might be a cold turkey withdrawal, but eventually, such proponents assert, domestic industries would arise to fill the needs previously met by foreign produced goods.

That conclusion could be debated endlessly and might ultimately be answered by people like one of the "typical" Americans scrutinized in a 1986 *New York Times*/CBS poll which reviewed the U.S. import "addiction." The head of a family earning $15,000 a year was asked if imports steal American jobs. "No," came the reply, "Americans wouldn't settle for sitting behind a sewing machine."

That answer was perhaps more profound than the pollsters or even the respondent may have guessed. We cannot return to the self-sufficiency that our country may once have enjoyed; that self-sufficiency would involve sacrifice and denials our society would never accept. The global economy is among us, inextricably intertwined with our lives, and it can never be divorced from our existence. That fact is undeniable, although it may be ignored—and is, by millions, including many business leaders.

The Global Paycheck

Our consumption of imports is only the most superficial evidence of our integration into the global economy. The funds we use to purchase those goods, the paychecks we bring home, the dividends and interest we receive, and the loans we obtain also are often directly linked to that global environment.

Hundreds of thousands of Americans are employed in foreign-owned businesses, ranging from the chemical worker in Louisiana (approximately one half of all American workers in the chemical industry are paid by foreign owners) to Barbra Streisand and Michael Jackson, both of whom get paid by CBS Records, owned by Sony. The 25,000 U.S.

workers of American National Can began working for their new owners, the French government company, Peichiney, in 1988. In Washington state, trade with 105 nations is the source of 20 percent of all jobs in the state. North Carolina reported in May 1989 that international trade accounted for 200,000 jobs in the state. In Virginia, which is trying to play catch-up with states having much greater foreign investment, 40,000 workers are employed by 340 different foreign companies.

Several million more Americans work for enterprises producing goods or services for foreign markets. In 1987 the Department of Commerce calculated that 4.1 million Americans are thus employed in export businesses.

The lives of workers at a company like Boeing would be very different indeed without the exports that account for a major segment of revenues. At Boeing, for example, exports typically represent over 40 percent of the company's income (its global underpinnings are further underscored by the fact that 25 to 30 percent of its parts are imported). Revenues, and therefore jobs, have substantial overseas roots at many of the country's largest employers. In 1987 total foreign revenues for Exxon amounted to 75 percent of its total revenues, for IBM 54 percent, for Citicorp 48 percent, for Dow Chemical 55 percent, for Procter & Gamble 32 percent, for Digital Equipment 46 percent, for NCR 54 percent, for Alcoa 39 percent, for Pfizer 46 percent, for Gillette 63 percent, and for H.J. Heinz 40 percent.

Those global jobs can be found throughout America's social strata and geography. The worker making 747s for export is only one of the more conspicuous of our export workers. Several dozen citizens of a northern Minnesota hamlet earn their living by making chopsticks that are shipped to Asia. Seattle fishermen are operating their trawlers under contract with the Soviet Union. Whole new industries in the Northeast United States have been built around harvesting and selling sea urchins and raw tuna to Japan. Even the sport fisherman off the coast of Long Island has a new perspective knowing that the large tuna he catches today may be purchased by Japanese brokers at the dock for $8 to $10 a pound; the fish, bringing up to $10,000 apiece in recent months, are air expressed to Tokyo's eager sushi eaters. The bluefin unloaded at Montauk may fetch up to $100 a pound only hours later in a Japanese restaurant.

Ownership of enterprises in the United States by foreign firms acting on a global basis is, moreover, much more common than most suspect.

These pages detail many such connections, although even a simple listing of all such company ties would have the appearance of an urban phone book. Such a list would include many familiar, firmly American names, such as Sohio, Kennecott, Central Soya, Baskin Robbins, Ball Park Franks, Chicago Pneumatic Tool Company, Ex-Lax, Fotomat, Standard Oil, Pillsbury, Smith & Wesson, Good Humor Ice Cream, Howard Johnson, and Keebler Cookies, as well as the many others revealed elsewhere in this chapter.

A Global Resuscitation

Many of the examples of foreign ownership in America provide revealing testimony to the global adeptness, or lack thereof, of American enterprises. A number of those examples are discussed in detail in subsequent chapters. One of these can be found in Fontana, California, where the Kaiser Steel Corporation, founded primarily to provide materiel for war efforts in a more violent age, fell casualty to international economic warfare in 1983 and shut down its plant. Two years later an American entrepreneur joined with Kawasaki Steel of Japan and a Brazilian ore supplier in a joint venture that reopened the plant on a more efficient, globally coordinated basis. *Being 100 percent American meant being 100 percent closed.* With the integration of companies active in the global economy, the Fontana plant was back in business. When asked to comment on the reopening, the head of Shearson Lehman Brothers commodities research simply remarked, "We're living in a world economy now, not a U.S. economy."

Similar tales can be found throughout the United States. In the Tennessee countryside, for example, the first impression for many visitors has been made by loud and disgruntled workers from textile, machine tool, and other plants shut or scaled down primarily as a result of competition from more efficient overseas plants. A closer look would reveal that the state has bounced back vigorously. The reason: foreign investors who have built new factories, or moved into the idled ones. In recent years, 60 Japanese companies alone have pumped in over $1.5 billion into Tennessee, creating more than 10,000 new jobs. Many attribute the decision of General Motors to place the largest industrial investment made by a U.S. firm, its $2 billion Saturn plant, in Tennessee to the presence of the many automobile parts factories established in the state by Japanese investors.

In 1989 a new Japanese high school, operated by the Japanese government, was opened in the Tennessee countryside to accommodate the state's new globalization.

The Invisible Global Connection

Even if we have thus accounted for the millions of people involved in businesses that export goods or services, that are owned by foreign enterprises, and those making domestically consumed products that rely on foreign components or materials, a question still might be raised about the millions of others who seem to remain outside those economic spheres. What of the teacher, the banker, the dentist, the construction worker, or the undertaker?

In reality, the segment of our population that lives in true economic isolation is marginal. Many of the industries that might appear on the typical list of "totally domestic" enterprises have global connections that are not as apparent but just as direct as those in the consumer electronics or auto industries. The cement and gravel industries are prime examples. Surely these industries, constrained to using local materials and selling in local or regional markets, would inevitably be purely domestic in nature. This is not so. Such businesses still can greatly benefit from global approaches to financing, management, and technology, as can be evidenced in communities throughout the country. The list of foreign-owned companies, and U.S. companies active overseas, in these sectors would span the continent. Kaiser Cement Company in California, Cherokee Crushed Stone, Kentucky Stone Company, Hoosier Stone & Concrete, Tulsa Concrete Co., Sterling Stone & Gravel in Wyoming, and Adelaide Brighton Cement in Florida are but a few of the foreign-owned firms in the local cement and building materials business. Lone Star Industries operations in Alaska, Washington, and Oregon are a 50/50 joint venture with Onoda Cement of Japan. Total foreign ownership in the cement industry has been estimated at 50 percent. Some of the earliest U.S. foreign investments, moreover, were by U.S. cement firms, including the first Portland cement factory in Argentina, built in 1915, and the Cuban Portland Cement Company, formed in 1916.

The truly domestic industry has all but disappeared. How about dentistry? Not when one finds operations like Dental Health Services of Tampa, Florida owned by a British firm. Opticians? Pearle Labs Vision

Centers is also owned by a firm from the United Kingdom. Janitors? Buildings across the country are cleaned by ISS/AS of Denmark, which supplies janitorial services in 15 countries; ISS has 16,000 employees providing janitorial services in the United States alone. What of that local equipment rental store? Many do-it-yourselfers rent ladders and steam cleaners from Rent-A-Center, owned by Thorn EMI of the United Kingdom. Or the forester in the Oregon interior? The National Forest Products Association reports that $5.3 billion worth of forest products were exported in 1988.

Certainly jobs can be found that are divorced in any direct fashion from the global economy. But they are few indeed, and in a broader sense the international economy plays a subtle but significant role even in many of these lives. As economists will readily attest, the economic multiplier effect of the export worker should not be underestimated. A U.S. Chamber of Commerce study in 1988 reported that for every 100 manufacturing jobs created in the United States, 64 additional new jobs are created in education, construction, and other service sectors. The bankers, mechanics, housepainters, and many others in a small West Virginia town might laugh off the idea that they rely on the global economy. They would soberly change their minds if the coal mine that provided the primary source of revenue for the town had to lay off half its workers because it lost its supply contract with a Japanese steel mill.

The Planetary Cash Flow

The global economy reaches all of us, including the most domestic of us, in another way that few ever consider; in the financial markets. The mortgage rates paid by would-be homeowners in Boise, Birmingham, or Boston are determined in large part by the bond markets, as are basic rates for business loans and general consumer credit. Those markets are indisputably world markets, in which the capital such homeowners seek to use shifts freely across borders.

In early 1987 consumers across the United States, riding the crest of what they saw to be a rebounding economy, were in a bullish mood. Many were ready to make the move into a mortgage loan, others ready to refinance their homes due to unusually attractive interest rates. Suddenly, all bets were off, interest rates rocketed into the double digits. Housing starts slumped. Economic growth slowed to a 2.6 percent rate for the second quarter, compared to 4.4 percent in the preceding quarter. Would-be homeowners and many consumers generally put plans on hold, in frustrated confusion over the behavior of their bankers.

Their bankers had little say in those financial events. The real explanation lay on foreign shores. For years Japanese investors had purchased U.S. bonds and quietly held them, often until maturity. As a result of the dollar's plunge of 45 percent against the yen in 1985 and 1986, however, these investors lost over $10 billion due to their heavy U.S. holdings. It was primarily the seemingly endless supply of this conservative Japanese capital that had kept U.S. interest rates so low. When the Japanese suffered such huge losses they moved into European markets. The temporary withdrawal of new Japanese funds from U.S. bond markets coincided precisely with the rise in U.S. interest rates, and the frustration of potential homebuyers in Mobile and Minneapolis.

Over $650 billion, an amount nearly equal to the entire international trade of the United States, is represented in Japanese pension funds which are moved around the planet by Japanese banks and insurance companies. Whether those institutions choose to buy bonds in New York or in Frankfurt is a major factor in whether mortgage rates will drop in Hamburg or Boise. Will the high school teacher in Des Moines be able to buy a long-sought house next month? The answer may depend on whether a Japanese funds manager decides to protect pensioners in Osaka and Kobe by investing in New York instead of London. At recent U.S. Treasury auctions Japanese investors bought up to half of all the 10-year and 30-year Treasury bonds sold.

In August 1988 *The Wall Street Journal* tracked the course of the single family home mortgage of a California couple, a scaffolding equipment salesman and his wife who sold class rings. The couple received the loan from a small local bank, "the sort of neighborhood S&L that might belong in a sentimental Jimmy Stewart movie." The mortgage was sold to a federal agency which integrated it into a pool which, among others, was sold in turn to a commercial bank in London.

An important factor in the availability of mortgage funds for buyers in Topeka and Albany is the functioning of this global finance market, and the monthly payments paid by the California couple in the above example may subsequently have a role in financing a new home in Wales. The global mortgage connection took on a more obvious posture in 1988 when Great Western Bank of California became the first U.S. thrift to tap

Euromarkets directly, with a $250 million issuance of floating notes in Europe.

Utility Lifelines from Overseas

Local and state bond issues are also increasingly entering these global markets. The California real estate developer may find that a new project hinges on the sale of local sewage authority bonds in the Tokyo securities market. In November 1988 Los Angeles County was provided a 10 billion yen loan ($81.8 million) by the Nippon Life Insurance Company and Long-Term Credit Bank of Japan. This was the first-ever direct foreign yen borrowing by a municipality but certainly not the last. A number of other cities, including Seattle, and states, including Mississippi, Ohio, Kentucky, and Washington have been aggressively pursuing the same avenues to finance new schools, roads, water systems, and other projects. Such foreign loans often provide funds at costs 50 to 75 percent lower than credit packages from U.S. banks. With the Congress nibbling away at tax-exempt fundraising by such entities, the role of foreign funds in state and municipal growth will be expanding commensurately.

Obtaining dollar-denominated funds is not itself new to public officials. In 1982, as thousands of local carworkers railed against Japanese imports, the state of Michigan was rescued from bankruptcy by a $500 million loan from Mitsubishi and five Japanese banks.

Foreign banks are also leading the way in selling letters of credit (L/C) to municipalities, a device which in effect extends to the borrower the credit rating of the bank. While U.S. banks offer the same service, it has been at much higher rates; also, there are many more foreign banks with top credit ratings than in the United States. The City of Boston estimated a savings of up to $400,000 through the use of foreign bank L/Cs in 1986. The Arkansas Development Finance Authority estimates a savings of $1.8 million in fees and reduced costs by using an offshore bank in a recent $110 million bond issue.

Real Estate: Saved by the Global Connection

International capital flows not only have helped finance large amounts of U.S. real estate; a surprising number of U.S. owners of commercial real estate have begun to depend on foreign parties as purchasers of their properties. The entire commercial real estate market in some cities and regions was kept alive during some lean years by the activity of overseas buyers.

In commercial real estate markets one of the biggest events of 1986 was the sudden appearance of the privately held, virtually unknown, Shuwa Corporation of Tokyo in U.S. markets. In August of that year, Shuwa astounded industry observers by agreeing to pay $620 million in cash for the Arco Plaza in Los Angeles. A month later the company bought the New York headquarters of Capital Cities/ABC Inc. Today Shuwa also owns such high profile sites as the Paine Webber building in Boston's financial district and the U.S. News and World Report building in Washington D.C.

By arriving on the scene of commercial markets that in some instances were comatose due to lack of available capital, Shuwa and many other foreign companies that followed in its footsteps provide a good example of how foreign capital has become a major catalyst in our real estate industry. It was in the early 1980s that parties on both sides of the Pacific began to awaken to a startling reality: U.S. markets were shriveling on the vine, due to a lack of available capital. U.S. investors were demanding, but not getting, short and midterm investment properties that would provide an easy 8 to 10 percent yield. Meanwhile investors in Japan were growing increasingly disenchanted with a market that typically returned 2 to 4 percent. With land values in Tokyo exceeding $29,000 a square foot, moreover, yields were even lower than those figures for many companies. Prices in some districts, such as the Marunouchi banking district of Tokyo, were so high that no building had changed hands in 20 years. Meanwhile, as the trade deficit with Japan grew, Japanese companies had vastly increasing dollar accounts that demanded investment. With the much longer-term investment perspective inherent in Japanese firms, the projects that Americans had been rejecting as inevitable failures looked like pots of gold to the boardrooms in Tokyo and Osaka.

Today, Japanese investors own the headquarter buildings of Exxon, Mobil, Citicorp, and ABC, among others. Tiffany & Co., the Department of Justice, the Federal Communications Commission and thousands of other tenants pay rent to Japanese landlords. One Prudential Plaza in Chicago and One Montgomery Street in San Francisco are among some of the prominent addresses owned by the Japanese. Since early 1986, most of the U.S. office buildings selling for over $100 million have been sold to Japanese interests. Salomon Brothers reported that the Japanese spent $4.1 billion on U.S. real estate in 1986 alone.

On the other side of the Pacific, New York developers are staging seminars in Tokyo to sell their projects. Recently a random check of Tokyo newspapers revealed Japanese language ads placed by a Riverdale, New York homeowner trying to sell his $2 million home and a Mississippi broker trying to sell 185 acres of farmland. Madison Equities of New York spent $600,000 on a promotion in Japan to sell Manhattan penthouses; the promotion paid for itself within days. Trammell Crow and Morgan Stanley sell limited partnerships in Japan to finance U.S. shopping centers and warehouses.

As Jon C. Minikes, a partner at Jones Lang Wootten, an international real estate consulting firm said of this trend, "We are in the beginning of an international movement of money of historic proportions, something on the scale of the Marshall Plan after World War II or the British influence after the First World War." A manager of real estate research at Salomon Brothers was even more direct about the saving role that Tokyo has played in U.S. markets, "The Japanese are the driving force in real estate pricing in America's first-tier markets."

Louisiana Purchase to the Watergate

The Japanese are not alone, but only the most conspicuous, on our list of foreign investors. If asked to name the single most powerful entity in North American real estate markets, many in the real estate industry would name the Canadian firm Olympia & York, for many years the largest landlord in New York. Canadian firms played a similar saving role in New York when Manhattan office real estate markets began to freeze up several years ago.

The British have been providing capital for U.S. development ever since they financed the Lousiana Purchase and the expansion of many major American railroads in the 19th century. French, Dutch, German, Saudi, Hong Kong, Philippine, Belgian, Italian (the Vatican owned the Watergate Hotel when it became the venue for Washington scandal), Swiss, and South American capital can also be found behind significant portions of U.S. real estate. At last report, foreign owners held 46 percent of the commercial property in Los Angeles, 39 percent in Houston, 32 percent in Minneapolis, 28 percent in New York, 18 percent in Atlanta, 10 percent in Boston, 17 percent in Dallas, 19 percent in Denver, 18 percent in Miami, 12 percent in Philadelphia, 11 percent in Portland, 17 percent in San Francisco, and 12 percent in Washington D.C. The development of Hawaii has been accelerated by the investment of over 800 different foreign enterprises.

Much of the foreign equity contribution in Hawaii, of course, has been in the hotel sector. That involvement is by no means confined to the island state. Many Americans who might insist they never stayed in a foreign hotel would be surprised if they were shown a list of those U.S. establishments owned or managed by foreign companies, a list that would include Westin Hotels, Vista International, Intercontinental Hotels, the Ramada Inn chain, the Algonquin in New York, the Parker House in Boston, Omni Hotels, Dunfey's Hotels, Stouffer's Hotels, Travelodge, the Palace Hotel in Philadelphia, the Princess Group, the La Costa Resort and Spa, the Dunes Hotel in Las Vegas, Hilton International, and the Aladdin Hotel in Las Vegas.

The World Banker

Mortgage financing represents only one element of a much broader financial front which is inextricably global in nature. Foreign banks routinely participate in major financings; frequently they provide a third or more of the funds committed by bank syndicates for the multibillion buyouts, restructurings, and other megadeals which have become almost commonplace. When Kohlberg, Kravis, Roberts & Company engineered their $25 billion takeover of RJR Nabisco in December 1988, one of their first steps was to travel to Tokyo to meet with Japan's cash rich lenders and potential buyers of "junk" bonds.

Even more traditional commercial lending for many companies has now transcended national borders. When the maker of Lee and Wrangler jeans, VF Corporation of Reading, Pennsylvania, needed a $50 million loan in 1987, Fuji Bank of Japan provided the funds. Hartz Mountain Industries has financed many industrial developments through Japanese banks. When the Ritz Carlton hotel in Boston needed credit in 1987, Tokyo's Sanwa Bank loaned it $65 million. Foreign banks are participating in everything from the rebuilding of Times Square, through underwriting of a bond issue, to fund raising for Boston College, which has utilized guarantees from Sumitomo Trust & Banking Co. for that purpose. The building of the rapid transit system of Dallas is another example; a foreign bank has backed nearly $100 million of debt incurred by the transit authority. A survey released in March 1989 revealed that the average number of U.S. banks used by large U.S. companies dropped from 15.5 to 9.7 during the preceding 5 years, while the foreign banks used increased from 3.2 to 5.6.

Likewise, those foreign institutions are shoring up struggling U.S. banks and providing important growth capital through myriad U.S. acquisitions. National Westminster Plc. of the United Kingdom has embarked on a $40 billion growth campaign in the former colonies. Two Japanese banks have poured over $1 billion into U.S. acquisitions since 1986. Marine Midland is owned by the Hong Kong and Shanghai Bank; the oldest commercial bank in the country, First Pennsylvania, has agreed to be acquired by the Hong Kong bank as soon as regulatory relaxations take effect. Foreign ownership can also be found in such financial institutions as First Maryland Bancorp (Allied Irish banks), First New Hampshire Banks (Bank of Ireland), Harris Bankcorp Inc. (Bank of Montreal), and the commercial factoring firm Heller International Corporation (Fuji Bank Ltd.). Not surprisingly, the insurance industry is beginning to match this pace, through such networks as that of Aegon NV, owner of Monumental Life Insurance Group, National Old Line Insurance Co., and Equity National Life Insurance.

The venture capital sector has also developed vital foreign links. Foreign venture capital being channeled into U.S. enterprises now equals that supplied by U.S. pension funds, which historically has been the largest source of American venture capital. Boston-based TA Associates manages over $700 million of U.S. venture capital, partly supplied by foreign institutions such as the Scottish Investment Trust Co., as well as another $600 million outside the United States through partnerships in 14 countries.

Hang Seng to Nikkei

So much has been written about the internationalization of our securities and brokerage businesses that it seems almost redundant to discuss it. Twenty-four hour trading by now seems almost traditional for the many securities firms with offices in New York, Tokyo, and London. Many brokers speak of the Nikkei index of the Tokyo Stock Exchange with the same alacrity—and emphasis—as they do of the Dow Jones index. A sizable number of them also follow such stock indices as the Hang Seng in Hong Kong, the Ordinaries in Sydney, or the Fraser Industrials in

Singapore almost as closely as they do the New York figures. U.S. Treasury debt is traded without stop around the clock by brokers in Tokyo, London, and New York. The Philadelphia Stock Exchange today opens at 4:30 A.M. to maximize its contact with European markets.

Not surprisingly, foreign equity markets are becoming very important to many U.S. firms. In the first half of 1986, for example, U.S. companies sold over $605 million in equity shares in European markets. When Black & Decker issued 8.5 million new shares in 1986, two million of those shares were sold in Europe. At Shearson Lehman Brothers, 5 to 30 percent of every initial public stock offering is now routinely sold overseas. "Our international efforts are not a nice side deal for us," noted the head of First Boston's international division. "We can't survive without them. The global market is a reality."

The door swings both ways. Over 55 foreign companies are listed on the New York Stock Exchange, and over 250 foreign equities are traded in the over-the-counter markets. In 1986 the biggest performer on the American Stock Exchange was the Philippines Long Distance Telephone Co.

Major securities firms have internationalized not only by opening foreign outposts. They have also yielded sizable blocks of their own equity to foreign owners. Blocks of stock ranging from 12 to 27 percent are held by various European, South African, Saudi Arabian, and Japanese investors in Drexel Burnham Lambert, Smith Barney Harris Upham, Lazard Freres, Salomon Inc., Shearson Lehman, and Goldman Sachs.

Investment funds emphasizing, or exclusively devoted to, foreign stocks have also become a common fixture of brokerage and financial management firms. Closed-end single country funds, ranging from the India Growth Fund to the First Australia Fund, have created new specialties at some brokerage houses. Likewise, the pension funds which provide security for so many retirees are often heavily invested offshore, including the Arizona state retirement fund.

The Chicago Mercantile Exchange offers a computerized trading system, Globex, which enables customers at all hours to conduct transactions from dozens of financial centers around the planet. The electronic trading system is itself an international joint venture between the Mercantile Exchange and the United Kingdom's Reuters Holdings Plc. Meanwhile, U.S. exchanges routinely trade Japanese stock index futures.

The internationalization of the "invisibles" trade has extended far beyond the financial sector. A leading company in the temporary worker business, Manpower Inc., was owned by the British firm Blue Arrow Plc. for several years. Consulting, marketing, advertising, and public relations are sectors broadly integrated with foreign-owned operations such as The Hay Group, Hill & Knowlton, J. Walter Thompson, and the many advertising firms controlled by the vast Saatchi & Saatchi empire of the United Kingdom (e.g., Ted Bates Worldwide Inc.).

THE GLOBAL AMERICAN

The pervasive reach of the global economy into our daily lives may be most sharply brought into focus by some "snapshots" of Americans from all walks of life. Our integration into the global economy is not proven by looking at investment bankers who spend half their lives on the New York/London shuttle or multinational corporate executives whose telephone bills may read like the index of a world atlas. It *is* proven, however, in a significant measure by the daily activities of Americans who have lower profiles but who comprise the heart of our economy.

Little League in Ohio

Jill and John B. are finally building their long-awaited house in the suburbs of Columbus, Ohio. After several frustrating years in which Jill held the only job in the family, John landed a well-paying job as foreman in a new auto parts factory. The factory is wholly owned by a Japanese company and over 90 percent of its production is used in vehicles produced by Honda Motor Corporation at its automobile plant located northwest of Columbus in Marysville. The house they are building, like many across the country, incorporates insulating materials, pipe, vinyl siding, heating control systems and a variety of other elements produced by CertainTeed, a U.S. producer owned by St. Gobain of France; Indal, a construction materials firm owned by RTZ of the United Kingdom; and Robertshaw Controls, also owned by a British firm. The couple chose Delta Faucet fixtures for the bathrooms and kitchen; Delta uses over 247 imported components in making its products.

As the day begins for Jill and John, they get their children dressed for school. They seldom look at labels, but if they did they would find that their son's flannel shirt was made in Bangladesh, his cotton trousers in Turkey, his socks in the United Kingdom, and his sweater in Israel.

Their daughter's blouse is from Guatemala, her skirt from Hong Kong, and her sweater from Mauritius.

After dropping the children at school in their Nissan sedan, Jill heads for her office, where she works selling office equipment made by AB Dick (unknown to her, the company is owned by General Electric Plc. of Great Britain). She is considering an offer to take a more senior sales position with a start-up company that hopes soon to be making automated accessories for photocopy machines. The entrepreneur behind the company only needs two final pieces to fall into place before he can commence operations: patent licenses that are expected from Japan and the venture capital company that is financing him needs final clearance from its home office in the Netherlands.

After a long day of work and school the family returns for a meal hastily prepared in their microwave (produced in Singapore). Their meal includes fish fillets (New Zealand), broccoli (Mexico and Brazil supply one fourth of all consumed in the U.S.), and Green Giant corn (produced by Pillsbury, owned by a British company) that they just picked up from their local A&P (the entire chain of stores is owned by a sole proprietor in West Germany named Tengelmann). The reason for the rush is that John Jr. is playing in Little League tonight. By the time he has arrived at the field in his father's Toyota he has slipped on his baseball shoes (Korea— it's almost impossible to find a boy in the entire league with shoes made in the United States), then grabs the baseball glove (95 percent of which are imported) he recently bought at Herman's Sporting Goods (owned by a British grocery chain), and charges off to field an errant fly ball (made in Haiti—no baseball has been made in the United States for many years). John Jr. is excited about his team's prospects this year due to a hot new pitcher who just joined. His last name is Yamada, and his father recently arrived from Osaka as a senior executive in the Honda plant.

Big Sky Meets the World

Samuel R. lives on a large ranch in Montana. His livelihood comes from raising grain and beef cattle. His chores are piling up on the ranch because their youngest son recently left for a job as a mining engineer with a well-known American minerals company, Utah International Inc. (owned by Broken Hill Pty. of Australia). To compensate for the lost productivity, Samuel just purchased a new compact tractor for use in and around the barn. He bought a John Deere, after looking at similar Ford and Kubota models, all three of which were made in Asia.

A typical work day finds Samuel in one of his massive grain fields atop a huge tractor that bears a label "Made in the U.S.A." In fact, the vehicle incorporates a French-made transmission, a British engine, and a Mexican axle. The crops exist only by virtue of heavy irrigation; the water is transported by foreign-made pumps.

Samuel pays much more attention to U.S.–Soviet relations than many Americans since he is aware that much of the wheat harvested from his acreage has in the past eventually been consumed as Russian bread. One of every three acres of U.S. agricultural production is sold overseas. The amount is likely to increase greatly as protective barriers are lowered in foreign markets.

Recently, Samuel and his middle son have been branching into the latest in agro-technology, trying to emulate the neighbor who paid for a new pickup last year by selling bull semen. The customers are several large communes in the People's Republic of China. Even if that effort fails the beef business is looking better and better. Beef buyers seem more numerous since the summer of 1988. That was when the Japanese responded to pressure to relax their beef import restrictions. If he were to discuss this with his buyers, Samuel would learn that beef sales to Japan from the United States are expected to explode, likely to reach at least $1 billion annually in the early 1990s. Thousands of cattle are already being shipped to Japan to fill the otherwise empty car carrier ships which deliver Japanese cars to the United States. Samuel also hears that many of his neighbors' children are flocking to the huge 80,000 acre Selkirk Ranch near Dillon, where heavy hiring is expected due to new ownership. The owner, unknown to him, is the Zenchiku Company of Japan.

On weekends Samuel and his wife visit their oldest son, who manages a motel near the interstate highway. When his son mentioned that the motel was owned by an Indian, Samuel assumed he meant a local Blackfoot or a Sioux. Only when he met the man did he discover that he had missed by a hemisphere. The man was from India (according to one recent study, 28 percent of all hotels and motels in the United States are owned by immigrants from India). Samuel asked him if he was related to any of the doctors in the local hospital (one in ten anesthesiologists in the United States are also from India).

At the end of a long day in the rolling hills of his ranch, Samuel and his wife sit down in front of their Sony television with their evening meal. The Big Sky country breeds big appetites, but his wife keeps trying to get him to eat lighter, so tonight they are eating Lean Cuisine (Nestle of Switzerland). She bought the entrée with one of the many discount coupons she clips from magazines. Unknown to her, like most such coupons, after she used it the piece of paper was sent to a massive processing facility in the Caribbean where its use was recorded along with millions of other coupons by a company under contract with the product manufacturers. For dessert their diet is broken; Samuel is surprised by a birthday cake, bedecked with Betty Crocker cake decorations (owned by a German company, Schwartauer Gmbh.).

Starting Life Globally

Sylvia L. is a student in the Washington, D.C. area. Her day starts with a quickly sipped Carnation instant breakfast (Nestle of Switzerland), then she's off to school in her Volkswagen. On the way she remembers to stop to buy some Lego toy blocks (produced by a Danish company) for her nephew's birthday and some Chesebrough Pond cosmetics (owned by Unilever of the Netherlands) at one of the People's Drug stores (owned by BAT of the United Kingdom) which seem ubiquitous in the Washington D.C. region. After class she starts her split shift as a cashier at the local Giant Supermarket (owned by the Dutch company Ahold NV).

Sylvia hopes to get married soon but her fiancee is waiting for a job in oil exploration, his field of training. He had an offer in his senior year that was withdrawn after the bottom dropped out of the oil market. In all likelihood only a drastic pricing decision by a group of oil officials sitting in a conference room on the other side of the planet could turn the situation around enough to precipitate the job offers in his field. He did just get an encouraging letter about new jobs in South American oil fields from Citgo (50 percent owned by the Venezuelan government oil company, Petroleos de Venezuela). To celebrate, he's going to offer Sylvia a choice of a box of her favorite chocolates from Fannie Farmer (owned by Midial of France) or a banana split at Baskin Robbins (owned by Allied Lyons Plc. of the United Kingdom). She'll be glad to see him; they haven't been together since he accompanied her to New York where she had to do some research in the computerized catalog system of the New York Public Library (data entry and coding for which was done in the Philippines).

Buying American, Meeting the World

Walter V. is a steelworker in western Pennsylvania. He hates foreigners. He is fond of saying they have "screwed up" the economy with worthless goods and put thousands of good union members out of work, including himself for several months. Walter now has a good job with the National Steel Corporation, where he operates a forklift, moving product to inventory. His company seems to be doing well as it just opened a new processing plant near Detroit. Walter drives a big General Motors station wagon with Firestone and Goodyear tires, drinks Colt 45 malt liquor, and when he buys something he always makes sure it's from a "good American company."

Walter is a weekend mechanic, but he refuses to buy those imported auto parts that seem to be everywhere, instead he always asks for a U.S. product like those made by the Budd Company. When he's not in his garage he can be found either at the racetrack, where he avidly follows the thoroughbreds, or fishing on a local lake. In his house he uses a Frigidaire in the kitchen, shaves with a Norelco, watches his four hours nightly of television on a Magnavox or his RCA VCR, and makes sure his wife buys dishes from the local Libby glass factory. He smokes Lucky Strikes, which he lights up with his Bic lighter. His favorite food is a "good ole' American hamburger," that he often buys at the local Burger King. On his way home from his burger today, his thoughts turn to his mother, who is recovering from an automobile accident. She is mending well from her bone repair surgery but she is fretting over the insurance claim she just submitted.

Walter is oblivious to the global facts of his existence. His employer is actually a joint venture between National Intergroup Inc. and Japan's NKK Corporation; its new Detroit plant is itself a joint venture with Marubeni Corp. of Japan. The forklift he drives at work is made in a foreign factory. It doesn't matter if it carries any of the U.S. labels such as Caterpillar, Clark, Yale, or Hesston; until recently all forklifts sold in the United States for many years were made overseas. His General Motors car had 30 percent foreign content in it the day he drove it from the dealer, and when he installs new Budd parts, he's buying them from a company owned by the Thyssen Group of West Germany. The maker of his Firestone tires is owned by a Japanese firm; all of his Goodyear radials are made with steel wire from Belgium or Japan. The stables that produce many of the horses he bets on are supported by foreign capital; in most years foreign buyers spend more than domestic parties at the big thoroughbred auctions in Lexington and Saratoga. And as for his second pastime, 85 percent of the rods and reels sold in America are imported. Walter's malt liquor is made by an Australian-owned firm, his Frigidaire by a Swedish-owned company, his VCR by an Asian producer, and his Norelco shaver and Magnavox television by firms owned by a Dutch company whose name he couldn't begin to pronounce (Gemeenschappelijk Bezit van Aandelen en Philips Gloeilampenfabrieken N.V.). The family dishes and his cigarettes both were made by companies owned by BAT Industries Plc. of the United Kingdom. His disposable cigarette lighter was made by Bic S.A. of France. With respect to his American hamburgers, Burger King is owned by a British company.

The synthetic bone used to reinforce his mother's hip was made in the Soviet Union, and the stapling device used for her surgical stitches, as many others in the United States, was made from Soviet technology. Finally, her insurance claim is in good hands. The claim was put on a plane to Ireland the day it was received, where it is being processed in Castle Island, 60 miles from the Shannon airport, by specialists who are more efficient and less costly than their American counterparts. The response to the claim will be transmitted electronically to a computer in New Jersey within days, from which a check or letter will be automatically mailed. Such Irish processing arrangements are used today by both New York Life and CIGNA.

The Global California Professional

William K. is a young lawyer in southern California. He drives a German car to his office in a building owned by a Japanese development company, where his practice is local divorce and real estate work. On his desk is a console that lets him access the widely used Lexis computerized legal data base for researching California law. Unknown to him, much of the data he utilizes has been inputed in Taiwan, by workers who cannot even speak English. Beside the console are two legal treatises he had been reviewing the previous night, one published by Aspen Publishers and another by Kluwer Law Book Inc. (both owned by a Dutch firm).

After reading the morning paper (like many, printed on Canadian newsprint), William starts his day by jotting a note to his secretary with his high-tech Pilot pen (made in Japan) to renew a magazine subscription. It's a McGraw-Hill publication, which means the renewal request will be sent to a global processing center in Galway, Ireland. On the way back to his desk his secretary asks for the ticket stub from his recent American Airlines flight to Dallas to assure that he will get his frequent flyer credit. The same information was typed into a computer several days earlier in the Dominican Republic (all passenger flight data is processed for American by keyboard operators in Barbados and the Dominican Republic). At the same time he asks for a reservation for the following week at the Stouffer Hotel in Washington D.C. (owned by Nestle of Switzerland). While in the nation's capital he hopes to purchase a new suit from Brooks Brothers (owned by Marks and Spencer of the United Kingdom).

After a hard afternoon working for the manager of a local real estate office (owned by a Tokyo firm), William heads for his health club. He spends 30 minutes with the Universal Gym equipment (Hanson Plc. of the United Kingdom) and then hops into the Jacuzzi (also Hanson Plc.). By the time he leaves the pool he has made a date to see a just-released movie later that night. The film is a 20th Century Fox release (owned by News Corporation Ltd. of Australia); afterwards they plan to stop at Shakey's Pizza (purchased in February 1989 by a Singapore company).

Global Linkage

The effect of the global economy is likewise felt in countries around the world. Economic events in the United States often have a dramatic effect on the lives of people on other continents. Developments in Europe may sharply affect lifestyles in Asia or Africa. Decisions taken in Tokyo or Hong Kong may reach to the worker in Mexico or India. The global economy reaches all corners of the planet.

Japanese housewives refuse to believe a visitor's claim that the 7-Eleven convenience store near their homes is an import from the United States; over 3,000 7-Elevens are scattered throughout Japan. Japanese tourists are relieved to see the familiar golden arches of "Makudonarudo" when they make one of their increasingly frequent visits to the United States. Hamburger eaters at Burger King in the United States find new menu items because a Japanese firm, Seibu Saison, agreed to buy Intercontinental Hotels from Grand Metropolitan Plc. (Grand Met) of Great Britain, which gave Grand Met the cash it needed to buy Pillsbury. The new British owners replaced the management of Pillsbury's Burger King unit.

The Belgian dentist protects his family's future with pension fund investments in the United States. A blue-collar worker in Dusseldorf, West Germany, is able to buy a new Japanese television for his Brazilian girlfriend. She came to his city as a result of a joint venture between their two employers, and the money he spends is the overtime pay he received because Americans have become enamored of the German sedan for which he makes components.

Coca-Cola is as familiar in Bahrain and Beijing as it is in Boston. Kellogg's cornflakes are eaten from Belize to Bali. Some workers in the People's Republic of China find their incomes quadrupling because department stores in Lansing and Milan have developed insatiable local markets for cloisonné spoons, while others find themselves idle because an agency in Washington has increased the duties on canned mushrooms. Thirsty people around the world drink American soft drinks labeled Canada Dry which are actually produced by the British firm Cadbury Schweppes. Egyptian workers produce Soviet tractors and Chrysler pickups in the same American-made plant in the North African desert. Securities brokers in Australia become wealthy because Wall Street becomes temporarily infatuated with mineral deposits in the Outback.

Orchard farmers in Taiwan totter near bankruptcy due to imports of cheap American apples. Rents in Bangkok go out of the reach of many local citizens due to the massive influx of foreigners from firms trying to establish new Thai plants. Brokers in New York scramble to develop mutual funds with exclusively foreign holdings to satisfy investor demands. Pepsi-Cola slakes thirsts in Tashkent, Minsk, and Tbilisi with product produced at one of Pepsi's 16 bottling plants in the Soviet Union. Sweet toothed consumers in Asia buy Haagen Dazs ice cream, a product developed by a Polish family living in New Jersey with a name intended to sound Danish, produced by a company headquartered in Minnesota that is owned by a British conglomerate.

The impact of the severe drought in the United States during the summer of 1988 sharply illustrated the global underpinnings of our economy. Farmers in Brazil, Argentina, and Australia immediately began planting more crops due to the shortfalls in the United States, knowing they would be rewarded with much higher world prices for their harvests. In Korea, producers of shoes celebrated a sudden windfall when hides from American cattle, slaughtered prematurely, were arriving at their factories, at sharply reduced prices and greater quantities. Meanwhile the Korean government fretted over food supplies since nearly all the country's agricultural imports come from the United States.

When U.S. farmers faced the prospect of being unable to meet their export commitments, European trade negotiators were able to more forcefully resist U.S. demands for elimination of European Community (EC) farm subsidies. EC bureaucrats also paid close attention to reports from the Chicago Board of Trade for another reason. They were trying to calculate the windfall to the EC treasury that resulted from reductions in those same subsidies, designed to bridge the gap between production costs and world prices.

Sales of steel and iron to the United States were disrupted as well. Shipments typically are sent up the Mississippi on the barges that bring grain down from the Midwest to New Orleans elevators. Lower harvests and low water levels prevented movement of those barges, quite a few of which belong to shipping giant Consolidated Grain and Barge, owned by the Japan National Federation of Agricultural Cooperative Associations. Meanwhile steel factories and other facilities in South America and Asia that use U.S. coal faced disruptions due to the fact that Appalachian coal could not move down the river to the ocean vessels waiting for it in New Orleans.

Accepting Our Global Context

This entire volume could easily be filled with the countless ways in which we are all bound to the global economy. The preceding discussion may only scratch the surface of our global character, but hopefully it is sufficient to establish the reality of our global interdependence. Perhaps a state-by-state, job-by-job review would be required to make every reader fully grasp the point; certainly such a review could be done and come to the same inescapable conclusion. But most will have absorbed the above points sufficiently and applied them to their particular lives and environments. Our economic life is global. Our businesses are global. Our personal surroundings are linked to the rest of the globe. *We* are global.

Global characteristics are not something we observe only by watching vessels unload at harbors or airports. Today, to even perceive them as just consisting of imports and exports or symmetrical exchanges is a great oversimplification. Our global context is a vast engine driven by planetary flows of technology, capital, production, materials, currency, ownership, marketing, ideas, and people. A vital fact of our global existence is that the interrelationship of these factors predominates over national borders.

Many may have mixed feelings about the global context of their lives, feeling perhaps that it reflects some sort of compromise of control. Likewise, many may have mixed feelings about living in the age of the automobile, or hanging in the sky for hours on end in a jumbo jet. But that doesn't mean we deny the existence of autos and jets, or for the most part, refuse to enter them.

No one could deny that the United States is, and long has been, a global entity in the political sense. Our massive foreign aid programs, our overseas military networks, our embassies in every corner of the planet, and for better or worse, our involvement in wars on foreign shores have long attested to the global context of our political existence. Yet for many Americans, and American enterprises, it has been too great a leap to reach the same conclusion about our economic existence.

A perspicacious man once told an audience in New Orleans that "It is not possible for this nation to be at once politically internationalist and economically isolationist. This is just as insane as asking one Siamese twin to highdive while the other plays the piano." Those words may have sounded like prophesy when they were first spoken by Adlai Stevenson in October 1952, but today they should only be taken as criticism of a country that has denied itself so much by shunning the global perspective.

CHAPTER 3

THE MYTHS OF TRADE

In dealing with the global economy, America has run out of gimmicks. For years, we have cajoled, jawboned, and pointed fingers to avoid responsibility for our global shortcomings. Many American businesses seem to have resorted to the simplest of all artifices, that of ignoring the rest of the world. But even when we have chosen not to disregard the global economy, we have obscured our vision of it with so many crutches, excuses, and prejudices that it is seldom seen clearly.

We let U.S. high technology take care of our trade problems. We decide that trade problems are problems for our government, not our individual enterprises. We decide we can fix our economic shortcomings by punishing foreign producers. We delegate our international business to the megacorporations who know best how to conduct it. We decide that in the international arena we are victims of uncontrollable economic forces and trends. We convince ourselves that all trade problems and international business skills originate with the Japanese. In short, we have covered ourselves with a fabric woven through with so many delusions and gimmicks that many would not be able to recognize a global opportunity or a global threat when it was squarely in their paths.

Accepting the global context in which we economically function, as discussed in the preceding chapter, is only the first step to winning in the global economy. If we are unable to cast aside our distorted perceptions of that context then our acceptance of it will be meaningless.

Getting Launched

To assume that mere acknowledgement of our global environment will lead to global success is equivalent to assuming a mission to Mars will be successful simply because we have proven that gravity can be defied. Such a recognition would be vital, and may have been almost enough in itself to get the Wright Brothers into the air, but certainly it was not enough to get Neil Armstrong on the moon. Likewise, acceptance of our global reality may be enough to make some businesses export sensitive or at least cognizant of their world competition. But it is the barest of foundations for the successful global enterprise.

Landing on the moon required expanding the premise that we are not prisoners of gravity into extravagant refinements of rocket fuel chemistry, radio telemetry, microcomputers, and myriad other technologies and skills. Winning in the global economy likewise requires highly tuned skills and techniques founded on the basic acceptance of our global existence.

Those skills and techniques are unattainable without first discarding our global gimmicks. Ingrained in the thinking of many Americans are a number of ideas, principles, and even "rules" that are as false as the thinking held by many in the not so distant past that man could never travel beyond the speed of sound.

Just as that widely held idea restrained and distorted early efforts at space travel, these false tenets relating to international business are wreaking havoc with many international efforts. Men would not have walked in space or dispatched probes beyond our solar system if the speed of sound myth had not been cast away. Likewise those preparing to survive, and succeed, in the global economy must reject the modern myths that block global understanding and global action.

THE MYTHS OF INTERNATIONAL AMERICA

The perceptions that are distorting our global view and our attempts to cope with the global economy span a spectrum that ranges from business technique to geo-politics. Those distortions, and the degree to which they are believed, vary from individual to individual and enterprise to enterprise. If all the false premises that are handicapping America's international involvement were to be inventoried, the list would be lengthy indeed, perhaps endless, since so many new myths seem to be rumored every month. An all-encompassing list might start with many of our national/ethnic stereotypes and span the perceptions held by at least some Americans that "customers in communist countries are never reliable"; the Bermuda triangle swallows container ships; or as documented in a recent North Carolina geography survey, that the U.S.S.R. adjoins Panama and Africa is part of North America.

The most common, and most damaging beliefs, however, can be reduced to a relatively short list. These critical myths include:

The United States enjoys high technology supremacy which will guarantee success in the world trading system.

The United States dominates both the world economy and key world industries.

Foreign investment in the United States is an evil to be avoided.

The U.S. domestic market is so large that international business efforts are unnecessary.

Trade deficits are certain indicators of international failure and efforts to succeed in the global economy must be aimed primarily at eliminating them.

Foreign firms succeed at global business because they have inherent cost advantages over U.S. firms.

The most effective remedy to trade deficits, unfair trade, and import threats is protection through high tariffs and other barriers.

Japanese enterprises are the most effective international entities in the world and must be emulated by the U.S. private sector.

Japan as a nation has used the global economy to maximum advantage and its policies should be adopted by U.S. political leaders.

U.S. multinational corporations are uniformly sophisticated and leading participants in the global arena.

Success in the global economy requires massive investment and therefore is reserved only for the largest companies.

Several of these involve three common themes, which underlie much of America's international mythology. In a broad sense these three themes might be reduced to "number juggling," "protectionism," and "Japan." These themes are treated in the three following chapters. The remaining points are discussed below and, to the extent they relate to strategies for winning the global economy, throughout the remainder of this volume.

LOSING THE HIGH TECH INITIATIVE

One of the most fundamental reasons for global myopia in the United States is the assumption that no matter what setbacks we may have in the international arena, our country will always be able to fall back on its invincible technology. Yankee ingenuity will always set things right.

In Chapter 1 the discussion of the Atari Syndrome briefly explained how an apparent overconfidence in a U.S. high-tech product led to disaster for one firm. That example was symbolic of a much broader trend. Almost without regard to industry, technology has moved into global channels. No longer does the United States sit as a vast depository of innovation which it can selectively disperse around the planet.

A generation ago, and earlier, in this country the technology issue did not exist. As early as 1911 International Harvester had five foreign factories trying to meet a seemingly insatiable appetite for American farm equipment. American locomotives pushed into the jungle of tropical countries around the equator. American telephones rang profound changes into the lives of millions on every continent. American television introduced awed populations from La Paz to Latvia to the electronic age. Sewing machines and elevators, light bulbs and lasers, telephones and typewriters were identified with America throughout the world.

In the 1920s popular lectures were given in Europe on "Fordismus," in which the wonders of American manufacturing and technology, as epitomized by Henry Ford's factories, were extolled. Major electrical systems in Latin America were run by U.S. firms like General Electric. Shanghai was illuminated by a U.S. firm. Overseas telephone systems were operated in many regions by ITT and other U.S. companies. During the 1920s a single U.S. firm, Jersey Standard, provided one fourth of all refined petroleum products purchased overseas. Citizens of London received their electricity from a U.S. company, Utilities Power & Light Corp. of Chicago.

A British writer complained in 1901 that "these [American] newcomers have acquired control of almost every new industry erected during the past fifteen years. . . . What are the chief new factors in London life? They are, I take it, the telephone, the portable camera, the phonograph, the electric street car, the automobile, the typewriter, passenger lifts in houses, and the multiplication of machine tools. In every one of these . . . the American maker is supreme."[1]

Such technology drove many U.S. industries to rapid prominence. Additionally, it fueled seemingly endless growth. It was concluded in a study by the Brookings Institution that 44 percent of America's postwar

---

[1] F. A. McKenzie, *The American Invaders* (1901), p. 31.

increase in productivity could be attributed to American technical innovations.

As this path of development began to digress with radios from Taiwan, cameras from Japan, and talking dolls from Hong Kong, our society made a subtle but profound verbal shift. In a very unimposing fashion, as though the terms had been in Webster's original dictionary, we began to speak of *high-tech* and *low-tech*. This new dichotomy marked the first real public acknowledgement that America's stronghold could not last forever. The implication was that a piece of the technology pie had been purloined, but we had convinced ourselves that America was better off without such low-tech production.

America then jealously guarded her revised self-image not as the technology leader, but as the high technology leader of the world. For many years the rest of the planet cooperated, looking at rocket launches, mainframe computers, semiconductor chips, moonwalks, and even Disneyworld with almost the same awe exhibited by prior generations over American telephones and televisions.

Still American business didn't bother with "technology policy." New products seemed to pour from a seemingly inexhaustible wellhead of technology. Customers around the world enthusiastically grabbed them. If a buyer in Sydney or Milan wanted a computer, if the world wanted jumbo jets, if a Brazilian factory owner needed new process controls, then the first step was for the buyer to obtain a U.S. visa for his passport.

High technology not only balanced our trade account, it guaranteed a surplus. As recently as 1980, the United States enjoyed a $27 billion high technology trade surplus. For many years this high tech surplus was so high that it alone kept the U.S. trade account out of the red. Silicon Valley became a 20th century Jerusalem for delegations from foreign governments, universities, and private companies questing for the high tech grail.

Apparently they found that grail.

The Lost Grail

Today, the high-tech power structure is vastly different from that which existed even as late as 1980. Not only Asian or South American but even U.S. airlines shop in Europe for jumbo jets. Mainframe computers are as readily available in Europe and Asia as in the United States. The American will to lead in the vitally important space technology race seems to have exploded along with the Challenger shuttle in 1986. The Japanese have taken the initiative in semiconductor production. Even Disneyworld clones can be found in Japan and, soon, France.

Our high technology surplus has evaporated. In 1982 that surplus dropped for the first time to the point where it no longer erased the red ink in the U.S. export account. By 1986 the United States suffered a high technology trade deficit for the first time in its history, in the amount of $2 billion. That deficit is growing almost as fast as the surplus had disappeared. From 1980 to 1986 the high tech balance declined by 97 percent. The drop was much more severe in the context of certain relationships; for example, the deficit with the newly industrializing nations of Southeast Asia *soared by 2,900 percent* during that period. As several economic studies have shown, this decline cannot be passed off as a result of exchange rate fluctuations or changes in overall national growth patterns.

The story by no means ends with a few numbers in the deficit column. High technology is, after all, the strategic underpinning for much of our industrial development. In 1987 the National Academy of Engineering reviewed the competitive situation in 34 critical technical areas, including systems controls and artificial intelligence. It concluded that the United States had lost the lead in 25 of those areas. The U.S. is not even participating in several major new technical research thrusts.

With respect to the overall computer industry and the critical production of semiconductors, Charles H. Ferguson, a former IBM software analyst now with the MIT Center for Technology, Policy, and Industrial Development captures the situation well; "Five years from now Japanese companies will market very competitive computers based on high-performance semiconductor technologies, which then will not be available to the U.S. industry."

When IBM decided to build a state of the art semiconductor chip factory in Fishkill, New York, it asked Shimizu of Japan to build it. The sale by Monsanto Electronic Metals Company of its silicon wafer production operations in 1989 left the United States without a major American-owned producer of silicon wafers, the basic material used in computer chips. Today Asian companies also hold 75 percent of the world market for dynamic random access memory chips (DRAMS), the type of integrated circuit found in most computers. America's overall balance of trade surplus for computers dropped to $3 billion in 1987 from $7 billion as recently as 1981. The U.S. world market share for semiconductors slumped from 85 percent in 1980 to 15 percent in 1989.

In 1987 the top three firms receiving U.S. patents, in terms of the number of patents granted, were all foreign. The fourth place firm, General Electric, had previously held the number one spot for 25 years. In that year, which dramatically reflected the new trends of world technology development, 47 percent of all U.S. patents went to foreigners as compared to 20 percent in 1967 during the closing years of America's technological "golden age." In 1987, Japan received 17,288 new U.S. patents, West Germany 8,030, and France 2,990.[2] Herbert Wamsley, executive director of the Intellectual Property Owners trade association, does not seem too far off the mark when he notes that the "level of patents is a sign of corporate virility. This is yet one more indication that America's technology leadership is slipping." When patentholders were compared on the basis of how often patents filed in the United States were cited by inventors, a strong sign of the value of a patent, Japanese patentholders were cited 26 percent more often than American patentholders.

There is no reason to believe this trend will reverse itself. More than 20 percent of the staff in U.S. research and development labs is foreign. Fifty percent of the Ph.D. candidates now graduating from U.S. schools are foreign. In 1986, the People's Republic of China alone had 15,000 graduate science students in the United States. In 1986, the last time such figures were reported, 5,677 foreigners were working in the top 50 U.S. government labs. In the critical areas of engineering, physics, and mathematics, foreign students today receive more U.S. Ph.D. degrees than American students.

Perhaps the biggest reflection of this seeming deemphasis of the future in the United States is its lack of commitment in research funding. In 1988, John Young, president of Hewlett-Packard Co. warned that U.S. nondefense research outlays as a share of GNP were significantly "behind West Germany and Japan, and the gap is growing." When the Congressional Budget Office analyzed this point in a 1988 study, it concluded that "Despite the greater competition from foreign firms, the portion of gross

---

[2]U.S. Patent Office.

national product devoted to research and development is lower now than it was 20 years ago."

The VCR Bust

Perhaps the classic high technology defeat of America has been in the consumer electronic market, where U.S. producers are also-ran entries even in their own $40 billion-plus home market. The most dramatic and highly representative chapter of that defeat is that of the video cassette recorder (VCR). A California company, Ampex, invented the basic VCR technology. It underwent further development at RCA. But it was two Japanese companies, Sony and JVC, that saw the long-term potential of the technology. After legally acquiring it and making 10,000 patented improvements to it, they brought it to market. The rest is history, a history that has seen several other producers rise to participate in a world market that has brought them hundreds of billions of dollars in revenues. None of them are U.S. companies.

A major reason why RCA, of all U.S. firms probably the best prepared to capitalize on the VCR, decided not to do so was the company's confidence in its new videodisc technology. It believed that videotape technology could not be used in mass production. RCA's competing videodiscs, read by light beams to produce a screen image, flopped disastrously under competition from VCRs. The final note to the story, however, was that the Japanese then began to look at disc scanning technology. Before long they had also turned that into a multibillion dollar market for compact disc players. Again, U.S. companies have essentially been spectators. That widely successful consumer electronics initiative has been without a single U.S. producer.

The next chapter in the global electronics battle, almost inevitably, will be that of high density television. This market is projected to hit a minimum of $100 billion by the year 2005. The Japanese are once more in the driver's seat, although European industry groups are also beginning to take up that technical challenge. Meanwhile the United States continues to ignore the obvious fact that consumer electronics has become a vital high-tech industry of the 20th—and the 21st—century, one which creates an economic engine capable of pulling a long train of other high-value, high technology activity. Many American firms seem to have the attitude that if they need new technology they can simply buy it by acquiring another company.

Technology—high, low, or middle—is no longer the exclusive preserve of any country. The world has become technologically integrated. No country is going to climb into the former U.S. position as the sole technological powerhouse of the world. But neither are foreign enterprises going to stop and wait for U.S. firms to keep up with them in the high stakes technology race.

A LOSS OF DOMINANCE

Shifting the focus from technology to a broader stage, a second myth can be identified: the continuing perception of U.S. domination of the world economy. A vast overconfidence in the international perspectives and activities of many firms, and even entire industries, has been bred by that perception.

The loss of high-tech leadership, and the huge flow of revenues accompanying that leadership, are major elements of the loss of bygone broader dominance. A best-selling book of 1988 was one which focused on Britain and the United States as modern examples of *The Rise and Fall of the Great Powers*. Author Paul Kennedy made the point well from the broadest of socio-economic and political perspectives. Yet the point can be starkly evidenced by our international business posture alone. As already detailed in Chapter 1, the United States has suffered profound losses in its export market share, its representation in the top ranks of global corporations and banks, and its international business role generally.

A New World for New York

Nothing reflects this point better than the case of New York, which served as the unrivaled center of world commerce for decades. Today other cities around the world have been attracting international business at a faster rate than the one time leader. Some key rival locations such as London, already have more branches of foreign banks than New York.

Much of this trend is simply a matter of the broad decentralization occurring in the closing years of this century. "Will New York be the dominant financial center in 1992?" asked the vice chairman of Merrill Lynch and Company in 1988, John G. Heimann. "The answer is no. New York won't dominate, nor will London, nor Paris, nor Tokyo." Due to the advent of around-the-clock financial trading "the dominating factor will be when people work, not where they work," in the view of Heimann and many other financial leaders.

BURROWING IN THE U.S. MARKET

Closely related to the U.S. dominance myth is the one that many companies use to justify their disregard for the rest of the planet: "The U.S. market is so vast that the economy outside the U.S. borders is irrelevant." The same idea may be expressed in a number of other ways: "We can make so much money in the United States, why worry about the rest of the world?" Or, "It's difficult enough in the United States, why worry about the rest of the world?" Or even, "As long as we control the United States we control the world industry."

On the basis of this mentality, huge numbers of U.S. enterprises see the global economy out of focus. They preoccupy themselves in fights over market shares in Kansas City and Buffalo. Some burrow themselves so deep in their domestic production in Ohio and sales in the Mississippi Valley that a "foreigner" is someone from Massachusetts.

Pointing out the flaws in this mentality is a basic premise of this volume. The age has passed when any significant economic act could be undertaken in American isolation. Whether or not we recognize it; we buy, we sell, we earn, and we manufacture as players in the global economy. Choosing to ignore that fact is also an "international" act in itself, one that sends a loud and encouraging message to competitors overseas.

THE FALLIBLE MULTINATIONAL

Americans may have much to say about their multinational corporations (MNCs), some good, some not so good. But, as briefly reviewed in Chapter 1, when they think of international business most Americans look to the Fortune 500 multinationals. To the extent that U.S. professional schools focus on international business, it is almost exclusively on the role of these firms as the archetypal international enterprises. In the collective mind of the American business community, international business means Fortune 500 business.

For all too many enterprises, one consequence of this perspective has been a total abdication of international business to the large multinationals. Even for those smaller businesses endeavoring to make their own way internationally, the large MNC is often the primary role model. When a company wants to begin to export, it looks to how it is done by the big guys. When it wants to invest overseas, it follows the example set by Fortune 500 predecessors. Even the lesser sized 500 firms often look to the top ranks in a similar fashion.

The problem with this practice is that it is based on the premise that what the Fortune 500 MNCs do is uniformly correct, prudent, and profitable. That premise is fundamentally flawed. As mentioned in Chapter 1, many MNC "emperors" often have no clothes. While the last half of this book closely scrutinizes the global performance of many of the largest MNCs, a quick look at some of their experiences will show the credibility of the infallibility myth.

Giant General Motors' loss of $2.2 billion outside North America in the early 1980s is one of the more conspicuous examples, but far from the only one. Sears Roebuck took an embarrassing misstep in trying to create a Sears World Trade unit. The subsidiary fell flat on its face and was closed down after four years with a loss of at least $60 million. Procter & Gamble watched its 90 percent Japanese market share for disposable diapers shrivel to 15 percent in just a few short years. Big Blue, IBM, was humbled in that same country in the early 1980s. It saw its number one position fall to number three and its 40 percent market share fall to only 15 percent today. Many believe this was due to a failure to adapt to local business culture. Chrysler had such difficulties in Europe during the 1970s that it finally closed shop and sold its European operations to Peugeot in 1978.

Misjudgments overseas by America's biggest organizations is hardly a new phenomenon. In 1917 Citibank (then First National City Bank) opened an office in Moscow one week after the October Revolution, simultaneously investing heavily in bonds issued by the Czarist government. It was adamant in its conviction that the Bolsheviks represented nothing more than a temporary fad.

Parker Pen Ltd. put blind faith in consultants who touted the virtues of global marketing techniques and suffered such large losses it ultimately sold its entire pen business. As established in public records, Ashland Oil Company, in a misjudgment of epic proportions, was found to have systematically paid bribes of over $30 million in oil producing nations, a global strategy which inevitably backfired with profound consequences for officers and shareholders. U.S. construction equipment maker Dresser Industries had such problems in the world market that in 1988 it finally turned over control of its U.S. manufacturing operations to its competitor Komatsu Ltd.

Financial giant Merrill Lynch decided to become an instant major player in Asia by surrendering the largest single block of its stock to a Hong Kong entrepreneur in exchange for his securities firm. After a few painful years and losses reportedly in the scores of millions, Merrill Lynch quietly called it quits.

Certainly such records are not confined to U.S.-based megafirms. Less than 20 years ago the German auto producer Volkswagen enjoyed a 10 percent share of the huge U.S. automobile market. Through a combination of poor marketing, misguided production and design, and inability to cope with labor problems, VW saw its share stripped away by other foreign competition. At the same time it was announcing closure of its only U.S. plant, the world press was reporting that the firm had lost over $250 million as a result of foreign exchange mismanagement.

Deutsche Bank, the megabank of West Germany, leapt into "Euro-equities" without testing the waters during the mid-1980s. In one offering alone, that for shares in Fiat, Deutsche Bank incurred losses of between $100 and $200 million.

BEING SMALL, BEING GLOBAL

As the experience of many megacorporations shows, big doesn't always mean smart. Nor does success mean bigness. The greatest untapped global potential in the United States, and many other countries, lies with firms outside the Fortune 500 and their foreign peers. A fraction of the firms that might be characterized as small or midsized are exporting today, and many of those are doing so without the direction or deliberation that a global firm must have to remain a winner over the long term.

In recent years a multitude of studies have demonstrated that America's small businesses are the primary source of new jobs. One study, documented in the 1987 book *Job Creation in America* by David Birch, showed that the formation of firms employing fewer than 20 people generated nearly all of the country's net employment gain from 1981 to 1987. Likewise, in Germany the most efficient and highest growth international firms are those of the *Mittelstand*, the ranks of 350,000 medium and small companies that supply two thirds of that country's jobs. Despite the high-profile posture of the larger German multinational companies, it has been these smaller firms that supply the majority of the country's exports.

Dun & Bradstreet Corporation tracks U.S. exporters by monitoring trade statistics kept in 70 industries. The figures show that more than half of those exporters employ fewer than 100 workers. After participating in Commerce Department trade missions in 1987, 3,000 companies, most of them small, generated $200 million in new export sales. Yet America's small company exporters, which are at least beginning to assume a global perspective, represent only 8 percent of all small firms in the country (those with fewer than 100 workers). More than 35 percent of those small firms not participating in foreign markets, as reported in a recent Dun & Bradstreet survey, said that they did not do so simply because they believed they were too small. Many stories of global winners among the ranks of the country's small and medium sized firms refute this point.

Super-Glue to Car Washes

A small, $7.5 million in sales, maker of electronic paging and voice messaging equipment, Spectrum Communications & Electronics of Hicksville, New York, began a few years ago to broaden its perspective beyond the U.S. Today half of its sales are offshore. American Natural Beverage Corporation of New York, the small company which makes Soho brand soda, perceived that market prices prevailing in Japan were 50 percent higher than those in the United States. Today it is selling successfully in Tokyo. Hetero Chemical Co. of Valley Stream, New York has 40 employees and sells 20 percent of its products to overseas customers from Singapore to Argentina.

The Small Business Administration estimates that there are at least 30,000 small firms, with potential to successfully participate in global markets, who are not even trying to export today. Many midsized firms are likewise denying themselves vast opportunities by failing to consider the global economy. After three years of efforts to promote U.S. exports by small producers, Briton David Ward, working in New England's

Chemarketing International, commented with frustration in a 1989 interview that "the silence is deafening from small companies clamoring to export."

Molex Inc. of Lisle, Illinois is an example of what can be done by a small or midsized firm. When many large producers migrate offshore, such as those of the automobile industry, their U.S. component suppliers usually have done little more than raise an occasional political protest, scale back, or even shut down. At the same time, again as demonstrated in the auto sector and as discussed later in these pages, many loudly object when foreign component suppliers follow their large customers into the United States to maintain their relationships. Molex didn't complain. Molex acted by perceiving that what was critical to its business was not a particular location but particular relationships and did everything necessary to preserve those relationships. When large customers for its electrical connectors moved off the continent, it traveled with them. Today the company has 38 small factories overseas. Well over 60 percent of its $290 million revenues are from overseas.

In 1988, LIXI Corporation, an Illinois medical technology firm, made 55 percent of its $3.5 million in sales offshore. Ambrose Co. of Redmond, Washington made 20 percent of its $1.5 million in sales to foreign customers. Indiana-based Weaver Popcorn makes much of its $40 million in popcorn sales outside the United States; the company sells in 30 countries, with 60 percent of the market in Japan and 90 percent in Sweden. From its base in rural Nebraska, Lindsay Manufacturing sells pivot irrigation systems to 50 countries, sales that account for two thirds of its business.

The maker of Super-Glue, Loctite Corporation, is a midsized firm that has become a global winner. By targeting global markets for the company's products, Loctite's management was able to nearly double its sales to $267 million. Today, the firm has factories in Ireland and Brazil and sales in 80 countries. When Hanna Car Wash Systems of Oregon found Asian and European competitors arriving in the United States in the mid-1980s, it moved offshore; today half of its $100 million in sales comes from 71 foreign countries.

Although the United States doesn't carry its proportionate share in this area, according to research by the *Economist* one half of all companies with operations outside their home markets are "small or medium sized." In 1983, for comparison, more than 75 percent of the British firms with direct overseas investments employed fewer than 500 people.

THE "INHERENT COST ADVANTAGE" MYTH

Too many companies think that the only reason for pursuing overseas production is to take advantage of low labor and other overhead costs. In the simple world that they perceive, U.S. firms are the victims of unfair competition from abroad because foreign firms operate more cheaply than their American counterparts. Asia in particular is viewed as having an endless supply of cheap labor. In that simplistic world view, millions of souls in places like Taiwan, Korea, Hong Kong, and even Japan are believed to be clamoring for the privilege of receiving a few cents an hour to turn out products for the West. Low costs, in this make-believe world, are something of a god-given natural resource that was not bestowed upon the United States of America.

Such observers loudly bemoan the fact that from 1980 to 1987 U.S. unit labor costs increased by 7 percent. They fail to comprehend that this figure is by itself meaningless. It is relevant only when placed in a global context.

Fifteen years ago and more it was at least true that there was a radical differential between wage rates in the United States and the countries of the Pacific Rim and some European nations. In 1960, for example, U.S. average wages were 10 times those of Japan and 3 times higher than those of Germany. But whatever the past experience, these perceptions have been rendered into myths by two critical developments.

First, wage levels have reached effective parity in many of the primary producing countries, or, in some cases, wage trends have even reversed themselves. That 7 percent increase lamented in 1987 should have been compared with parallel figures among key international competitors. During the same period labor costs increased by 50 percent in Japan and 18 percent in West Germany. Indeed, in 1987 U.S. wages were reported by the U.S. Bureau of Labor Statistics to be lower than those of eight other industrial nations and 20 percent lower than the weighted average of 13 trading partners.

The second important point in this regard is that overall wages are becoming an increasingly irrelevant factor in the world economy. Hard, irrefutable evidence shows that labor costs, especially blue collar production labor costs, have been shrinking rapidly as a percentage of total production costs. A generation ago such costs were often a third or more of total costs. Today in the United States, such costs are on average 18 percent of total costs and still dropping. The efficient minimills that are the wave of the future for the steel industry typically have production labor expenses of 10 percent or lower. The textile sector, which has been perhaps most vocal of all in complaining about overseas competition with low labor costs, has reduced labor costs to 10 or 12 percent of total costs.

This means that for many industries wages are not a primary factor in measuring strength. The unfair edge that many Asian firms in particular are supposed to enjoy has been virtually eliminated for many sectors. Many American firms—often without knowing it—have reached a common denominator with the countries of Asia with respect to labor costs and, increasingly, manufacturing productivity overall.

The trend in raw material costs, pushed down by constant innovation, further demonstrates the point. The raw materials which are in the control of many developing countries are increasingly less of a cost factor. The International Monetary Fund has calculated that the amount of raw material needed for any given unit of production has dropped at a rate of 1.25 percent per year (compounded) since 1900.[3] The raw materials cost for *the* archetypal product of the 1920s, the automobile, accounted for 50 percent of its total cost. The corresponding figures of the archetypal products of the 1980s is dramatically lower: for semiconductors, 1 to 2 percent; and for fiber optic cables, 10 to 12 percent. Innovation in use further slashes at material costs. The ton of copper wire needed to transmit telephone messages from one city to the next in 1960 has been replaced by 50 pounds of fiber optic cable.

Even in countries where wage and material costs may remain markedly lower, offsetting infrastructure expense often exists. A recent survey conducted by the United Nations in 17 developing countries found that wage costs, for example, may be low in such countries, but that their differential was totally overshadowed by expenses for electricity, transportation, telecommunications, and similar infrastructure factors. In many countries these were found to be double the level prevailing in the United States.

With costs so far reduced, or at least reduced to common denominators, American firms have lost a primary crutch used in apologizing for not keeping up with their overseas counterparts. The most meaningful assets that determine global success today—productivity, management,

---

[3]D. Sapsford, *Real Commodity Prices* (IMF Research Paper dated May 17, 1985).

innovation, skillful marketing, and strategic perspective—are as readily available to them as to any enterprise on the globe.

ABANDONING THE FOLKLORE

The American business community's conduct in the global economy has been based on mountebankery of a vast scale. It is at once the propagator, the audience, and the victim. Accepting the global underpinnings of all modern business may be a vital first step to winning in global economy, but that step will be futile unless American business casts off the delusions that distort the way it perceives and responds to those underpinnings. The patient may accept the illness, but that acceptance may be followed by a fatal and false step if remedies for indigestion are taken when in fact triple bypass surgery is needed.

Once we have thrown off these myths, the path lies open to bold new global opportunities for American business. But those opportunities will be denied us if we keep behaving as though we lived on some remote island, measuring the rest of the planet by what we hear in drumbeats, flotsam off the beach, and the folklore of our forebears.

CHAPTER 4

ASSESSING GLOBAL PERFORMANCE: THE NUMBERS GAME

Many of the most widely held misbeliefs regarding our status in the global economy, and the means for improving that status, stem from our obsession with numbers. We enthusiastically tally exports. We grudgingly count imports. We uncomfortably mark the statistics of foreign investment in the United States. We establish major international policy directions and try to navigate through fast moving tides of global competition on the basis of deficits, surpluses, and current accounts.

Recently, after a frustrating week of unsuccessful joint venture negotiations in Boston, a German executive offered his analysis of the situation to one of his U.S. counterparts: "We take too long to make decisions—that is difficult. But you want to reduce everything to a number—that is impossible." He may have been speaking of one specific international negotiation but he may as well have been addressing the U.S. international trade perspective generally.

The numbers approach to trade perhaps reflects the character of a nation that lives by the quick fix. A college student interviewed in one of the recently conducted national "geography IQ" polls gruffly defended his inability to locate the People's Republic of China on a world map. "If I need to find it," he snapped, "I'll go to the library and look it up in a book." If a company is floundering, the emphasis in revitalizing it all too often simply focuses on generating a profit in the earliest quarter possible. In a curious fad of the 1980s, seminars were given in shopping center parking lots on the art of walking over hot embers. The lure used by promoters was that they have been able to condense 20 years of teachings by Indian yogi hermits into a quick two hours. If a school is turning out too many D-minus students, the answer is to give it cash. Do we want to see how our country is doing in the international economy? Simply see if the boats and planes leaving U.S. ports are heavier than the ones coming into U.S. ports.

Strictly by the Numbers

The way in which a country or an enterprise measures its performance in the international economy is vital to its self-identity and to the decision making necessary for winning in the global economy. Focusing almost exclusively on import/export accounts or deficits, however, can lead a country, and a company, astray. Certainly in recent years the U.S. government and its business community have been led far astray by their obsession with reducing America's complex shortcomings in the global economy to a simplistic balancing of trade accounts.

This chapter and the next look at this counterproductive obsession, the overall validity of our focus on deficits and the protectionism that is a natural outgrowth of that obsession. For a full comprehension of the system that fuels this mentality, the starting place must be with the apparatus that generates the numbers.

THE DATA MACHINE

With a population of only 800 and one of the most remote locations in the continental United States, the citizens of Pembina, North Dakota often don't have much to do but count the ice floes on the Red River or traffic accidents on Interstate 29. It's no wonder they sometimes get a bit excited about the monthly reports their town sends to Washington. The excitement is in a fashion reciprocal because what Pembina dispatches the world anxiously awaits.

Pembina is not alone. It is the smallest of the 300 customs ports where merchandise officially enters and leaves the United States of America. The monthly exercise in Pembina is repeated from New Orleans to Long Beach, Providence to Anchorage.

That exercise is the compilation of the monthly official trade account prepared by the U.S. Customs Service and the Commerce Department's Census Bureau. The month-by-month tabulation of imports and exports records dollar-for-dollar trade transactions totaling in excess of $700 billion yearly. When network news anchors report the latest trade deficit or the president quips about reassuring trade reports from the Department of Commerce, these are the figures to which they refer. Nearly everyone in American business is at least vaguely familiar with these reports. Unfortunately, few could explain what they really signify, how accurate they are, and why they should be considered as such important benchmarks of our performance in the global economy.

The Waiting Game

The trade account figures are important because everyone treats them as important. As the population of Pembina counts truckloads, the rest of the world fidgets over their numbers. As this chapter details, it is far from clear what the trade numbers mean or whether they are even remotely accurate. What *is* clear is that we have convinced ourselves that they are an important part of our national identity.

During the middle of each month, perspicacious readers of *The Wall Street Journal* or the business pages of any major newspaper will frequently find headlines such as the following, which appeared during 1988:

- As Trade Report Looms, Investors Seem to Think about Little Else
- Stocks Retreat as Narrower Deficit in U.S. Trade Stirs Inflation Fears
- Shares Decline Across Asia and Europe as Vigil for U.S. Trade Data Continues

The story that follows such headings is usually focused on Wall Street, although, as the last of the headlines implies, they can be repeated for the investment communities in Chicago, Los Angeles, Tokyo, Hong Kong, London, Paris, or Frankfurt. Month after month, the trade reports that start in many out-of-the-way places like Pembina are anxiously awaited as primary economic indicators that will send buy or sell signals burning across telephone and telex lines.

In January 1988 the trade account mania grew so severe that traders who were waiting for the January 14 release of the figures started referring to the "Robinson Crusoe" market because "everyone was waiting for Friday," the day of the data release. During that month, and in several others in the recent past, investors became infatuated with the trade reports and many did not move until the trade data was released each month. The chief foreign exchange dealer at Continental Illinois National Bank & Trust in Chicago reported that business had been reduced to a two and one half week trading period. Each month everyone would wait for the Department of Commerce figures, and would "sit on their hands" until they got the figures.

On the morning of the trade data release, brokers across the globe often modify their schedules to be awake for the trade report as soon as it is flashed across their computer screens or telexes. In particularly sensitive months, when brokers and investors have convinced themselves that the U.S. trade data is the "maker or breaker" of markets, the Tokyo Stock Exchange has all but closed down in anticipation of the reports.

Spinning the Trade Account Wheel

Reporting the numbers *to Washington* is in reality a euphemism. The eagerly awaited data from Pembina and Portland actually travel in two ways and to two sites. Automated reports, from those districts such as Baltimore which at last have entered the computer age, represent about 45 percent of all transactions; these are transmitted to the main Customs Service computer in Franconia, Virginia. Astonishingly, the remainder of the data which seems to play such a large role in America's self-identity is processed by hand. These reports are mailed to the Census Bureau's central processing facility at Jeffersonville, Indiana. Eventually the two sets of figures are combined at their final destination; a tan-brick, innocuous Census Bureau building in Suitland, Maryland.

The process at Suitland is subject to Fort Knox-type security. In a sealed and guarded package the final numbers are carried to the chairman of the Council of Economic Advisors the day before their public release. The Chairman will brief the President and senior White House staff by early the next morning regarding the contents of the confidential pouch.

Meanwhile, in an atmosphere of high drama, reporters gather at the Department of Commerce awaiting an 8 A.M. release. Then, in a locked room, the monthly data is distributed and ravenously digested until 8:30 A.M., when a Department employee releases the reporters from their chamber and they sprint away to inform the world.

From such outward appearances, these trade reports would seem to rank among the most vital documents of 20th Century civilization. Indeed, investments cumulatively valued in the hundreds of billions of dollars are made on the basis of the data every year. But the veracity and relevance of the trade data do not live up to the drama and awe with which it is disseminated and received.

Historically, these figures, which the world awaits with rapt attention, have been rife with error. As late as 1985, the monthly numbers excluded as much as 50 percent of the reported imports. This was due to the many problems involved with accurately tracking all imports in a timely fashion. Today that gap has been reduced, although certainly not eliminated. Currently the deletion factor is closer to 15 percent, which means the government may as well report import statistics for a typical month as $30 billion, "give or take $4.5 billion."

In a typical year of the early 1980s, as stock brokers, bankers, accountants, economists, and investors frenzied and moved massive blocks of funds about on the basis of 4 or 5 billion dollars difference in the trade account, the actual figures could easily have been $100 billion more than they were told by the government. Today, with improved reporting methods, the annual figure may be off only by a mere $50 or $60 billion. Such an amount, of course, could be more than enough to trigger a major bull or bear market. Major trade wars, sometimes souring relations between trading partners for many months or years, have been ignited often over markets worth only $50 or $100 million.

The problem of timely reporting is far from solved. Some shipments still may not find their way into the official statistics for as long as eight months after entry.

Even without the delay factor, how accurate are the numbers? With the advent of the U.S./Canada Free Trade Agreement, the data for U.S./Canada trade was put under a magnifying glass. As a result the Commerce Department had to swallow its pride and report that the trade deficit reported with Canada for so many years had been vastly overstated. For 1986 alone, the Department was forced to correct the books by adding $10.7 billion to the U.S. export column. As a result the deficit figure had to be reduced *by 41.7 percent*.

International Monetary Fund (IMF) data concerning imports of U.S. goods by its trading partners in the Group of Seven industrial countries (France, Germany, Italy, Japan, United Kingdom, Canada) is used annually to verify U.S. data. Every year a severe understatement is found. Since 1981, the average correction for those countries alone has been $12.5 billion a year, or nearly 13 percent of the total U.S. exports to those countries. From 1981 to 1986, the U.S. trade deficit with the Group of

Seven nations was found to be *27.6 percent* lower than that shown by U.S. data.

When a senior economist at the Federal Reserve Bank in St. Louis used this IMF data to verify the official U.S. figures, the conclusion was that it is likely that U.S. exports are typically understated by $20 to $25 billion. In some years this has amounted to roughly 10 percent of our total export shipments. Major swings in the dollar, significant shifts in investment to or from United States and foreign funds, and substantial direct investment decisions have been based upon changes of but 3 or 4 percent in the reported figures. In sensitive months the trigger, and the reaction, can be much more acute. When trade figures for August 1987 showed a change in the monthly deficit of only $.79 billion, the Dow Jones Industrial Average plummeted 95.46 points.[1]

Nothing reveals the unreliability of the trade account data prepared by the U.S. and many other nations better than the "global audits" conducted from time to time by various international economists. Since one country's exports are another's imports, if all surpluses and deficits around the globe are combined into one data base, they should balance out to zero. But such audits invariably find huge discrepancies.

When a comprehensive study of this nature was done in 1983, it demonstrated that the world's current trade account discrepancy amounted to *$100 billion.*[2] That same year a number of U.S. protectionist measures were being proposed on the basis of a $11 billion deficit that could easily have been accounted for by one or more of the accounting mistakes or oversights creating this $100 billion mystery.

Massaging the Numbers

To make matters worse, the trade figures have not been adjusted for inflation or seasonal variations. For this reason alone many economists consider the numbers to be unreliable indicators. Seasonal factors alone could gin the numbers by a $1 billion or more. Trade in such commodities as oil, corn, and automobiles sharply fluctuates during the course of a

---

[1]When such effects of the trade reports on stock markets were examined for the year 1987, it was found that on four different occasions trade data reports moved the Dow on a single day by + 1.3 percent, − 3.8 percent, + 3.2 percent, and − 2.5 percent. "A Monthly Announcement That Makes Wall Street Sweat," *New York Times*, January 15, 1988.

[2]Based on global trade audit conducted by the Bank for International Settlements.

year. September figures, for example, usually reflect a billion dollar-plus strengthening in the trade balance simply because imports of autos from Japan are very slow in that month and U.S. manufacturers, on the other hand, tend to ship heavily in September.

Furthermore, the fact that the figures represent what the Commerce Department calls a *statistical month* means that the monthly figures merely reflect the import and export documents that are processed during that reporting period. A national longshoreman's strike could paralyze U.S. ports for the period and the trade account figures for that month would, in all likelihood, not reflect it. The anomaly might show up a year later in reports that correct that period. Records showing actual months of entry and shipment are compiled once a year and published in the 3rd quarter of the following year.[3]

Also, the dollars used by the Department of Commerce to tally the trade account are what economists refer to as *nominal* dollars, that is, unadjusted for any inflation effect. When the Department calculates Gross Domestic Product, on the other hand, it uses *real* dollars with inflationary effects factored out.

Another gap in the official figure is caused by the method of calculating actual shipment values. The government has typically published import data based on the CIF value, which includes costs, insurance, and freight incurred in moving the goods into the country. The actual customs value, typically a FAS (free alongside) value, is prepared but withheld for 48 hours after release of the CIF figures. Exports, on the other hand, are reported solely on a FAS value basis. Naturally this makes imports appear significantly higher, as much as 5 or 6 percent higher in an average year. Thus, depending on "whose ox was being gored," the protectionist could always refer to the higher CIF figures when complaining of imports, while other commentators and politicians could, and have in the past, selectively chose CIF or FAS numbers to create any number of imaginative trends. In 1988, when measures to try to resolve this dichotomy were announced, a new emphasis on FAS figures allowed a number of commentators to compare those lower figures with previous year CIF figures so as to demonstrate significant improvement in the trade account.

Apart from its questionable raw import/export data, the government records do little to help business identify trends, weaknesses, strengths,

---

[3]The Conference Board, Economic Analysis Program, *World Economic Monitor* (Spring 1987).

and general strategic movements in our purchase and sale of goods and services. They fail to identify shifts in quantities versus values in export shipments, so that trends in price or shipping cannot be easily identified, or clues found to indicate tendencies in foreign markets. One international economist, Leonard H. Lempert, who believes that the "monthly figure is virtually worthless," explains the U.S. preoccupation with the trade numbers philosophically. "It is man's insatiable quest for what he thinks is knowledge."

The government trade data efforts are, unfortunately, on a level with many other efforts of the federal government in the trade sector. Compared to Belgium, France, Canada, Germany, Italy, Sweden, and the United Kingdom, the United States ranks dead last in export promotion spending per capita, last in export promotion spending relative to GNP, and last in export support spending relative to total government spending. In 1988, Canada maintained 91 government trade experts in the United States while the U.S. has 15 such experts in Canada. In real terms, the money allocated for such efforts in the Commerce Department dropped 20 percent from 1985 to 1988.[4]

Our Deficit Anxiety

Since that distant age when groups of people first began to function as nations, every nation has sought to export more than it imports. Some day, perhaps equally distant in the future, governments are going to discover that it is virtually impossible to realize that goal. *It is a mathematical certainty that all nations will never be able to generate a positive trade balance at the same time.*

Yet as a nation we pull out our collective hair; we flagellate ourselves into numbness; and we agonize endlessly over the trade deficit. We convince ourselves that deficits are inherently bad, and surpluses inherently good. Lamenting the deficit and postulating ways to overcome it have almost become a national obsession. Finding a political speech or article about international affairs or the economy without some conspicuous reference to the trade deficit has become as rare as hearing a Washington's Birthday speech without a reference to a cherry tree.

---

[4]*Journal of Commerce*, September 21, 1988.

The common theme of such references is that the deficit is an evil which has been foisted upon us by foreigners. More specifically, we as a nation seem to have persuaded ourselves that:

- The trade deficit causes a major loss of jobs in the United States.
- Fixing the deficit by attaining a balanced trade or net export account will bring greater output and growth to our economy.
- The way to fix the deficit is to simply export more.
- The primary reason for our deficit is our long-term consumer import buying binge.
- The deficit is caused by foreign producers taking advantage of American generosity.
- The most important item in our international agenda must be to fix the deficit.

As a result of these perceptions, each of which is gravely mistaken, the international mandate for many United States policymakers has become elimination of the trade deficit. Elimination of the deficit has been shouldered as a sacred responsibility by countless politicians and business leaders. Some large companies are even afraid to take an active role in the effort for fear that they will be accused of importing as well as exporting.

To such minds deficits simply mean we are losers, and if we are losers the blame must lie with someone else. That ubiquitous bumper sticker that inspires honks of approval across the continent accurately sums up this mentality: "Hungry? Eat Your Import." Of equal vacuity is the "thinking man's" version of this slogan: Our trading partners must buy their "fair share" of U.S. goods.

Never did such a profound example exist of trying to cure a disease by solely treating its symptoms. Those who believe that America's global performance will improve if the U.S. deficit is fixed might as well convince themselves that they can reverse the course of a weather system by the use of an umbrella.

The real issues of international business should relate to the acquisition and effective use of global management, marketing, production, and financial skills. For many that effort has been eclipsed by the deficit and the myths surrounding it. Therefore a vital step in becoming global is the debunking of these myths.

The Bumper Sticker Scholars

The conventional wisdom about the deficit, accounting for much of the political panic that seems to surround it, is that it has decimated the

American work force. Our international trading activity, such "bumper sticker professors" reason, is selling out American jobs.

The many social scientists who have exhaustively studied the employment dynamics in our trade account do not receive the same media coverage as the union bosses and senators who speak to smokestack industry audiences. But their conclusions are certainly more founded in fact.

Nobel prizewinning economist Wassily Leontief was one of the first to analyze trade and employment interconnections. His work was updated recently by senior economists at the Conference Board and the U.S. Office of Technology Assessment in Washington. These experts confirmed Leontief's findings. Specifically, they found that every $10 billion increase in U.S. exports generates approximately 193,000 new U.S. jobs, while a $10 billion increase in U.S. imports eliminates about 179,000 jobs.[5] *Trade is not eliminating American jobs. Instead trade is shifting American jobs.* Sales into international markets proportionately bring much greater employment benefits than employment lost by imports.

Exports create more professional, managerial, marketing, and other high-paying white collar jobs than are lost by a corresponding amount of imports. Imports strike hardest at the blue collar production worker and laborer, which is typically a more cohesive political constituency than any white collar constituency. In final analysis, however, the effect of exports registers much more heavily in the positive column than imports show on the negative side.

Rebuttal of the job loss myth also lies in the fact that during the years in which the U.S. economy piled up its record trade deficit that economy has been the most prolific job producing machine ever recorded in any peacetime era. Since 1980, the country added more new jobs, 13 million in total, than the combined nations of Europe have added in the last 30 years.

Indeed, in 1980, when the country's employment stood at 100.9 million, the United States had an appreciable trade surplus. By 1985 the U.S. trade deficit was up to $130 billion but employment was up to 108.1 million. As the deficit mounted during the late 1980s, employment levels continued to climb and unemployment rates continued to drop. No one even seems to ask those who vigorously bemoan the deficit and clamor

---

[5]The Conference Board, *Across the Board* (September 1987).

for protection if they really would like to return to 1980 when we had 10 million fewer jobs with a trade ledger entry in positive column.

While a number of other industrial nations were accumulating trade surpluses, they weren't patting themselves on their backs. They were looking enviously at the high rates of growth in the United States and with bewilderment at those Americans who chronically complain to them about its trade deficits.

The "Simple" Export Solution

Reality has confounded those who take the position that we can solve the trade deficit simply by exporting more. Interrelationships in the global economy do not function simply.

Policymakers in Washington have tackled the deficit through campaigns to drive the dollar downward and encourage economic stimulation in other important import consuming nations such as Japan and Germany. The underlying goal is to stimulate the U.S. economy, which will increase demand for goods and services on the part of U.S. domestic businesses.

The problem with this approach is that, as in so many aspects of American government and business, it fails to acknowledge the great degree to which the U.S. economy has already become globally integrated. The U.S. has been successful in dramatically raising exports in recent years. What was not foreseen, however, was that our consumer and industrial sectors function in large part on the basis of imports. As exports have risen, so too have imports. The dollar decline has meant little for trade with newly industrializing nations such as South Korea and Taiwan, since those countries have maintained their currencies at parity with the dollar to avoid major disruptions in sales; this should have been predictable for anyone who understood how vitally important the U.S. market is to those nations.

The Nightmare of "Fixing" the Deficit

In the world of the "deficit-obsessives," once the deficit is fixed by creating a net export balance, the United States will enjoy greatly increased output, higher employment, higher GNP, and a higher standard of living. That world is as imaginary as one created by Aesop or Dr. Seuss.

Our latest trade deficit amounts to slightly less than 4 percent of the total U.S. gross national product of roughly $4.4 trillion. To eliminate that deficit we would need to somehow divert 4 percent of our labor and production into making new goods to either export or substitute for imported goods. This means reslicing that $4.4 trillion American pie.

Who will take the smaller pieces? Unless there is major reduction of government spending, new construction, and/or overall private consumption; unless broad sectors of the American economy agree to accept a smaller share of the national product; the idea of a 4 percent diversion is nothing but an academic postulation.

Nobel Laureate and economist Franco Modigliani of MIT has stated the case well. ". . . We should recognized that reducing the trade deficit is not a patriotic exercise of reclaiming what foreigners have sneakily taken away. It will not result in larger output . . . Instead, balancing our current account will mean a lot of sacrifices, as we will have less resources available to us and will be paying more for what we continue to buy abroad."

Ultimately, we will have to accept that deficits don't get fixed, any more than other ledger entries get fixed.

Don't Blame the Consumer

As mentioned above, it is not simply the American consumer sector that relies on imports. Much of the thunder over our deficit may be targeted at Sonys, Toyotas, and European wines. But in reality, capital goods and industrial supplies contribute heavily to our import figures and in many years have represented the single largest segment of our import account.

From 1981 through 1987, such industrial products accounted for 56 percent of the total merchandise trade deficit. It has been calculated that two thirds of the trade deficit with Asian nations is attributed to components made for U.S. manufacturers, that is U.S. designed products made under contract in Asia, and capital equipment for U.S. factories.

These same figures may add a new dimension to the focus that many have on foreign producers as the root of our trade problems. Slightly less than half of our imports *are* consumer products. Who sends all those items to our store shelves? The biggest exporter from Taiwan is not some anonymous Chinese mandarin. It is General Electric. Taiwan's other largest exporters include KMart, J. C. Penney, IBM, Mattel, Schwinn, and Wilson Sporting Goods. The U.S. bicycle market illustrates this with the five million-plus bicycles that flow into the U.S. from Taiwan annually, but Jay Townley, vice president for purchasing at Schwinn, has noted "there isn't any Taiwan bicycle company that competes in the U.S. . . . It's only American brands and American companies. The competition from Taiwan is us."

Even when the importer of goods is clearly a foreign based entity, appearances may be deceptive. A number of foreign firms contribute heavily to both the U.S. import *and export* accounts. The trading firm Mitsui & Company typically exports approximately *$1 billion* more from the United States than it imports.

BLACK MAGIC DOLLARS

In the minds of those who equate deficits with failure there lurks the impression that imports constitute an irrevocable loss to foreign producers. To such minds, when we buy imports, we are surrendering hard-earned American greenbacks to foreigners. At this point mysticism would seem to enter the picture and create the perspective that those dollars disappear, fall into a netherworld, or vaporize as if by magic. Foreigners have pried our precious currency from our grip and left us with a pile of rapidly depreciating electronic toys.

America will never be able to fully cope with the global economy until it exorcizes this black magic from its view of the world. It must learn that the deficit is simply an accounting entry, one of several by which our international transactions are recorded. It doesn't reflect an imbalance itself. The dollars sent overseas by our import purchases inevitably must come back.

The dollars we spend for an Asian cassette player are not used as fuel in a distant hibachi grill or as confetti in a Hong Kong parade. They continue on their inexorable course through the world economy. They may be used to buy a steak imported from the United States. If so, the dollars return as part of the U.S. merchandise trade account. The money may help pay for a U.S. process design for a new factory. If so, the dollars return as part of the current account, which reports payments for intangibles. They might buy a share of stock in IBM, in which case the dollars fall into the investment account in our balance of payments. Perhaps the dollars are used for a trip to Disneyworld; then they would fall into the current account, like royalties and other invisibles. There is, in final analysis, nowhere else for these dollars to go. Of course, in their transit these dollars may be exchanged a number of times overseas and even be accumulated by banks or other financial institutions. But ultimately the dollars must come home.

Only in one of the transactions described above would the dollar return be used to offset the so-called deficit in the U.S. trade account. If the seller bought the steak, the funds would return in the corresponding ledger entry and balance the import figure. Otherwise, despite the fact that the dollar finds its way back, another deficit has been created, fueling the protectionist clamor. That perennial debate over trade deficits thus amounts to nothing more than anxiety over which ledger entry is used in recording our returning dollars.

The likelihood that the dollars could offer much greater economic benefit to the country if they return as investment is a point generally ignored by the deficit-obsessives, but one discussed in detail in the next chapter.

Measuring Global Performance

The time has come for American business to cast off its preoccupation with the trade deficit. The trade deficit, or even the broader trade account, has become more than an ineffectual benchmark of global performance; it has become a barrier to sensible analysis of global enterprise.

It may be true, in the words of a German CEO visiting the United States in 1988, that "the only place the U.S. export deficit is really a problem is in the minds of American politicians and journalists." But those in the U.S. private sector who prudently nod agreement with that sentiment must recognize the pervasive way the deficit obsession has altered their own world view, their own interface with their government on international business issues, and their own efforts to become global winners.

Focusing on the deficit as the centerpiece of our trade policy may be appealing as a way of simplifying our trade issues and even polarizing political sentiment over U.S. international business problems. But if it has become such a symbol, it is a hazardous one indeed, for in final analysis it is a symbol of shallowness, of a hollow economic policy, of self-doubt, and a gross misunderstanding of the global economy. A value system that places exporting *per se* at the pinnacle of global performance is a system doomed to eventual failure. In many ways this has been the

Japanese value system, one which is beginning to haunt many Japanese firms, as discussed in Chapter 6.

If there is to be a "numbers game" that plays any constructive role for the global firm, then it must be focused on devising meaningful methods for measuring global performance. Assessing the global enterprise or globalism of an enterprise may prove no less complex a task than establishing the global enterprise itself. Ultimately economics may never be able to create a system that can reduce the global strengths and competitiveness of an enterprise to mere numbers. But it is global competitiveness, not deficits or export races, that must be the concern of the enterprise determined to become a global winner.

Defining global success may be a major test of the global perspective. To say that global success means being adept at the movement of goods and intangibles across national borders is axiomatic. But it should also be abundantly clear by now that the global firm is not simply an exporter. As explained later in examining the elements that establish global winners, the global company also must be able to produce within its key markets, whether through direct investment or contractual relationships. It must be an insider in its key markets around the planet. But simultaneously it must be able, in the most unrestricted fashion possible, to adjust its insider strengths to match ebbs and flows in markets and production values.

If sales are to be a measure, then sales in one country, or the balance of purchases and sales in one country, become relatively meaningless. An individual global company does not gauge itself by whether its total sales in one country exceeds the total purchases in that country.

It is not unreasonable to extend the same reasoning to a nation. Those who spread the alarm over deficits may be quick to point out that in 1986 the U.S. suffered a $152 billion merchandise deficit. From a global perspective, however, it must be added that in that same year U.S. companies sold in foreign markets $640 billion worth of goods made by overseas units. That number, which represents a clear benefit to the global United States, was more than four times the published deficit figure. U.S. imports from those related offshore U.S. units, moreover, amounted to one half of the total deficit. Each of these figures represent important global strengths and important global benefits to the U.S. which are ignored in the deficit debate. Ultimately the goal of a nation as a global participant must be to promote and sustain a steady international flow of capital, merchandise, and services. This is not compatible with a slavish focus upon keeping specific trade numbers in balance.

For most of the first century of its existence, the United States ran a trade deficit. The economy didn't disintegrate. To the contrary, it grew into the mightiest engine of growth on the planet. During the Great Depression, on the other hand, the U.S. produced trade surpluses. More recently, many of the countries which run large trade surpluses, such as Japan and Germany, have suffered from low growth and low job creation rates.

Still we are supposed to accept that imports of Honda automobiles and Sony VCRs are inimical to our lives, that by contributing to deficits, they in effect make our nation poorer. In the same accounting system, the IOUs from Peru and Argentina that are counted in our international assets column are supposed to enrich us. Ultimately, it's not the accounting system that makes this so ridiculous; it is the value system that we have overlaid on those ledgers. No enterprise, and no government, is going to become a global success until it learns to abandon those false values and assume a global perspective. They will then quickly learn that when efforts are fully turned to nurturing global growth, the trade figures always take care of themselves.

CHAPTER 5

PROTECTIONISM: THE ANTIGLOBAL MENTALITY

In the third century B.C., the Chinese emperor Qin Shi Huang Di completed the most spectacular public works project the planet has ever known, a project which quickly became a symbol of the power of the Middle Kingdom. The Chinese called the massive structure the "Long Wall of Ten Thousand Li," and for centuries based their society on the principle of isolation it embodied. Today we know that ancient monument by its Western abbreviation, the Great Wall, and we can see it as a very different type of symbol in global society.

Since that time other such walls have been erected: by Hadrian to keep out the Picts of Scotland, and more recently by the French, under Maginot, to barricade against the Germans. Each of these involved vastly different technology, and vastly different construction, but identical results: They were doomed to failure. Those who are preoccupied with the trade deficits discussed in the preceding chapter perennially offer what they consider the perfect cure for deficits: erecting a contemporary Great Wall constructed not of stone but of tariffs and laws. In their minds, deficits and protection are essentially two sides of the same simplistic coin. Their facile reasoning says a trade deficit is a debilitating hemorrhage, and protectionism is the only way to staunch the wound. Anyone who took the time to consider the lessons of the national walls of the past—Great and otherwise—would find the effects of such physical impediments and those of political and economic walls ultimately are the same. They all breed false confidence, weakness, and uncompetitiveness.

The global business perspective and protectionist sentiment cannot coexist. While the most important tasks of the company dedicated to winning in the global economy lay in acquiring totally new management, production, and marketing perspectives and skills, it is fruitless to turn to those tasks until this fundamental point is understood. *Free trade is not a form of foreign aid.* Furthermore, *foreign investment is not a betrayal of the homeland.* They are the foundation of success for a company, or a country, in the global economy. No nation, not even the United States, can go it alone today.

Much has been written on the subject of protectionism. A great deal of it has been insightful, well-researched analysis by economists and other experts, almost invariably demonstrating how the erection of barriers to perpetuate unsuccessful businesses carries huge penalties for any economy. Unfortunately, such tracts are usually just read in the circles of such writers, meaning for the most part they are preaching to the choir. Public attention, on the other hand, goes to the impassioned statements of politicians, union managers, and others with vested interests in the protection "racket." Those who are going to survive, and succeed, in the global economy, must learn to look beyond those editorials. Protection is bad business.

FOREIGN INVESTMENT PARANOIA

A major target of protectionist sentiment is foreign investment in the United States. The issue has preoccupied many editorial writers across the continent as they publicly debate America's international posture. Investors from Tokyo, Perth, London, Amsterdam, Toronto, and elsewhere are portrayed in this debate as having "bought up America." We have "lost control of America," we have "mortgaged our birthright," we have "traded our forefathers' legacy for Sony Walkmans" in the rhetoric of many of these observers.

Such thoughts seem to be readily embraced by a large segment of our population. When a national cross-section of over 1000 adults was asked in 1988 if the United States should limit foreign investment, 78 percent favored restricting investment beyond the existing controls on investment in airline, communications, and national defense industries. It therefore comes as no surprise that politicians have frequently joined the crowd in opposing foreign investment. For anyone who appreciates the seriousness of the issue enough to give it close scrutiny, it will also become clear that such attitudes and efforts are based on profound misconceptions of the global economy.

From the Champs Elysees to Main Street

For much of its existence, the United States has been a country in which opportunity has far outstripped available capital. Our country would wear a very different face, one far less prosperous, today if the engineers of its development had been denied the use of foreign capital. In the 19th century, funds from Europe—over $2 billion in its last three decades alone—were used to build many of the railroads and ports which became indispensable elements of the American infrastructure. Foreign funds likewise were funnelled heavily into the construction of American factories, production of machines, and even the development of that archetypal American institution, the cattle ranch. Many an American cowboy rode in a saddle purchased with wages paid by a London firm and across rangeland financed by British pounds sterling.

Yet one would be hard pressed to find a picture of a wrangler bearing a placard stating "Brits Go Back to Queen Vicky," or a "Say No to Dutch Money" slogan painted across an 1870s boxcar. Today, such is not the case. It is popular to label foreign investment in the United States as a defeat for the country, in much the same way the trade deficit is viewed.

In this respect we are behaving very much like the French did 20 years ago, when they railed against foreign investors, especially American, and clamored for their leaders to slam the door shut. American participation in European industries during that period was at levels that in retrospect might lend new meaning to "the good old days" for contemporary managers. U.S. firms held 80 percent of the growing computer market, 50 percent of telecommunications markets, and up to 40 percent of the European markets for elevators, tires, petroleum, pharmaceuticals, and automobiles. A widely read French book of the time, *Le Defi Americain*, or *The American Challenge*,[1] by Jean Jacques Servan-Schreiber painted a gloomy picture of a Europe that was succumbing to the control of U.S. investors. In this 1968 best seller, Servan-Schreiber railed against U.S. companies who were buying control of European businesses. He

---

[1]The *American Challenge* was only the most prominent of several popular books published in Europe in the same genre, including Edward A. McCreary, *The Americanization of Europe*; Francis Williams, *The American Invasion*; and J. McMillan and B. Harris, *The American Takeover of Britain*.

argued that the foreigners from across the Atlantic were turning the fledgling Common Market into an American Common Market.

Americans reacted with fury. We called the French paranoid. We called them insecure. We called them scared of the future. We called them xenophobes. Today across America may be heard cries that are virtual echoes of what was heard on the Champs Elysee a generation ago. We call ourselves patriotic.

Those who would slam the door on foreign investment should introduce themselves to the facts surrounding that investment:

> Ownership of U.S. assets by foreign interests represents only 2 to 4 percent of total U.S. corporate assets.
>
> The pace of investment abroad by U.S. firms is roughly equal to that of investment here by foreign firms ($38 billion by U.S. firms overseas in 1987, compared to $41 billion by foreign firms in the U.S.).
>
> Due to the substantial investments made by U.S. firms 10, 20, and more years ago, the total of American investment abroad exceeds the total of foreign holdings in the United States by well over $250 billion.

We are far from being invaded by alien aggressors. Only a small fraction of the acquisitions made by foreign interests of existing companies have been hostile. We are not owned by the Japanese or anyone else. Foreign investment is widely dispersed among companies across the globe. Japanese investments, which seem to attract the most criticism, are only a third in relative size compared to much larger holdings by British and Dutch firms.

The fact that most U.S. firms have global shortcomings is not the result of foreign investment in the United States. Those who want to attack foreign investment, like the trade deficit, as a cause for those shortcomings are in strong need of a dose of global perspective.

The Numbers Game, Part Two

As with trade account data, to understand our foreign investment figures the process for compilation of those figures must be appreciated. The statistical games played with respect to our trade deficit are played with equal alacrity in preparation of our foreign investment figures. The most commonly published figures with respect to foreign investment in recent years state that foreign investment in the United States outweighs U.S. investment overseas by several billion dollars. This implies that such an investment deficit is inimical to America's health in much the same fashion as the trade deficit. Even if that implication were accurate, which it is not, such reports have still grossly misrepresented the facts.

The official investment figures compiled by the Department of Commerce are based on original book value for U.S. investments overseas. The Department has on occasion acknowledged the misleading nature of these figures but defends itself by stating that this representation is the easiest method of developing such reports.

Although many U.S. investments overseas have expanded dramatically since their original acquisition, the government looks no further than the original investment number—often 5,10, even 20 years old—in trying to assign a value to it. This is equivalent to the U.S. government practice of valuing its gold reserves at the official price of $42 an ounce when calculating net U.S. assets (another practice which grossly distorts the international investment figures). In calculating such international statistics, as in trade deficit accounting, the government follows practices which no responsible corporate controller would tolerate in even the rawest of recruits.

Beyond the Numbers

Even if accurate data could be developed with respect to foreign investment in the United States, bare numbers will never tell the entire story. To focus on statistics implies that assessing foreign investment—or foreign trade, as discussed in Chapter 4—is strictly a quantitative exercise. Some numbers, such as the 2.5 million Americans employed by foreign enterprises in the United States may indeed be significant. But the qualitative aspects of foreign investment are vitally more important to private enterprise.

In any of the industrial nations that constitute the source of active foreign investment, the attraction of private investment to any enterprise is a sign of strength. It is a sign of confidence, a ratification of success and expression of optimism for the future. Yet protectionists would have us believe that we must spurn capital from offshore, that we should turn defensive when funds are offered from Europe or Asia, solely due to their offshore origins. If pressed to explain themselves, such individuals typically wrap themselves in the flag and tune out the realities driving foreign investment in the United States.

When a Dutch, British, Japanese, or British firm determines that it is more attractive to invest in the United States than in its own country, it is a clear indication of the strength of our nation. Arguments that such foreign investment reflects weakness of the United States are patently wrong. Foreign investors are not forced here by their governments in some grand political conspiracy. They are attracted by the forces of free enterprise and because prospects in the United States are brighter than at home.

Such investments show not the power of the investors' home countries, but rather the strength of the individual enterprises making the investment. No one can deny that the foreign company that pays $600 million in cash for a U.S. office building has inherent strength. Yet the very dollars they wish to spend have been generated by trade with the United States. This is another point on which the forces of protection have been noticeably quiet.

As explained in Chapter 3, dollars are not magically conjured in a foreign kettle. U.S. dollars, inescapably, are generated by a U.S. source. Simple arithmetic dictates that the dollars spent by foreigners in purchases of U.S. goods, assets, and services must equal the dollars spent by the United States on imports and foreign assets. If the current account was matched dollar for dollar, with total import/export parity, no dollars would be left for investment. The trade deficit makes available dollars for investment in the United States, meeting a commensurate need in the U.S. capital account. America always gets its dollars back.

The Reverse Marshall Plan

It is difficult indeed to understand how foreign investment is destroying the United States when the plain facts show that it actually has been providing the wherewithal for growth in our economy. Foreign investment played a major role in establishing the United States as the sole major country on the planet to have been able to raise its fixed investment level as a share of GNP during the last decade. The great interest of foreign investors in America compellingly demonstrates that the investment problem is not a U.S. problem. If it is a problem at all, it is primarily for their home countries. Economists at California's Claremont Economic Institute have characterized these foreign investment trends as evidence of a "reverse Marshall Plan" in which other countries have chosen to invest in the reindustrialization of America, probably at the expense of their own home industrial structures. During the 1980s the additional capital made available in the United States as a result of such investment was approximately $700 billion.

The fact that such large numbers of typical Americans have expressed support for restricting foreign investment in the United States fortunately does not mean that all decision makers have accepted that premise. In the same poll mentioned above, a second target group of 100 public officials and business leaders were asked to express their views on the subject. Ninety-nine percent opposed a ban on foreign investment, and 86 percent opposed any controls beyond those which already exist.

Many of these leaders apparently share the view of the United Kingdom's Lord Lever, the statesman, lawyer, and industrialist who has stated that he doesn't "give a damn who owns my industries as long as they're successful." The foreign investment xenophobia also doesn't extend to many state and local governments, moreover, state overseas delegations to solicit investment have become almost as common as governors' visits to state fairs. Indeed, many localities battle fiercely to attract new foreign-owned factories. In final analysis, these investors from overseas have recognized that to be global they must be in America.

Attacks on foreign investment are shortsighted, harmful to the vigor of U.S. competition, inimical to U.S. economic growth, prejudicial to U.S. employment expansion, adverse to U.S. international relations generally, and generally contrary to efforts to become global. Anthony M. Solomon, former president of the Federal Reserve Bank of New York, has summarized the point well: ". . .the recent rush to condemn foreign investment as politically motivated and threatening to so-called American sovereignty or independence is misguided on every conceivable level."

PROTECTION FORTRESS, PROTECTION PRISON

Limiting foreign investment, of course, is only one weapon in the protectionist arsenal. Protection comes in many colors, sizes, and shapes. Traditionally protection meant high tariffs. But today it may mean not only high tariffs but quotas, voluntary restraints, orderly marketing agreements, and myriad other measures that limit the free flow of goods over borders.

Our trading partners have exercised great imagination in developing nontariff barriers that might be invisible to the casual observer. Japan rejected French surfboards in 1985 as being unsafe—on the grounds that people could fall off them. France once decided that Japanese VCRs could enter the country only if every unit was separately inspected—in the interior of the country at a small warehouse in Lyon. One of the more notorious, though shortlived, efforts was the Japanese attempt to block U.S. skis on the grounds that they would not function on Japanese snow. A multitude of so-called safety, health, and technical measures can be found around the world which bear many labels but share a common purpose: the protection of local firms from competition.

Whether in sheep's or wolf's clothing, protection remains alive and well in the United States and elsewhere across the planet.

Living High Off Taxpayers and Consumers

Those who have urged protective restraints in the textile, steel, auto, and other sectors have been successful primarily through scare tactics. Without protection, they argue, we will live in a country of empty factories and unemployed workers, a world in which Americans would all be serving as domestic staff for the foreign owners of their country. Such arguments have been markedly successful. At least 25 percent of the products entering the United States are subject to some form of special protective measure such as voluntary restraint, high tariff, or quota.

The protection that the United States has erected in those industries has extracted a heavy toll. In the textile sector, where quotas today restrict the importation of 1,400 categories of goods from 40 different countries, every job saved costs the U.S. consumers $42,000 a year, according to analysis done by the Institute for International Economics. Protection in the automobile sector costs us at least $160,000 annually for each job saved, and in the tuna fishing industry, each job represents $76,000 added cost to the consumer. In the protected dairy industry, each job represents a cost of $220,000 to be absorbed by consumers. In the shipping industry the figure is $270,000, and in the meat industry, $160,000. In the carbon steel sector every job saved has cost Americans a walloping $750,000. In the specialty steel the figure is $1,000,000 per year per job saved.[2] Taxpayers and consumers would have come out far ahead if instead they had simply paid for many such workers to retire at full pay.

The available evidence indicates that tampering with international competition in these industries has introduced costs so high that many more jobs have been destroyed than were saved. A 1987 study by the Center for the Study of American Business[3] found that protection to the steel industry temporarily saved 17,000 steel jobs, but 52,400 jobs were lost in steel-using industries. The 1977 Orderly Marketing Agreement to restrict Japanese television imports was intended to bring back television production to the United States. Instead Japanese imports dropped from 90 to 50 percent of the market but imports from other Asian countries increased from 15 to 50 percent, more than making up the difference. The actual jobs saved by protection are always far fewer than promised by the protected enterprises in their protection "bargains" reached with the Congress.

Inevitably, job loss occurs even with protection. U.S. automakers have eliminated over 130,000 jobs in the last 10 years. Textile makers have improved productivity to such a point that employment has dropped well over 30 percent from the level when protection was first imposed. Investigations by the Institute for International Economics have shown that textile industry job losses, overall, have been primarily the result of such productivity gains, not import competition. Despite the huge cost to American taxpayers and consumers for protecting steel jobs, a study of the U.S. steel industry in 1988[4] demonstrated that over the long term, during the steel protection imposed in the 1980s, protection did not permanently preserve any steel jobs—although it permanently destroyed many others.

When the Federal Reserve Bank of New York studied the cost of protection in 1984, it determined that U.S. protection for clothing, sugar, and cars alone was the equivalent of a 23 percent income tax surcharge for families with income below $10,000, or 10 percent for the then "average" family earning $23,000. That same study showed that due to U.S.

---

[2]Institute for International Economics (1987) and the Brookings Institution (1989).
[3]Arthur Denzau, "Can Trade Protection Save Jobs?" Washington University (1987).
[4]International Labor Organization, *Structural Adjustment in the United States Steel Industry—A North-South Perspective.*

protection, the price for imported clothing is twice what it would otherwise be. Studies from economists in Washington, London, and New York have found that the U.S. population is paying annually $700 million extra for its shoes and $20 to $27 billion extra for its clothing as a result of protective measures. The corresponding cost for steel restraints is placed at $7 billion. In 1987 *The Economist* reported calculations showing that, were Americans unable to continue to purchase imported goods, their real incomes would effectively be reduced by 20 percent due to the higher prices they would pay.

The total price for the protection favors granted to a few U.S. industries is now at least *$65 billion annually*. Meanwhile, the Congress does contortions to find a way to squeeze out a mere $500 million in taxes or trim $100 million from a budget.

Without much of the protection they demanded, the "hollowing" of our economy promised by protectionists has failed to materialize. Year after year, manufacturing of hard goods continues to represent 20 percent of our GNP, as it has for 40 years at least. Manufacturing jobs are on the rise. The U.S. job machine needs no help.

The Protection Windfall

Protection of an industry, we are always assured, is intended to save the industry, to permit a period of recovery, to allow for new investment that otherwise wouldn't be possible under the siege of imports, and to maintain jobs for workers who would otherwise be on the street. Has this happened?

Impassioned pleas for the chance to retool, reinvest, and rebuild were made by the giants of the steel and auto industries in the late 1970s and early 1980s. When they finally received the protection they demanded, what did these firms do?

General Motors, in a move that continues to be hotly criticized by many, used much of its protection pot of gold to buy EDS Inc. and pay huge bonuses to its executives. Ford began a buying spree that left it owning the second largest savings and loan institution in the country. USX began its reinvestment and revitalization of its steel business by acquiring Marathon Oil. Chrysler bought one of its major competitors, American Motors, as well as a major defense contractor.

In 1986 the Congressional Budget Office studied the results of restraints and determined that the clothing and steel industries had essentially not used the periods of protection to expand investment in their businesses. In recent years, restructuring finally has been undertaken in most of these protected companies, but in most cases long after protection was given them and after protection windfalls went into other efforts.

What about the unprecedented opportunity to recapture market share that protection offers U.S. producers? When the voluntary restraint agreements (VRA) limiting Japanese car imports took effect in 1981, the prices for Japanese cars shot up. It would have seemed a "no-brainer" for Detroit to capitalize by aggressively recovering some of the market share it had lost to the Japanese. Seldom is management presented with such a black and white decision. Behind "Door Number One" the carmakers knew they would find the regained market share they, and the huge network of support industries feeding the auto industry, needed for long-term growth—the retrenching they had effectively promised the government leaders who negotiated the protection. Behind "Door Number Two" they would find quick profits.

Anyone who made a study of protected industries would not be surprised that the carmakers leapt for the second choice. Prices for U.S. cars were raised, almost dollar for dollar, in sequence with the Japanese increases. The U.S. International Trade Commission (ITC) concluded that *in 1984 alone, as a direct result of these import restraints, consumers paid an additional $5.2 billion for U.S. cars and an extra $3.3 billion for Japanese cars.* If those numbers are multiplied by all the years those restraints have been in existence, the total windfall to Detroit has staggering dimensions. A Brookings Institution economist who has specialized in the auto industry, Robert Crandall, noted. "What we did [by introducing the VRAs] was transfer billions of dollars from consumer's pockets into the Big Three" automakers. A 1987 report by IMF economists concluded that as a direct result of the Japanese VRAs the average price for a new auto in the United States has *increased by 50 percent since 1984.*

The chairman of Chrysler had mounted one of the most expensive lobbying protectionist campaigns ever to obtain the VRA arrangement, warning passionately in congressional testimony that if the protection was not given, Americans would find themselves left with nothing but "drive-in banks, video arcades, and McDonalds hamburger stands." After the restraints were imposed he began collecting a salary and bonus, which in some years has approached $20 million. As the cash rolled in with little change in market share except among the U.S. firms themselves, Ford rewarded itself with a $250 million executive bonus pool. The ultimate irony was that the protection initiated to restrict foreign competition had the effect of inviting new foreign competition. The new higher prices resulting from the restraints allowed new producers like Hyundai and Yugo to enter the U.S. market in the low-priced end of the market.

The Retaliation Reality

Protection has a ripple effect that can build to tidal wave proportions. Retaliation for protective measures is a fact of international political life. It is practiced regularly by the United States and its trading partners. Were the proponents of protection to have their way and the U.S. slammed its door on such major segments of trade as computers, steel, and general electronics imports, the results would be predictably disastrous. When battles erupt over trade, the ricocheting bullets will hit almost anyone—and sometimes everyone.

In the mid-1980s the United States placed a duty on Canadian shakes and shingles. Canada promptly placed high duties on U.S. shipments of books, magazines, computers, nursery trees, cider, oatmeal, and rolled oats. When the U.S. attacked pasta from Europe in 1985, U.S. producers of lemons and walnuts fell casualty to high retaliatory duties. U.S. buyers were denied the chance to purchase Volkswagen trucks when the U.S. slapped a 25 percent duty on them in the infamous "Chicken wars" of 20 years ago, caused by European reluctance to allow importation of U.S. chicken meat.

Although they often do not realize it, many U.S. industries are already on "retaliation lists" drawn up in many foreign capitals, like an advance military order of battle ready to be triggered when the U.S. slams the import door. Many Pacific Rim countries have quietly leaked their plans to target U.S. paperboard and pulp shipments when Washington tries to raise the trade stakes. These U.S. industries would be paralyzed by such a move; those Pacific Rim nations reportedly consume 15 to 20 percent of U.S. pulp and paperboard production. U.S. farmers are also an easy, and very vulnerable target, as has been vividly demonstrated in the past. One half of Japan's wheat consumption, and most of its soybean consumption, is typically harvested from fields in Montana, Kansas, and other U.S. states, but there are farmers throughout Canada, Australia, Brazil, and Argentina who would rejoice at the chance to displace the thousands of U.S. farmers who now derive their livelihood from such sales. Under the right circumstances, it might take but a slight political misstep against Japanese computer chips, televisions, or car parts to slam that door against U.S. farmers.

The first to suffer in any retaliation is the worker. The International Labor Organization (ILO), known for its staunch labor protection positions, has itself recognized that trade protection is not in the interests of workers. The ILO has determined that the U.S. loss of export markets during the 1980s accounts for up to 10 percent of U.S. unemployment. In ceremonies commemorating Labor Day in 1987, director general Francis Blanchard remarked that "research by the ILO and other organizations and institutions clearly shows that far more jobs would be created than lost by measures designed to reduce protectionist barriers, stimulate trade, and open up markets."

For most industries, the loss of healthy globally-based competition caused by protection may be "retaliation" enough. John Weinberg, chairman of Goldman Sachs, was thinking of this in the context of the U.S. financial markets when he stated recently: "You're going to have to let others in this [U.S.] market if you want to make it a major global marketplace. Otherwise, the global market will just go elsewhere."

Our relationship with Japan, fraught with tension caused by the current disbalance of trade, is one of the most vulnerable of all to possible paralysis from protection. Japanese investors have been financing roughly 10 percent of the U.S. budget deficit through purchase of government securities. The U.S. consumes 35 to 40 percent of Japan's total exports. When Washington talks tough to Japan, quite a few U.S. companies get scared; many more would share that fear if they genuinely understood the global underpinnings of their business.

Japanese suppliers provide the lion's share of the high-speed computer chips used in the United States; in 1987 they supplied an estimated 90 percent of the U.S. market. A cutoff of that supply would send not only computer makers but the thousands of companies who supply them with other parts into a disastrous tailspin. Soybean and wheat growers are not the only farmers with a big stake in Japan. The country annually buys over $5 billion worth of U.S. farm products, making it the biggest customer in the world for the U.S. farmer.

Sitting on the sidelines in misery throughout any trade wars will be the world financial community in New York, London, Tokyo, Frankfurt, and elsewhere. As doors slammed in the United States, the developing countries with the largest debts would be losing their biggest export market, and therefore their biggest source of hard currency to pay that debt. Indeed, the resulting freezeup of trade would dry up the export revenues of most nations, which are the source of currency to pay international obligations.

Protection feeds on protection. Antitrade maneuvering, once initiated, escalates rapidly, threatening the world with virtual gridlock in its trading system. Anyone who doesn't believe that point has but to look in the history books for proof. Many of the most inimical effects of the Great Depression can be traced to the simple fact that doors across the globe were slammed shut. As a result of an out-of-control sequence of retaliation and protection, protection and retaliation, epitomized by the United States' own Smoot-Hawley Act of 1930, trade evaporated. In retrospect, the protectionism that spawned that law played perhaps the biggest role of all in turning the Roaring Twenties into the Great Depression. After that 1930 legislation against imports, *U.S. exports plummeted 70 percent in four years* as a result of overseas retaliation.

The Quota Kings

Nothing illustrates the absurdity of protection better than the nature of the quota system which the United States uses to regulate the importation of textiles, sugar, footwear, and certain other products whose industry leaders were able to persuade Washington to insulate them from the pressure of foreign competition. The story of Hong Kong's experience under textile and apparel quota systems sharply reflects the lack of understanding U.S. policymakers have of the trade issues as well as their understanding of the industry they purport to protect.

In 1960, Hong Kong garment producers were essentially a group of small firms eking out an existence by making and selling into the lowest end of the U.S. garment market with clothing of poor quality and minimal fashion appeal. U.S. producers had a stronghold on high-value, high-quality, high-profit garments. Even then they were protected by a tariff which was five times greater than the average for most other goods. Yet those producers and their unions, flush with political power, convinced themselves and lawmakers that they were threatened by these factories on the other side of the planet. They then embarked on a course, which to an objective observer in retrospect, would seem to have been nothing less than a well-laid plan to strengthen and enrich those foreign producers. In 1962 the U.S Congress imposed a quota system to restrict imports of the cotton clothing being produced in Hong Kong.

The obvious and immediate effect of quotas is the shrinkage of supply. As any economics freshman could attest, the inevitable result of a limited supply is an increase in prices. There has never been a quota in the world trading system that did not result in higher prices to consumers. In Hong Kong, this meant that previously struggling producers who held U.S. quota rights began to realize not only large profits but, more importantly, profits that were virtually guaranteed as long as they held quota rights.

Garments of synthetic and wool fabrics had presented markets of interest to the Asians, but they previously had not had the resources to invest in new production. Since there was no significant production, such garments were not subject to quota limits. With their new cash windfall from the quotas that in the minds of the U.S. sponsors of this protection were supposed to limit Asian production, the Asians began to build new factories for synthetic and wool garments of much higher quality. These new garments were an even more direct threat to the U.S. industry, who had, in effect, created this new competition. Not surprisingly, new quotas on these products were established by 1972.

The cycle continued with breakneck speed. With the windfall profits brought to them by the second round of U.S. quotas, the Hong Kong producers moved into the remaining products not covered by the limits: linen, silk, and ramie garments. Within a few short years, Washington and the U.S. textile industry had almost single-handedly made Hong Kong the largest garment producer on the planet.

As the cycle continued, the now wealthy Hong Kong producers constructed new capacity in countries not covered by quotas, such as the People's Republic of China, Indonesia, and Malaysia. Doubtlessly by now many of these newly created millionaires were wondering when the Americans would come to their senses. It was the ultimate in U.S. foreign aid. The American government had given these Chinese producers guaranteed markets, guaranteed profits, and guaranteed longevity of sales for as long as the quotas continued.

Some of the Asian producers even left behind the "nuisance" of manufacturing, closing down and simply selling their quota rights for veritable fortunes. The Institute for International Economics has calculated that buying, selling, and auctioning of textile and apparel quota rights brings foreign producers $5 billion annually.[5]

---

[5]Institute for International Economics, *Auction Quotas and United States Trade Policy* (September 1987).

The U.S. industry and its political allies seemed hell-bent on continuing this aid program. When they demanded and obtained new quotas for the new countries and new products, the next round of profits to the producers allowed them to spread their network further. Layer after layer, the quotas, profits, and new foreign capacity continue to pile up. The latest development has been extension of these foreign garment empires into remote lands of the Indian Ocean such as Mauritius and the Maldive Islands. Who says the U.S. government bestows no royal titles? The Congress has turned Asian producers of apparel into virtual kings.

Similar patterns can be traced for virtually every quota the United States has ever tried. In 1984 when substantial restraints were imposed through voluntary quotas on steel imports, 14 primary producing nations sold to the United States and were included in the restrictions. By 1985 imports were pouring in from 76 countries. Producers in Eastern Europe, never serious world players in the past, were given new vitality by being able to suddenly ship to the United States at high prices. Factories in Romania, East Germany, Poland, Hungary, Czechoslovakia, and Yugoslavia accounted for 2.6 percent of U.S. imports in 1984; in the first half of 1985 they accounted for 35 percent.

When the U.S. government proudly announced the semiconductor accord in July 1986 to control Japanese invasion of yet another industry that had been invented by U.S. companies, no one seemed to have considered such past records. The accord sought to set minimum prices for Japanese products sold anywhere outside Japan. The arrangement immediately caused prices in Japan to sharply drop, hurting U.S. sales there. A gray market, moving chips through nontraditional channels (such as airline carryon bags stuffed with thousands of chips) quickly developed around the world. Not surprisingly, users across the globe declined to cooperate with the U.S. price fixing. Most U.S. firms only became weaker, accelerating foreign efforts to acquire them.

In 1986 the annual windfall to foreign producers from U.S. quotas was calculated by analysts at the Institute for International Economics and the Brookings Institution. The figures for *extra profits to foreign producers alone* were found to be $3.5 billion annually for apparel, $2.8 billion for steel, $2.5 billion for cars, $570 million for textiles, $560 million for sugar, $320 million for machine tools, and $300 million for dairy products. Not included in these figures were the huge corresponding profits to U.S. producers and indirect costs incurred in other industries (e.g., higher tractor prices due to the use of higher priced steel), all paid for by U.S. consumers.

Maginot Politics

The global economy itself is the greatest mediator of protectionism. There has never been a quota or similar restriction that could not be beaten, and beaten very profitably, by global competitors. Unfair trade can be beaten. Persistent dumping, subsidization, and similiar actions always come back to haunt those who practice them.

The shrewd global enterprise understands that protectionist restrictions mean two things: higher prices (and higher profits) and inattentive managers in the protected industry. The global enterprise always knows those managers are going to be behind their wall, patting each other on the back, and losing any competitive edge they may have had.

The moment the French completed the Maginot Line, the lives of German strategists became much simpler. They knew where the French opposition was going to be, what their priorities were, and what they were thinking. The moment the Chinese completed the Long Wall of Ten Thousand Li, their society began a long decline into decay. When the U.S. textile industry succeeded in erecting a protectionist Great Wall, life for Asian apparel producers became much simpler—and vastly more profitable.

Becoming Global by Competing, Not Hiding

In the global economy protection is no longer the mentality of the fortress, but of the prison. The protectionist wall doesn't keep the foreigners out. It keeps the domestic industry in. This is one of the most fundamental elements of global perspective. Another element, closely aligned, is the simple reality that over the long term international business problems will never be solved on a political basis. These perspectives have too often been obscured by widespread misunderstanding of the effects of our goods and capital deficits and the dynamics of protection—a major element in our fallacious trade folklore, our myths of trade.

A British manager in the electronics industry spent a day on Capitol Hill in 1986 listening to Congressional hearings on proposals to protect his U.S. competitors. When asked of his reaction to experiencing firsthand the sponsors of U.S. protectionism, he made a few diplomatic comments, then finally seemed unable to contain his true thoughts. "My God, they're playing with rules made for a world that no longer exists," he stated in frustration.

In another era, if Britain was peeved at Portugal, it could erect protective tariffs against Madeira and port; London wineshops could restock their shelves with other vintages and life continued as normal. Protection is never such a simple matter of refilling shelves from other inventories in today's global economy. In that economy capital, technology, merchandise, and legal rights move with interdependence like myriad gears of a complex machine. That machine has created a world far removed from that simple mercantile one in which trade protection was historically exercised. To interject protection today is tantamount to stripping the gears of that machine—or severing entire economic sprockets.

Protection is based on a perception that the ultimate goal of a country in the world economy is to increase its exports, that the essence of that economy is the import/export flow of merchandise across national borders. In today's global economy such a view is an anachronism.

From another perspective, protection is the preservation of the status quo. Vast political stakes are, in any system, vested in the status quo, meaning protective legislative proposals will always be made. But if maintenance of the status quo were always in our best interest, we would all be living in caves objecting to the suggestion of that radical device, the wheel.

It is wrong to leap to the opposite extreme and insist that totally unrestricted free trade benefits all people in all places. Free trade is unquestionably good for business and industries as a whole. But it can be very bad for a specific factory, a specific location, or a specific work force. Those factories, locations, and workers are, of course, those who are inefficient, overly costly, and often mismanaged. The free enterprise system weeds these out, whereas protection ensures their survival, at a grossly wasteful cost to society. If an industry is struggling with global competition, the problem must be squarely confronted, not delayed. In the worst cases, adjustment assistance may be needed from the taxpayers to cushion the blow to displaced workers and move them into more viable sectors. Such programs are already on the books in the United States and other industrial countries. In the United States we must learn to use them more aggressively.

Fortunately the most fervent of the protectionist "true believers" are slowly losing their religion. While the textile industry continued its perennial quest for added protection, many major producers have in recent years quietly bitten the bullet and restructured. U.S. textile and apparel companies are now spending 8 percent of sales for automated facilities and factory improvements. Links between retailers, clothing producers, and textile mills have been automated for vastly improved efficiency in ordering and inventory management. The U.S. industry has made a long-needed capacity trim of 10 percent. Although they still clamor for protection, U.S. textile producers now are among the most efficient in the world. Today they are exporting much of their production. Even the most zealous of textile protectionists would have a hard time arguing that such measures would have been taken had the import door been locked as tightly as they had hoped.

Such procompetitive measures are the ultimate answer for any industry feeling the pressure of global competition. The reverse course is that of the ostrich, burying its head to avoid reality, using rules made for an obsolete world.

Yet some industries cannot seem to break the protection habit. Certain members of the steel industry still clamor for protection. In 1988 a major campaign for protection was mounted in Washington, despite the fact that domestic steel mills were operating at 90 percent capacity, 1988 industry net earnings were computed at $2 billion, and shortages even existed for some products. U.S. autoproducers mounted a familiar campaign in early 1989 to seek a 25 percent tariff on imported minivans, despite the fact that Detroit was already making high profits on such vehicles and dominated the U.S. market for them. Letters from Detroit urging dealers to support the tariff emphasized not the need for protection but that the tariff's effect would be to impose a $2,000 penalty on imported vehicles.

The course of protection invariably is a course of insecurity for workers, management, and shareholders. In barest analysis, it perhaps represents nothing less than abject fear of the future. As then Treasury Secretary James Baker stated in 1987, "We can become competitive only by competing, not by closing ourselves off from the world."

This means that the greater distance an enterprise, and an industry, can obtain from government protection, the better. Ultimately, protection in today's economy amounts to a home for the desperate, constructed by the misinformed. It is never progress. That most unbusinesslike American, Henry David Thoreau, may not have been speaking of international business, but he conveyed the point exceedingly well when he commented over a century ago. "No government ever furthered an enterprise but by the alacrity by which it got out of the way." Chairman Robert Allen of AT&T, which has stumbled over protectionist pressures frequently around the globe, has described the problem in more contemporary terms. "Protectionist barriers are to economies what steroids are to athletes—a temporary fix and a long-term disaster."

CHAPTER 6

BLINDED BY THE RISING SUN

If the collective international business community were to lie on a psychoanalyst's couch to unravel the many knots entangling it, the first diagnosis inescapably would be "severe Tokyo-psychosis". The disorder would be classified in the analyst's text as a form of schizophrenia: A phobia of Japanese economic forces nervously coexisting beside an infatuation with Japanese business techniques.

For many policymakers and managers this disorder has become a crutch, an obsession, and a scapegoat all in one. For nearly everyone active internationally, it has distorted the way global business is perceived and therefore the perceived path toward success in that business. The only viable prescription for the malady is a strong dose of global reality.

Keeping Up with the Japanese

To a large segment of our population, international business issues are, for better or worse, Japanese issues. For managers across the continent, and much of the industrial world, if international techniques are studied at all, they are Japanese techniques. High-value, high-tech Japanese products equate to high-fashion around the globe. Japanese *kanban* just-in-time inventory procedures are discussed in reverent tones by consultants and CEOs. Japanese quality circles are hailed as a revolutionary idea in factories from Kankakee to Kuala Lumpur. The Japanese corporation, the *kaisha*, is spoken of reverently as the paragon of transnational enterprise.

A speaker at a recent New York seminar on exporting captured the popular sentiment. As he, and many others have bitterly convinced themselves, the U.S. trade problems all stem from the fact that the Japanese have "just been too damned good" at international business.

By being too good at dispersing their goods across the planet, the Japanese have struck sensitive nerves in broad segments of Western society. The wave of foreign investment in our country is, to the popular mind, Japanese investment. When we read about foreign investment in the headlines, it is the Japanese purchaser of an office tower, the contruction of a Japanese auto plant, or the acquisition of an American semiconductor maker (even when, in the must publicized case involving Fairchild Semiconductor, the U.S. company was already owned by a French firm whose original purchase had raised little public notice).

The net effect has been to make the Japanese investor in the United States appear as the most active of all foreign investors. Certainly the investors from the East have attracted much more attention than the more low-profile Dutch and British, whose respective investments still exceed those of the Japanese in the United States.

When governors send delegations to woo large international firms, it is more often than not to Tokyo. When states open up foreign outposts to solicit investment, the almost universal choice of venue has been Tokyo. At last report over 35 of them had offices in the Japanese capital.

Seminars around the industrial world on international business methods may have myriad titles but a large percentage of their themes could be reduced to a common denominator of learning the "secrets" of "how the Japanese do it." More specifically, the themes might be characterized as: How the Japanese have knocked the socks off American firms; How to beat Japan at its own game; How to join in transpacific alliances to capitalize on Japanese skills; How *the* country that "lives for trade" functions; or How Western *gaijin* managers must learn to think like their counterparts from the Land of the Rising Sun in order to succeed in the world markets.

Americans have been indoctrinated by countless professors, authors, consultants, reporters, politicians, and senior managers to revere the global alacrity of the Japanese. To the "right thinking" business mind, Japanese companies are the quintessential global players. Since the early 1980s, Americans who bought a book on how to forge the successful international enterprise were almost inevitably soon stumbling over names like Toyota, Canon, and Sony, as well as terms like *kanban, kaisha, zaibatsu* (Japanese industrial combines), *sogoshosha* (general trading companies), or *senmonshosha* (specialized trading companies). Just being able to pronounce such words turned many readers into self-appointed experts on international business.

Many managers in the United States and Europe have indeed fallen under the Japanese spell. Factories across North America are organized to be more Japanese. At a new Peugeot plant in France, over $100 million has been budgeted for the express purpose of training workers in Japanese-style assembly techniques. Many managers have convinced themselves that it is the height of folly to open a new factory without a strong dose of soy sauce and *sushi*. In a 1988 nationwide survey of U.S. CEOs, 86 percent said that Japan had the world's most competitive economy.

If the world of international business were gauged by the emphasis of the media, the subject of seminars, or the topics of popular books, then it would indeed seem that our planet is in the lockgrip of Japan, Inc. To those who reduce the complexities of trade to a bumper sticker mentality, this means we are supposed to anticipate a day when our children will all be washing the windows of Japanese executives, and cashing their paychecks in yen. At the other end of the spectrum, many international business gurus would presumably rejoice over a total assimilation of Japanese practices; certainly the idols they have been worshipping in the past years have had a distinctly Eastern cast.

Rising Sun, Blinding Sun

Without question, the Japanese economy enjoyed comparative advantages over the countries of the West for many years, advantages obtained through industriousness and sacrifice and a distinctly different internal economic structure. The country created an export machine unparalleled on the planet today or ever before in history. The "Japanese miracle" is well documented, and the island nation deserves great respect for having amassed such vast economic power in a land that was never blessed with raw materials. That economic power, based on hundreds of billions of dollars in export earnings, cannot be disputed. Nor is it reasonable to dispute that Japan and many of its corporations will continue to play a substantial role in the global economy for the foreseeable future.

The critical point of this chapter, however, and the point that is almost invariably missed in the chronicles of Japanese success, is that we have misinterpreted that success. This misinterpretation has perverted our perspectives on international business. The net effect of our emphasis on Japan, Japan, Japan has been to create a profound distraction in our international business efforts. In a nutshell, that distraction is our totally false perception of Japanese infallibility.

To lend unabated allegiance to the Japanese way is absurd. No national policy, no international enterprise, or group of enterprises is ever perfect. The belief that somewhere, behind a bamboo veil, exists a panacea for all international business problems may be a comfort, but it is a totally false comfort. There is, moreover, little evidence that most Japanese managers are proficient at handling anything more than an exporting enterprise. Their record of creating truly global enterprises is limited and, at best, mixed in its results.

Japan and its enterprises are in many ways ill-prepared for dealing with the rigors of today's changing environment. Cracks are appearing in the well-oiled machinery that has driven the Japanese economy for so many years. Recognition of those flaws, as discussed more fully below, is a vital first step in stepping away from the Tokyo-psychosis that is handicapping the global efforts of many Western firms.

Without question, valuable lessons can be learned from Japanese companies and Japanese government practice. But those lessons include both the negative and the positive, examples of how to do things wrong as well as how to do them right. The truly accurate compendium of Japanese international practice would contain as many chapters on failures as on successes. Japanese companies are far from perfect. Otherwise thousands of them would not fall into bankruptcy every year, and the country for many years has suffered from one of the highest rates of corporate bankruptcy in the world.[1]

The truly realistic assessment of the Japanese phenomenon must also underscore the fundamental point that what may have worked for a Japanese firm in its non-Western home environment may easily prove disastrous when emulated in the West. The Japanese system and the Japanese corporation offer no cure-all for the Western firm in its effort to succeed in the global economy. In many cases their examples may be as relevant to the Western firm as that of a used yurt seller in Outer Mongolia. The best lessons for the enterprise attempting to join the ranks of the global successes are not from any government, not from any set of companies, but from individual enterprises which have truly mastered the global economy. A few of these are Japanese. Most are not.

---

[1]"Behind the Export Explosion, A Battered Home Market," *Forbes*, July 2, 1984.

CRACKS IN THE STRUCTURE

Many of the "Japan" books so ravenously consumed in the West are clouded by such passion over the "Japanese conspiracy" or the supposed "Japan, Inc." juggernaut that they border on the "yellow peril" mania that swept the West in a bygone era. Several of these volumes continue to be released every year. A recent one which sold widely in the United States described the Japanese plot to acquire the state of California, thereby eliminating the Western computer industry by taking over Silicon Valley.

As might be expected when emotion rules, such reports, in creating an impression of Japanese omnipotence, gloss over many critical aspects of vulnerability in the Japanese system. In the past, Japan as a nation reaped the benefits of an unparalleled export machine, a hardworking, self-sacrificing work force, and a stable, harmonious internal market structure, all of which were supported by a unique government/business interrelationship. Compelling reasons exist today to question the current viability of each of these cornerstones that have supported the Japanese businessman around the world.

Maekawa Report: The Kudohka Threat

A document of profound importance to Western businesses was released over two years ago in Tokyo. Unfortunately, its issuance was noted in the back pages of a handful of magazines and otherwise widely ignored in the West. Inside Japan the document was broadly circulated but few Japanese were interested in sharing it with the West. When pressed they even characterized it as being of no relevance to the West. Some observers said instead that the Japanese were simply embarrassed by it since, in looking to the Japan of the future, the government sponsored report pointed out a number of self-destructive flaws in the Japanese economic structure.

Certainly the document should have been, and still should be, of great interest and concern to anyone in the West. The analysis was entitled the *Maekawa Report*. Its subject, by its own terms: "economic structural adjustment for international harmony." In more direct terms it may have been characterized as "how to mend the cracks that threaten to destroy the engine of Japanese prosperity."

The *Maekawa Report* provided some of the first explicit warnings that all is not well in the Land of the Rising Sun. Since then events have overtaken those warnings. Many of the country's smokestack industries are staggering along, introducing the specter of wholesale unemployment in the country of *shushin koyo*, or lifetime employment. Laments over the *kudohka*, or "hollowing" of the Japanese economy are regularly heard in the corridors of Japanese government and business. The nation's cumbersome distribution and retail structure is emerging as a major handicap to growth. The real estate markets of the country are running amok, creating widespread social problems and threatening the stability of not only the Tokyo Stock Exchange but the financial markets of the West as well.

Meanwhile, the government quietly amasses a public debt that is among the largest in the world, a practice which seems to be one of the best kept secrets on the planet. Amid all of this the average Japanese consumer in this seeming storehouse of wealth is emerging both as a victim, forced into a standard of living below that of the United States, and as the strongest hope for rationalizing the country's structure and its role in the world economy. That role is an increasingly important one. The day is past when any of the above economic ills can be characterized as merely Japanese domestic problems. In the global economy, the economic ills of Japan, just as those of every other region of primary production and consumption, are ills suffered by the entire planet.

The Japanese Rust Belt

The scene is a somber one: Grim-faced, middle-aged men gather under a grey sky outside an aged, mammoth factory building. They exchange painful goodbyes. Some fight back tears. Many are numb with the news as they walk along abandoned railtracks. They watch with disbelief as more and more of their coworkers stumble out of the building with the same shocked expression. One thousand of them have lost their jobs on this bleak winter day.

The venue for this scene might be a 1970s West Virginia or Pennsylvania coal and steel town. But in reality it is one of the industrial cities of Japan. It is a face of Japan that has been too long obscured to the West.

Between November 1985 and November 1986, Japanese manufacturing industries eliminated a total of 260,000 jobs. The cumulative effect of the strong yen, shifts in markets, new technology, competition from newly industrializing countries, and inefficient industries created by government protection is expected to double the Japanese unemployment rate in the next five years, pushing it up to 5 percent and more. This is not merely troublesome, it is revolutionary change in a nation where for the past 30 years the unemployment rate has never surpassed 3 percent, the nation in which *shushin koyo* promises workers a job for life.

Towns centered on coal, steel, shipbuilding and other heavy industries are developing broad sectors of empty houses. Many more are being abandoned. The Japanese Labor Ministry has determined that 2 million workers will need to shift out of manufacturing industries by 1993 to take stress off the economy. In the coal industry less than 30 years ago 622 coal mines operated, employing over 230,000 workers; today only 30 mines remain, employing less than 15,000.

In the Japanese press a town that frequently is cited as a symbol of the hollowing of the Japanese economy is the industrial city of Muroran, on the northern island of Hokkaido. The population of the city has dropped by nearly 20 percent since its boom days of shipbuilding and steel production. Its once bustling shipyards are closed. Its steel furnaces no longer light the night sky. The city's mayor often reminisces publicly about the days when 500 workers were employed at the local train station to handle the crush of shipments. Today the volume of products through the station requires 10 workers.

Japanese planners once were able to move workers from "twilight" industries into the production created as new markets were opened overseas. This outlet is no longer available in today's slow-growth economy. The Japanese psyche has never taken defeat well, meaning restructuring is a long, drawn out, and overly costly affair. Losses of $2.5 billion were incurred before the nation surrendered its aluminum smelting industry.

In the past, under the *shushin koyo* system, many redundant workers were also shuttled into the *shukko* network in which interrelated companies accepted excess workers to avoid layoffs, or firings, or forced retirement. That system has been stretched to the limits. It has been calculated by Sanwa Bank that Japanese companies are paying $26 billion a year to support an estimated 900,000 displaced workers through such inefficient devices. The Japan Railways company has attempted to branch into the fast food and bookstore businesses in order to find work for 60,000 displaced employees.

In a major departure from tradition, some major companies such as Nissan and Mitsubishi Motors have announced that they will no longer accept other companies' laid-off workers. Other heavy industry firms such as Nippon Steel are turning to arrangements whereby workers are in rotating layoff for a few days each month. Even with such measures Nippon Steel in 1987 closed five major blast furnaces, eliminating 19,000 jobs.

As in the United States and anywhere else such restructuring occurs, the human toll sometimes becomes tragic. Families are split up as bread-winners must move away to find gainful employment. More than a few suicides of distraught union officials and unemployed workers have been reported.

The Closet Debtor

In the West we have concluded that Japan is a frugal nation. Anyone who reads even a fraction of the voluminous "us versus them" commentary comparing the United States and Japan is aware of the fact that the Japa-nese save more than the freewheeling Americans. Japanese companies, takeover shy and accustomed to conservative, long-standing financial re-lationships with banking members of their extended corporate "families," are often contrasted with their profligate debt-happy counterparts in the West.

At the bottom of this structure, however, can be found a government that is anything but frugal. Japan's public debt burden is one of the heav-iest of any industrial country, imposing a burden on its government and taxpayers that far exceeds, on a proportional basis, that in the United States. In 1985 Japan's public debt represented over 69 percent of its GNP, compared with only 48 percent in the United States. In many years interest on that debt has absorbed one fifth of all public spending. In the West any knowledgeable voter knows that budgets could be easily bal-anced—and debt avoided—but for the necessities of defense spending. Japan has found ways to build up staggering debt without any substantial defense spending, relying as it does on the umbrella protection of the U.S. military forces.

The Japanese private sector reflects a similarly high reliance on debt, borrowing at levels that their Western counterparts would consider un-healthy. In 1989 trading company giant Mitsubishi, for example, had a debt equity ratio of 324 percent. Its megacompetitor, C. Itoh, had a ratio of 479 percent.

Bullet Train Relics

Although the Japanese Diet, the national congress, has pursued its own style of Gramm-Rudman budget cutting—through its "minus zero ceiling" policy of setting absolute ceilings then cutting from that fixed point—such efforts are totally undermined by public works spending in the country. The government has decided that the stimulation of the domestic economy so desperately needed requires massive channeling of funds into public works. Another perspective is that the federal government in Tokyo is addicted to pork barrels of such vast proportions that they wouldn't even fit in the fantasies of a U.S. Congressman. The Liberal Democratic Party that has ruled Japan for many years has perhaps learned far too well the link between shiny new schools or train stations and local voter support.

When economists in Japan complain about their nation's inability to address the restructuring it so desperately needs, they often do so by pointing to public works. A tiny hamlet of 55 families, Ushiroyama, received a $16 million tunnel to make it easier to navigate winter roads. 1988 marked the completion of the 86 mile long tunnel under Tsugaru Strait, completing the direct road link between Tokyo and Sapporo. As a result, if anyone is so inclined (few are, since frequent air service is available), they can make the drive in 12 and a half hours instead of the previous 14 hours. The cost for this great time saver was $8.4 billion. The first of three bridges to the lightly populated Shikoku Island was also completed in 1988. Traffic has been only half that projected. Still work continues on the next two bridges. The cost of the first was *$9 billion.*

With all the tunnels, schools, public halls, sewage systems, and bridges heaped upon the country by the ruling Liberal Democratic Party, Japan has used more cement annually than all of the United States. Officials have publicly stated that they expect the government to spend the equivalent of *trillions* of dollars for additional public works projects before the end of the century.

A vivid symbol of Japan's profligacy is its famed bullet train, which sucks in public funds the way an astronomer's black hole absorbs light. A tour of one of the most recently completed segments is an eye-opener to the observer trying to ascertain why the Japanese economy seems to be in gridlock. The Tokyo to Niigata line stretches for 170 miles northwest of the capital city. It cost $10 billion to construct. Extravagant stations were erected along the route, often in remote mountain towns; some cost $100 million. Forty percent of the line was placed in tunnels, the remainder in a specially constructed viaduct. Snow along the route is melted automatically by a system of hot water sprayers. The government paid farmers (only in the past could they be called "peasant" farmers) as much as $810,000 an acre for farmland in the rail corridor.

Indeed, a major portion of all public works spending is funneled right into the pockets of land owners, owners who often have already been made wealthy by the distorted real estate markets in the country, discussed below. This, of course, casts grave doubt over the traditional justification for such public works: that they broadly disseminate funds into the pockets of the Japanese consumer. For many projects, land acquisition costs exceed 90 percent of the total price tag to the taxpayers.

Such massive public works spending may have made sense when the Japanese infrastructure was weak, the government had no serious debt problems, and the rest of the industrial world could afford to be cavalier about events in Japanese consumer markets. That day is past. Infrastructure improvement in the form of basics—for example sewer lines and highways—are needed, but not extravagant high profile political monuments. In the words of one Japanese economist, with which many others nod agreement, the bullet train is nothing more than an "historic relic" of a former age in which Japanese economic growth seemed boundless, a symbol of Japan's inattention to the exigencies of the global economy.

Middleman, Middleman, Middleman

There is probably no greater handicap to the Japanese economy than its archaic distribution system. A long stream of foreign companies have stumbled upon the costly inefficient system in which layer after layer of distributor, subdistributor, sub-subdistributor, and other middlemen sell into industrial accounts they have "owned" for decades. Typically, these include tiny retail outlets. The average product in the Japanese home market passes through seven layers of distribution. In the United States and Britain, by contrast, three layers are usually utilized. Roughly 25 percent of the Japanese workforce is dedicated to distribution of products, compared to 5 to 10 percent in Western countries. Distribution costs in the country mushroom the final sales price of an import by as much as 300 to 500 percent. Even for domestic goods the distribution system typically adds at least 50 to 100 percent to the final price. The streamlined efficiency which characterizes Japan's export industries seems an alien concept in the country's domestic markets. *It costs a Japanese company less to distribute its products in the United States than in its native country.*

A 1988 incident sharply highlighted the burden shouldered by the Japanese consumer. During that year astounding bargains in cordless telephones were discovered by some consumers. The reason was that enterprising vendors had bought the Japanese-made phones in the United States, outside the cumbersome Japanese distribution system. Even with the 15,000 mile detour the phones sold for *one eighth* the prevailing Japanese market price. A nervous Japanese manufacturer finally solved the problem by buying up all the discount phones.

The victims of this system are first and foremost the 120 million Japanese consumers. Traditionally, the Japanese consumer often has been stuck with what was left at the bottom of the barrel, or the back of the warehouse, after export markets were satisfied. In the past, Japanese travelers outside their country have been awed by the diversity of products, and the diversity of prices, they find in foreign stores. Not infrequently the unfamiliar product they rush to buy has been made in Japan. Japanese companies have filled foreign markets with goods while treating their home market as if it were a developing country.

Without a strong consumer market, Japan's long-overdue campaign to pump up the domestic economy will fall flat on its face. Gradually the country is coming to grips with the issue. A new bureau for product distribution can be found in Ministry of International Trade and Industry (MITI). Government economic planners are investigating why agents and distributors must receive so much compensation for their services. Japanese seminars and Japanese media, perhaps prematurely, are hailing the "opening" of the Japanese consumer market much as they lauded the opening of China a decade earlier.

The Ministry of Posts and Telecommunications has even entered the fray by establishing catalog ordering operations at key post offices. Patrons can buy stamps and then order consumer goods directly from manufacturers' catalogs, to be paid for COD at the post office. In cities throughout the country, stores specializing in goods directly imported from the newly industrializing countries can be found, displaying embarrassingly large price differentials when compared to competing goods from Japan's traditional distribution channels.

Point of sales data systems are being installed in many stores. Western franchise operations are catching on, introducing important efficiencies, including inventory control measures which, ironically in the land of *kanban* inventory for manufacturing, have plagued the retail sector. The 7-Eleven chain has over 3,000 units in the country and has become a significant force in introducing the Japanese distribution system to the 20th Century.

Low-Tech Japan?

A surprising reflection of the way Japan's export preoccupation has distorted its domestic economy is the fact that much of the country is far
behind the United States in absorbing high technology electronic products. Simple devices such as telecopiers are plentiful in the country—and
commonly used to transmit maps in Japan's cities, where street numbers
follow no logical sequence and offer no clue of physical location. But,
despite the fact that many of them originate in Japanese factories, the
most sophisticated devices that are commonplace in the United States are
alien to many Japanese office workers.

Personal computers are used in only 20 percent of Japanese offices.
U.S. lawyers and others involved in investigations of Japanese sales to
the United States under the antidumping or countervailing duty laws are
shocked to find that major corporations often compile their sales data by
the use of the abacus and pencil. When such investigations require the
amassing of data on scores of thousands of sales, the effort is not infrequently made by using platoons of office workers who scurry about to
collate original shipping papers.

Even among the ranks of the companies considered high-tech, a ratio
of 11 workers to each machine has been calculated, compared to 4 to 1 in
the United States. Even without serious competition, Lotus Corporation
has sold only 100,000 of its 1-2-3 software packages in Japan. Its U.S.
sales exceed 4 million units. On a per capita basis the U.S. level of installed computer power is three times that of Japan.[2]

Some of the hottest high-tech competition in recent years has been in
sales of cellular phones. Matsushita and NEC Corporation of Japan have
been leading world suppliers. Although the electronic infrastructure is in
place, in 1987, as a result of the country's distribution system—including
the government regulations that help preserve it—56,000 phones were
installed in all of Japan. In the United States, with a population twice that
of Japan, the number was 1.1 million.

The $120 Melon

The penalty for Japan's inefficient internal distribution system and its
concommitant export focus is by no means confined to the high-tech sec-

---

[2]George Gilder, "IBM TV?," *Forbes*, February 20, 1989.

tor. Similar availability problems and/or high prices can be found throughout the consumer sector. For many basic commodities the worst of the Japan distribution formula is reflected in the country's Large Scale Retailer's Law. That law gives the small "momma-san and poppa-san" operations that predominate in the retail sector a total veto over the establishment of competitors. Not surprisingly, it has sharply suppressed the introduction of efficient retail operations. Any retailer seeking to open a shop larger than the size of the average convenience store (500 square meters) must be approved first by local shopkeepers. For any shop larger than 1500 square meters approval by MITI is required. The sole purpose of the law, not surprisingly, is unabashed protection of existing merchants and the multilayered system that supplies them. Sixty percent of Japanese retail sales are through these small, costly shops; for comparable operations in the United States the figure is less than 5 percent.

The result of such protection is predictable. The top 200 retailers account for only one fourth of total sales in the country. In the industrial West, one fourth of sales are typically conducted by a handful of large and efficient, inexpensive operators. In Great Britain, for example, only four retailers account for one fourth the trade.

The sharpest evidence of all is found in the price tags for consumer goods. A shirt with a price tag of $30 in New York may sell for $150 in Tokyo. A cup of coffee or soft drink may cost $4. A pound of hamburger often costs the equivalent of $20. And incredibly, some melons can be found in the grocery store with a price tag equivalent to $120. Of course, those are gourmet melons. Ordinary muskmelons are a mere $30. Japanese consumers must spend at least 26 percent of their income on food, compared to less than 15 percent for the average American.

The distribution system for foodstuffs incorporates the additional consumer penalties of import barriers and subsidies. With free entry of foreign goods, the Japanese consumers would pay one tenth of what they currently pay for rice. Japanese subsidies for farmers are the highest in the world, exceeding 100 percent for some products.

Yet the distribution system is but one aspect of the burden Japanese citizens bear. Their plight is caused by a tangled web of economic factors. While 90 percent of Japanese characterize themselves as belonging to the middle class, the description may be an exaggeration to many Westerners. As economics professor Kimihiro Masamura of Kawasaki's Senshu University has noted, "Japan's middle class is not really middle class by anyone else's standards, and it will probably never be rich by international standards. Japan's middle class is lower class."

The Real Estate Time Bomb

If the investors around the world who agonize over the U.S. budget deficit or trade deficit as distortions of the world economy want something to really fret about, they should look to the Japanese real estate market. The cumulative effect of dollar/yen manipulations, piecemeal market openings, and political jawboning as efforts to decongest the Japanese economy are more than offset by the effect of that real estate market. The simple reason is real estate prices that only can be characterized as near-lunacy absorb billions of dollars that desperately need to be diverted to the consumer sector, and thereby more diversely into the global economy.

In downtown Tokyo 2,200 square foot apartments sell for the equivalent of $10 to $15 million each. In the city's central districts a "Donald Trump in the making" might be found on every corner, some of them dishing out soup. It was reported in 1987 that the owner of a 450 square foot noodle shop in Tokyo's financial district sold the property for $14 million. Rental rates in downtown Tokyo averaged $650 a square foot in 1988, $250 higher than in Manhattan and nearly triple the rate on Rodeo Drive in Beverly Hills.[3] The average cost for a condominium, often half the size considered livable in the West, within a 90 minute commuting radius of Tokyo, was $570,000 in 1987.

When Argentine taxpayers protested in 1987 over the $500 million to $1 billion price tag of their government's plan to move the capital from Buenos Aires to Patagonia, the government announced a foolproof solution: The sale of the country's embassy in Tokyo would more than cover the expense of the move.

When Tokyo city officials studied the feasibility of building a simple 7 kilometer road to link the port area with the city center, the cost was projected at approximately $7 billion, with land acquisition representing 95 percent of that figure. In 1988, the total current market value of all the land in Japan, one twenty-fifth the size of the United States, was calculated to be *twice the value of all real estate in the United States.*

The payback period for a typical office building in Tokyo is now over 100 years. Japanese banks have been forced to introduce the multi-

---

[3]"Tokyo Ginza District Tops Global Retail Rental Study," *The Wall Street Journal*, February 9, 1989.

generational mortgage, by which Japanese couples are able to borrow the vast sums needed to acquire a house with the agreement that their children will complete repayment of the loan. The system gives a whole new meaning to the term *mortgaging the future*.

The phenomenon is exacerbated by the compression of available land in the country. Nature, through mountain ranges, has removed almost two thirds of the land from possible use. Farming uses one half of the remainder. Despite gross inefficiencies those farms are well-preserved by the politically powerful *Zenchu* farmers' organization. A significant part of the problem also lies in the country's tax system.

That tax framework penalizes sellers with a high capital gains tax on land but encourages holding of property through artificially low property taxes. The holder of a million dollar property in Tokyo pays between $1,000 to $2,000 annually in property taxes. Those playing the anachronistic, and socially costly, role of "urban farmer" (less than 50 percent of the land in Tokyo is developed) sit on individual parcels worth scores of millions of dollars and pay almost no tax at all due to the privilege of their status. Still the political will to change the system is slow in coming. Those who have been made paper millionaires enjoy their status. Japanese farmers, wielding wildly disproportionate clout in the nation, oppose changing the status quo for obvious reasons.

The Japanese farmer's situation epitomizes the way in which the country is dragging itself down with atavistic legal and business structures. The so-called urban farmers may keep their property tax exemptions, amassing further millions, so long as they promise to continue farming for 10 years. A common tactic for qualifying is becoming a persimmon farmer, which means planting trees and waiting eight years for them to mature. Another obscure rule exacerbating the real estate crisis is the "right to sunlight rule" vested in existing landowners, which has restricted many buildings even in downtown Tokyo to just three stories.

Double-edged Sword

Not only has this land lunacy cut off the use of hundreds of billions of dollars from consumer markets, with severe effects on the foreign producers who would largely benefit from consumer purchases, the system has also lent a new and dangerous vulnerability to the global economy. Investors have borrowed funds for up to 100 percent of their inflated land values, then moved this money into a vast range of offshore investments.

Billions have flowed into the U.S. stock markets in this fashion, pumping up U.S. stock values and bringing many other investors around the world "along for the ride."

Meanwhile the Tokyo stock market has become inextricably tied into this runaway real estate market. Much of the money borrowed on this precarious collateral is also being channeled into Japanese stocks. Where are many of the investors attracted? To companies sitting on valuable real estate. That joyride will not last forever. When the bubble bursts, the explosion will be felt from Wall Street to Walla Walla.

Domestic Trade Wars?

The trade wars between Japan and the West soon may pale compared to the war that is brewing in the country's internal economy. The Japanese population is beginning to understand that government and business interests have foisted upon them the most uncompetitive and overvalued consumer market in all of the free world. They have been persuaded that they have "beaten" the United States and Europe. But they do not feel so victorious when they have to pay a premium of 100 percent over the Western price to buy a television, computer, or VCR that was made in their own country.

Likewise it's not always easy to feel the victory won by their system when they find that it is precisely because of that system, they have to pay over $100 for the steak that would cost $10 or $15 in Dallas or Sydney. The Japanese man on the street gets little joy from the privilege of paying over $400 for the Sony compact disc player that he could buy in New York for $200, or pay $800 for the Casio electronic keyboard that costs $400 in Los Angeles. Why, he is beginning to ask, in the economy that supposedly rules the world, does he have to ask tourist friends to buy Japanese-made Fuji film in America in order to save 50 percent of the price he would otherwise pay in Osaka?

Golf club memberships in Tokyo are a prime example of the degree of craziness resulting when nonmarket forces distort a consumer economy. At several clubs membership costs several hundred thousand dollars. At one, the Koganei Club, memberships have sold for over $3 million.

Gradually, through painful facts such as these, the Japanese people are beginning to recognize that the country's obsession with exports has not necessarily served them well. In the future the island nation will be paying a huge liability for the way it has neglected its domestic market through closing it to foreign competition, focusing obsessively on export production, and even permitting real estate markets to become the "tail that wags the dog." A senior adviser to the Mitsui Research Center, Jiro Tokuyama, laments about what has happened, "The United States is a land of opportunity and Japan is a land of lack of opportunity."

Japanese Business: Global Novices?

The Japanese battalions of lean, mean global enterprises that are perceived to garrison the Eastern islands in reality have very shallow ranks. A vast number of these enterprises are considered global by Western observers only because their products are found on shelves throughout the civilized world. Many of the others who have at least stepped beyond Japanese production still have far to go before they might be considered as successful global enterprises.

Traditionally, the so-called international firm in Japan has been nothing but an exporter, or often not even an exporter but a firm that sold its goods to a *sogo shosha* trading company that handled the offshore market. When the rest of the world began to realize in the 1960s that the aspersions it cast on Japanese quality were ill-founded—and, concurrently, that their faith in the quality of U.S. goods was misplaced—those Japanese goods were hungrily consumed. The large producers in Tokyo, Osaka, Nagasaki, and Kyoto, only had to trouble themselves with production; for many businesses the markets took care of themselves, either due to the use of expert trading agents or irresistibly low prices, or both.

This system left an indelible mark on Japanese industry. That industry awed the world with its productivity and efficiency. It reaped vast profits in markets from Topeka to Tanzania. It commercialized new technologies with a speed that dazzled Western competitors. But it ignored the comparative advantages of producing overseas, the strategic importance of becoming true insiders in key markets, and the need to integrate the international perspective at the topmost ranks of management. Smug with their export wealth, they declined to be more than Japanese. The effect of that export mentality has been gravely underestimated by both the Japanese and their Western competitors. Many Western enterprises have also suffered from the same mentality.

As stated previously in these pages, exporting may add certain cosmopolitan sensitivities to a company, but it does not create a global enterprise. The company that is satisfied with exporting as its sole offshore involvement looks at the world, and reacts to the world, in a different fashion than the global company. Appreciation of these differences is vitally important in understanding the Japanese manager's state of mind.

A useful analogy is sometimes made by the more perspicacious of Japanese executives, usually when they are in a more relaxed environment outside their home country. The Japanese company approaches the world as in the traditional Japanese board game of Go, they say in confession-like tones. In Go, all the disc-shaped pieces are valued equally; the goal is to surround your enemy and capture his pieces until he is eventually eliminated. The game of Go is a game of market share.

If any game could be considered the archetypal Western game, it would be chess. In chess, pieces of varying value and strengths must be manipulated strategically for the purpose of diminishing your opponent's value and strengths. In essence, it is a game of profitability. The approach, the tactics, the values, and the goals in chess and Go vary dramatically.

The Japanese exporter produces, cuts costs, mass produces, and cuts costs again, always with pricing and increasing sales in mind. Japanese shareholders traditionally have been very patient with this constant, long-term effort to maximize sales; they are satisfied with very low dividend income, typically in the 2 percent range. The government has supported this approach by assuring that most capital gains on securities are not taxed, lending added emphasis to long-term market share enhancement over short-term profits. Japanese banks traditionally have likewise emphasized sales volume in evaluating creditworthiness. As long as low Japanese costs have guaranteed the competitiveness of Japanese goods, the system has run like clockwork—or more aptly, like a money machine. In today's much more complex world of the expensive yen and lower-cost production in the newly industrializing countries—or even in the United States in some sectors—this basic assumption of cost-competitive production in Japan is often not valid.

By putting all their eggs into the domestic factory basket, Japanese companies have built themselves into an intricate trap. They have denied themselves the global perspective that many of their competitors are gaining. They have lost the flexibility to readily adapt to the roller coaster exchange rates of today's economy. They have lost access to many of the strategic moves available from global production and management. Not only are these past practices not good models for the West, soon they will not even be valid models for future Japanese managers. A new generation in the Land of the Rising Sun must discover the global enterprise.

Those rare Westerners who take the time to look inside Japanese enterprises typically find a sharply parochial structure even in most of the country's largest international firms. Senior managers are uniformly Japanese even in the most entrenched foreign location. The experiences related by American managers who have left Japanese operations in frustration are so similiar as to assume a generic form. They complain of discrimination against non-Japanese and of the lack of upward mobility for non-Japanese. When the Boston Consulting Group studied the U.S. subsidiaries of Japanese corporations in 1988,[4] it found that decision-making processes left out American representatives in most operations. Kazuo Nomura of BCG, who worked on the study, commented on the "shadow system" of management: "Business is conducted at night on the telephone in Japanese between Japanese. They come back in the morning and tell the Americans what has been decided."

When the head of NECs subsidiary in America attempted in the early 1980s to turn the operation into a truly integrated U.S./Japanese company, he was replaced—reportedly for "trusting Americans" too much. Donald Moffet, president of Fujitsu Systems in the United States, is one of the few American CEOs of a Japanese subsidiary, but he complained publicly that he has no right to fire or set salaries for any Japanese employees in his operations. Those Japanese who really want to integrate themselves into the American operations, Moffet further stated, "must be prepared to bury their bones in America."

The many discrimination lawsuits that have been filed in the United States as a result of such practices is only their most obvious penalty; the real damage lies in the price paid in pursuing global pretensions while simply exporting the Osaka mindset.

In a few industries, such as the automotive sector, the primary Japanese producers have been global for many years. Yet only the surface has been scratched for Japanese businesses overall. Today less than 4 percent of the production of Japanese companies is located outside Japan, compared to 15 to 20 percent for many Western nations. Even globally oriented Toyota as late as May 1989 was producing only 12 percent of its cars overseas, compared to over 30 percent for General Motors.[5] In February 1989 Hitachi Ltd. conducted a massive corporate image-boosting campaign with full page ads in U.S. newspapers. Its theme: Hitachi is a

---

[4]L. Nathans, "A Matter of Control," *Business Month*, September 1988.
[5]"Japan's Growing Global Reach," *Fortune*, May 22, 1989.

global company and "citizen of the world." Reading the data presented in the ad carefully, however, revealed that 95 percent of the $45 billion firm's production was based in Japan.

Slowly Japan is awakening to the significance of this fact, and the difficulty of improving that figure. Shiro Miyamota, president of the prestigious Japan External Trade Relations Organization captures the situation: "The age of multinationalism has finally arrived in Japan. It won't be an easy transition."

Many of the factories represented in Japan's offshore production figure are new ventures which are still trying to assimilate to their new environments. Those ventures provide an enlightening benchmark for assessing the experience of Japanese firms in going global. Some of those global efforts have been successful, but a careful scrutiny of these offshore experiences reveals a picture of hit and miss decisions, and many fumbling efforts alongside the more highly-publicized successes. When the experiences of Japanese firms in the United States were closely studied in the mid-1980's, it was found that 85 percent of them were operating at a loss.

The Elevator Shaft

To those Japanese firms that realized they must become at least multinational, the largest Japanese elevator manufacturer, Fujitec, was admired for many years as a paragon of such operations. The company moved production out of Japan before most other firms had even considered offshore sourcing. Manufacturing was set up in South America, Singapore, and Hong Kong. Flush with money and prestige, the company confidently erected a plant in Ohio. Its apparent strategy was one familiar to many Japanese firms, that of buying market share through pricing.

Fujitec stumbled badly in the U.S. venture. Its production managers missed their U.S. startup by two years. Rushing to satisfy disgruntled customers, the U.S. unit decided to take the most un-Japanese step of hiring temporary production workers. Efficiency sagged and costs increased. When products were finally delivered, customers complained about lack of maintenance service for the equipment. The plant's financing unraveled due to the delay and exchange rate losses. The ultimate result was that the U.S. failure gave the company its first loss since being publicly listed in 1963. Its operating loss for 1986 was equivalent to 85 percent of its shareholders' equity and five times the company's capital.

Stumbling Over Computers

Executives at giant NEC Corporation, formerly Nippon Electric Corporation, are seldom quick to talk about the history of their company's efforts in the United States. Perhaps some have even forgotten the disaster of its first major effort in the United States, a campaign to sell telephone equipment in the 1970s which was an unmitigated failure. That effort misread the market and left the company with large U.S. inventories of equipment that, embarrassingly, had to be shipped to South America.

All of those executives, however, remember the battering the company brought upon itself when it began to market personal computers. The company began by attempting to sell its Japanese models in the United States without even adapting them to accept programs for U.S. accounting and business practices. Predictably, the company was ignored by the U.S. market. After spending millions to adapt them to the proper programs, NEC relaunched the product with only a skeletal sales organization. Those few who bought the product were impressed with its technical capabilities but became quickly disenchanted due to the lack of service support from NEC. Some purchasers, such as Federal Express, gave up on trying to get help from NEC and established internal service capability. Distributors of NEC products were even discovered to have replaced the company's computers in NEC telephone exchange systems with those of archrival IBM.

Showdown in Arkansas

In the late 1970s, the town of Forest City, Arkansas resounded with optimism and beamed with a newfound prosperity. The town's long-failing factory, once operated by Whirlpool to make televisions for Sears Roebuck, was being rescued by a deep-pocket, technology-rich firm of Sanyo Electric Company. Even those who criticized the entry of a Japanese corporation into the town began to mellow when the Japanese increased production, raising employment to over 2,000, and sharply cut the defects that had plagued prior operations. A new line to produce microwave ovens was added to the existing nine television production lines. A number of national news accounts raved over the way in which Japanese ingenuity had accomplished what American managers could not.

The turnaround did not end at the upswing, however. The intitial success proved to be almost totally driven by technological improvements. That honeymoon was soon over. Sanyo brought in managers who spoke no English to the little southern town. The company fired the union president when labor trouble threatened. It demanded major changes in benefits and job rules. After two strikes, one of them racked by violence, the operation began to unravel. By mid-1988 the new microwave line was gone and only two of the TV lines remained in operation. Of the 2,000 workers once employed, only 350 remained. The company had incurred nearly $70 million in losses in four years at the plant.

A similar experience can be found at National Steel, in which the NKK corporation of Japan bought a 50 percent interest in 1984. That investment issued a great hurrah, fueled by the announcement of a $1 billion modernization program and introduction of Japanese management techniques that would turn the firm around. By 1988 the company was under siege, with the lowest profitability in the industry, senior management squabbling and sometimes walking out, and Japanese-inspired devices such as quality circles being largely ignored by embittered workers.

Nissan: Motoring Downhill

The perception held by many in the West that the Japanese auto companies are nothing less than huge irrepressible cash machines is certainly not consistent with the recent history of Nissan Motor Company. In the past few years, with a few short-term exceptions, the company has had a history of sinking market share, severe losses, and forced austerity. Much of the problem can be traced to the company's international strategy.

During the 1950s and 1960s the firm seemed to do no wrong; its innovative engineering (e.g., first front wheel drive) at the time brought it the nickname of "the company of firsts" in Japan. In the 1970s, however, tenacious competition from Toyota pushed Nissan into a fateful decision: It would shift its emphasis to markets outside Japan. Nissan launched a huge drive to become global, with new plants in the United States, Mexico, Spain, England, and Italy, as well as several joint ventures in the West. Most of the expansion it financed with profits earned in the U.S. market, which had been made all the more lucrative by the imposition of import restrictions. Previously, like its competitors, Nissan had used those profits to underwrite its Japanese business, perennially a low-margin hotbed of competition.

For its ambitious expansion, the firm paid a price far beyond the initial multibillion dollar cost for its new international factories. That's not to say those construction costs weren't a major problem in themselves. The company paid $745 million for its plant in Smyrna, Tennessee. When rival Honda built a plant in Ohio shortly afterwards, it paid only $490 million for a facility that could build 50 percent more vehicles. Concurrently, the company launched a still controversial campaign to change its U.S. name from Datsun to Nissan, an effort which cost millions in advertising and which lent considerable confusion to its efforts to market vehicles which had become less and less attractive to consumers due to stodgy designs. The elimination of the Datsun name which U.S. dealers had spent two decades developing is still, years later, hotly criticized in the industry.

By 1986, the "company of firsts" had become the first Japanese automaker to report a loss since the days of the post-war recovery. For the first six months of 1986 the company had an operating loss of $121.9 million. U.S. market share dropped steadily. In just one year, from 1985 to 1986, the company lost over 10 percent of its existing market share. In the first quarter of 1988 the company sales in the United States dropped 22 percent. Its manufacturing plants around the world have typically lost millions in their first few years of operation.

Austerity programs became a sign of Nissan's plight. At its home office, pencils began to be doled out one-by-one. Discarded paperwork was ordered to be saved so it could be traded for toilet paper. Five thousand production workers were shifted into sales jobs, including door-to-door solicitations. Executives, stinging from salary and bonus cuts, began to stay in the company cafeteria at night to drink sake and beer instead of touring the expensive bars of Tokyo.

As discussed later in this volume, Nissan had failed to grasp a fundamental point. No firm becomes global by defining the globe to include everything but its home market.

High Technology Misconnection

In the mid-1980s, one of Japan's huge *sogo shosha* trading companies, Mitsui, launched a high technology venture in the United States that seemed guaranteed to succeed. Gallium arsenide semiconductor chips, already representing a $100 million market, promised to be the successor to the silicon chips' market. Over $1 billion in sales were projected for the early 1990s. The Japanese firm had the combination of a top scientist from Bell Laboratories, patent licenses from Japan's NTT for producing the chips, and a deep-pocket financial commitment from Tokyo. With great fanfare Mitsui launched Gain Electronics Corporation in Somerville, New Jersey.

The company quickly proved that a Japanese connection gave no immunity to the problems often endemic to such high technology ventures. It was run by scientists inexperienced in management, plagued by impurities in production materials, and unable to secure the defense contracts intended to provide a business base. Consequently, the company was unable to meet its original goal of attracting U.S. partners to the project. In 1987 the company brought on experienced management and even landed a contract to supply custom chips. It was all too little too late. After pouring over $30 million into the venture without a return, Mitsui closed down the operation. Today the once bright star in Mitsui's high-tech crown is an empty factory shell.

Hidden between the pages of the Japanese high technology annals also can be found tales of technology innovation gone haywire. Many millions have gone into the development of machines for which no viable market could be identified. Classic examples include: The multimillion development effort of a Japanese company to produce a machine that made different varieties of snowflakes, a machine with a price tag of $1.3 million; or the $110 million project to develop a nuclear powered blast furnace for steel production.

Beaten on the Home Turf

On the other side of this coin can be found a number of stories of success by Western firms competing with Japanese firms in their own backyards. The mentality that fosters the specter of Japan, Inc. conquering the world embraces the corollary that Western firms are denied the chance to do business in Japan. The Congress and the press will never let us forget— and rightfully so—that Japan still protects several key sectors from viable foreign competition. Yet in many sectors Western firms have performed admirably in establishing Japanese beachheads.

Schick, a division of Warner Lambert, learned how to make the best of a bad situation and put the Japanese distribution system to work for it many years ago. Today it sells $50 million worth of razors and blades in Japan, accounting for 70 percent of the country's wet shaving market.[6]

---

[6]*The Wall Street Journal*, April 6, 1989.

When the sales of another U.S. firm, Gillette, are added, the American market share rises to 80 percent. McDonald's fast food units in the country gross over $700 million annually. Brown-Forman of Louisville sells 500,000 bottles of its Jack Daniels whiskey in the Land of the Rising Sun, where a bottle of the Tennessee sour mash retails at $50 to $200.

As early as 1984, affiliates of Exxon, Coca-Cola, and Texas Instruments in Japan earned $174 million, $115 million, and $111 million, respectively. Avon has over 300,000 representatives in Japan conducting door-to-door cosmetics sales. Amway Corporation chalks up over $500 million in sales annually. A company in Columbus, Georgia, American Family Life, sells 85 percent of all insurance policies sold in Japan in its niche—cancer insurance. Michelin supplies 3.5 million tires to the Japanese a year, a third of which come from U.S. plants.

Japan Anti-Inc.?

The most fundamental element of the Japan, Inc. mentality in the West is the involvement of the Japanese government as coordinator, instigator, promoter, and protector of the Japanese enterprise in its conquest of the world. The image, however convenient to trade negotiators and Japan-bashers, has become obsolete, if it ever was true.

The complete proof of this fact can be found in scores of incidents in which the Japanese government handicapped and/or misdirected the Japanese private sector. The simplest evidence, however, and perhaps the most compelling, lies in the reaction that many Japanese business leaders have to the government's efforts. When allowed to privately, and anonymously, muse on the point, most take the same view that the typical free enterprise manager would have throughout the world, the view capsulized in the Thoreau quote at the end of the last chapter. They would prefer that the government would simply disentangle itself from their lives.

The mighty Ministry of International Trade and Industry (MITI) and its sister agencies have indeed made prominent marks on the Japanese economy. But those marks are not uniformly in the positive column. MITI was, for example, a primary force in propping up the Japanese steel, coal, aluminum, and shipbuilding industries long after most of their segments had lost all traces of competitiveness. The net effect of the efforts was to channel huge sums of taxpayers money into noncompetitive efforts when instead the money would have had much more positive social and economic impact if the government had bitten the bullet and used it in job adjustment and restructuring efforts. The effort not only proved expensive for the Japanese taxpayer but also cost the country much credibility overseas as the rest of the industrial world built up resentment over the huge subsidies being given those smokestack industries.

The sagacity and efficacy of Japanese government efforts in directing the country's international business, as MITI perceives its mission, is perhaps best reflected in the auto industry. One of the great struggles of industry and internal politics ever to take place in the country was waged more than 15 years ago when MITI decided that the Japanese automobile industry should consolidate into only two producers and, moreover, not focus itself offshore. Many companies whose car logos are today recognized around the world have been handsomely rewarded for having declined their government's advice.

The impressive story of one of Japan's most successful global firms, Honda, forcefully demonstrates how the judgments and interests of one company have diverged from those of the government. MITI strenuously fought Honda's initiative to diversify from motorcycles into automobiles. Another global enterprise of long-standing success, Sony, steadfastly refused aid and protection from the government as it developed.

The Missing Research Link

The rest of the world would not be quick to find fault with Japan's ability to innovate. But they judge on the basis of compact disc players, Walkman players, and maybe even the number of patents filed by Japanese firms (more than any other country on a worldwide basis). The research system that has created such devices, however, has been one preoccupied with applied and practical research. The Japanese system has converted the transistor into best-selling radios and American video recording concepts into global VCR products. When profit is in the wind, Japan's industrial labs are unequaled on the planet. The most recent example is the strides Japan has been making in the effort to commercialize superconductivity—after the development of the core technology in the West. Even in management and production techniques Japan often plays the same role. Many of the famous Japanese methods, such as quality circles, were first conceived in the West.

This system, however, profoundly shortchanges pure research efforts, the kind that led to the development of such items as the transistor in the first place. In the history of the Nobel Prize, only five Japanese scientists have received the award, compared to 140 Americans. The government provides little incentive for theoretical research, nor does it significantly engage in it itself. One of the Japanese Nobel laureates works for IBM. Another, Susumu Tonegawa, who won the prize for medicine in 1987, departed Japan in 1963 to pursue more original work in the United States. "Japan's science is definitely inferior to America's in terms of real creativity," he remarked to an audience in Tokyo in 1988. For original work, he advises Japanese students, "Talented scientists have no choice but to get out of Japan."

The Japanese government simply fosters research done by private enterprise, spending far less on government-backed basic research than in Western countries. While the United States and Germany increased government funding of such research 10.4 percent and 13.3 percent respectively from 1981 to 1985, the comparable figure in Japan was a paltry 0.1 percent.[7]

In the private sector, researchers enter the same lockstep inhibiting progression in which Japanese executives function. Rewards are based on seniority, not performance. Researchers in their prime years can thus be found cleaning equipment, punching time cards, and accounting for broken test tubes.

Kokusaika: The Uneasy International

It's difficult to travel as a *gaijin* in Japan today without prompting at least some discussion among local hosts, companions, guides, or new casual acquaintances about *kokusaika*. The term essentially translates as "internationalization." Strangers in Tokyo bars may hoist a glass to toast *kokusaika* when a Westerner appears. Managers may use the term in describing the significance of an American delegation visit to their factory. Bankers hear the word frequently in seminars about Eurobonds and Wall Street.

The observant listener may learn much in such Japanese discussions. They reveal a great deal about the Japanese view of the world and Japan itself, and much of why the common Western perceptions of the country are wrong. Many Westerners will be surprised to find most Japanese speaking of *kokusaika* as a new movement. The confident, seasoned global Japanese is largely a myth. The Japanese live in a country totally

---

[7]"Back to Basics," *Far Eastern Economic Review*, January 12, 1989.

intertwined in the global economy, but as a people they are no further than the citizens of the United States in assimilating that reality. They have, quite literally, been shielded by agents who carried the Japanese image only by proxy into the world.

Also found between the lines of the *kokusaika* colloquy is the innate Japanese sense of vulnerability, bred into most of the country's population at an early age when they are taught the cliché that Japan is a "small island nation with few natural resources." They know they are an economic superpower, but they also know that their personal standard of living is below that of most industrial nations.

As the *kokusaika* debate reveals the life of the *gaijin* more fully, their nation's wealth seems elusive to the man and woman on the street, whose personal lives are spent in cramped quarters paying sky-high prices for objects most Westerners take for granted. They suffer their own strange schizophrenia: the feeling of superiority in macroeconomic terms but often inferiority on a microeconomic scale. Japan must live with the certain knowledge that a country whose lifeblood depends on market access overseas cannot for much longer deny its own markets to foreigners. Its dependency on exports is a vulnerability of the highest order. "Japan," notes Chung Hoon Mok, president of the far-reaching Hyundai Construction Co. in Korea, "is like a thin bottomed pan on a hot fire—very vulnerable to external forces."

Nowhere is the Japanese struggle with *kokusaika* more apparent than in the attitudes of Japanese corporations when confronted with today's global exigencies. For all their reliance on offshore markets, not a single major Japanese company can be found with a foreigner on its main board of directors. In late 1986, Nomura Securities, one of the recognized leaders of the country's globalization efforts, withdrew the top two managers from its New York office on one day's notice; the reason, reported by a number of insiders, was that the executives were becoming "too American."

As mentioned above, Japanese managers indeed have little incentive to be international. There is ample evidence that Japanese managers who leave the country for long—ostensibly to lead the globalization effort— become tainted within their corporate hierarchy. Many are shunted aside into company backwaters upon returning to Japan. The rank of international managers in the vast majority of Japanese companies bears testimony to the lack of true commitment to becoming global. Executives who are responsible for supervising overseas activity in most companies are at a managing director level, equivalent to a division manager in most U.S. firms. Typically the most senior international position is at least three levels removed from the CEO of a Japanese company.

Time to Join the World

If *kokusaika* is an awakening, then it needs to be an awakening on both sides of the Pacific. Today's global economy little tolerates the superficial perceptions, fostered by distance and distrust, that gives Japan a false sense of superiority or the United States the impression that a conspiratorial complex of business superstars resides in Tokyo.

Past perceptions on either side of the ocean have been based on an export juggernaut that, for compelling political, social, and economic reasons on both a domestic and world scale, cannot continue. Japan's export machine has brought the country far too much of a good thing.

The Japanese people are beginning to understand that the real beneficiaries of their vaunted productivity have been consumers in foreign markets rather than themselves. Not only the *shinjiniui*, Japan's yuppies, but older generations as well are not abiding the status quo. What good is Japan's economic success, the young and the old are asking, if the Japanese people cannot participate in it? The pressure by no means comes solely from within. The industrial nations of the world will not be satisfied until the vast latent resources of the Japanese consumer are opened to them.

The resulting change, only in its embryonic form today, will change the face of Japan. For many of the interests vested in the export-obsessed industries of the country, these changes may bring a new crisis. An economist of the Industrial Policy Bureau of MITI, Keiji Miyamoto, captured the situation well: "Just when Japan is being admired for its economic power, major changes are taking place within the industrial structure. Japan's future economic performance is in danger." As the United States has vividly demonstrated, the macroeconomic power of a nation is not enough to assure that enterprises of that nation will be global winners, or even that the leadership of the country understands what is needed to build such winners. As R. Taggart Murphy, a Chase Manhattan executive based in Tokyo has stated, "Japan commands wealth but lacks a global vision."

Meanwhile Western firms must cast off their own complex about things Nipponese. They must cease being enslaved by the phobia of a mythical Japan, Inc. on the one hand and a far too worshipful sentiment about Japanese business technique on the other. Japan as a nation faces problems at least as severe as those which America has encountered in recent years. The country has produced numerous winners in the global economy, but quite a few losers as well. Many of the winners have reached their prominence not because of, but in spite of, the Japanese system.

That system that forged the modern Japanese enterprise is so different that to borrow their business techniques is tantamount to a right handed individual trying to learn a trade by borrowing the tools of a left handed person. The ultimate conclusion must be that it is meaningless for the enterprise aspiring to global success to look for Japanese solutions to problems that are uniquely American or, as the case may be, German, French, or British. The enterprise that shuts itself off from learning from other's experience closes the door on growth. Some Japanese firms, as pointed out in more detail later in these pages, do offer instructive experiences. Just as some British firms have lessons for U.S. firms or, for that matter, the North Carolina firm may have for the California firm. But no firm today is a successful global enterprise because it is Japanese, or because it is of any other national origin. In a 1981 interview that deserved far more attention than it received, the then general manager of international operations for Kikkoman Foods, Yuzaburo Mogi, shared some insight into the lessons learned at the Wisconsin plant that company has operated since 1973. His ultimate conclusion: "I'd like to dispel the myth that Japanese management is really all that good and will produce wonders if transplanted abroad. We should be very careful about applying either so-called Japanese-style management to America or American-style management to Japan."

Sound global business practice follows no flag. Likewise the truly successful global manager never makes a decision simply because it is "how the Japanese do it." Any firm, or manager, that assumes such a mentality has lost the global race before leaving the gate. Homer Sarasohn was one of the American experts who, during the postwar occupation of Japan, quietly taught courses on U.S. business techniques to the founders or top managers of such companies as Sony, Matsushita, and Fujitsu. Today Sarasohn is appalled at the attitude of U.S. managers toward Japan. "This present-day fad of aping the Japanese style of management is absolutely destructive of our own future," Sarasohn stated in early

1989. "We've got to recapture the enthusiasm, the pioneering spirit that made America a world leader."

The modern Japanese corporation certainly has as much to learn from the West as it does to teach to the West. In the changes that must inevitably sweep the Land of the Rising Sun, the Japanese enterprises that endure will be those that learn how to evolve into truly global enterprises. Japanese firms must learn to join the world, not *vice versa*.

CHAPTER 7

THE "GLOBAL" AMERICANS: INNOCENTS ABROAD

Toying with Tijuana

"Going international" seemed like an idea whose time had come for Lionel Trains when it shifted production to Mexico in the early 1980s. U.S. production costs were soaring and imports from foreign competitors were threatening the strong toy train market share of the then-General Mills unit. Wages of 55 cents an hour in Tijuana seemed to make the decision a "no brainer." With very short notice, the company's primary production plant in Michigan was closed. The last job assigned to its U.S. workers was loading equipment and parts into trucks bound for south of the border. Converting the company into a transnational operation didn't seem to require much planning. Once in Mexico, the company simply had to unpack the trucks, bring in the cheap labor, and turn on the power.

Trouble started even before the first box was offloaded. Fifteen truckloads of equipment were severely delayed by Mexican customs agents when the company couldn't find the proper tariff category for vertical milling machines and other production items. Boxes that did arrive on time were found to have been mislabeled by the distraught ex-workers in Michigan. Lionel had brought a handful of managers from the U.S., who were expected to quietly hire and train local managers and workers. It was soon spending thousands of dollars monthly to fly managers and engineers from the U.S. after it found that its plan to rush through such hiring and training didn't fit the realities of the local work force.

When, after arrival, it began to explore local sourcing of key components and services, the company discovered that a critical plating process could not be performed in Mexico. Parts had to be shuttled back and forth to subcontractors in California, with further customs entanglements.

Communications with headquarters, suppliers, and customers were severely disrupted by lack of local telephone service. The plant had to get by for a year with only two phone lines.

When the products that were supposed to delight children across America finally came off production lines, they were riddled with defects. The supply, production, and public relations problems quickly reached catastrophic dimensions. Production delays and quality problems grew so disastrous that Lionel couldn't fill two thirds of its orders. The company's share of the train track market plummeted from 75 percent to 25 percent. Its overall share of the mass-market toy train market dropped from 25 percent to 10 percent.

Less than three years after going international the company gave up. It leased back its former plant building north of Detroit, rehired many of its former workers, and began turning out U.S.-made trains again. Looking back with regret over the whole affair, chief executive Arthur Peisner candidly concluded, "There's nothing that says you can't make trains in Tijuana, just not the way we did it."

Misstep in McParis

When it began its aggressive conquest of the globe, McDonald's Corporation identified the lucrative French market as one of its priority targets. The fastfood giant signed a master franchise agreement for the Paris region with a Moroccan businessman and moved on to new frontiers. In a business where one rotten franchise can quickly spoil an entire region and eventually even the reputation of the entire franchise system, the company soon discovered its worst nightmare was becoming true in Paris.

Inspectors photographed dog droppings on the floors of the Paris restaurants. Raw french fries were found stored beside trash. The sign at the high profile Champs Elysees unit had the company's name misspelled. Open cans of pesticide were found atop boxes of food. French fries were being cooked in a substance that reportedly was the color of crankcase oil. Customers could enter one restaurant only through the arcade of a porno movie theater. The "ugly American" at whom some Parisians enjoyed poking fun was fast becoming the "ugly, greasy American."

Efforts to force the franchisee to observe company standards were fruitless. When the Illinois company finally took legal action to cancel the franchise, it wound up in a four year legal battle, while the company's reputation continued to decline in Paris. Even the judge in the proceeding, who referred to this "cancer" that had formed in the McDonald's international business, concluded that the company's efforts in the important Paris market were set back at least 10 years as a result of its handling of the initial franchise award.

Taking the Telephone out of International Telephone

For the first half of this century, if there was any U.S. company that could be identified as a truly international firm, it was International Telephone and Telegraph, later ITT Corp. As early as 1929 the company employed over 35,000 workers outside the United States, supplying phone systems in Europe and throughout the world.[1] Having begun life by the merger of two offshore phone companies in Cuba and Puerto Rico, its primary focus always was offshore. As everyone knew, ITT's core business was that American high-tech speciality, telecommunications.

When the telecommunications business began to attract global competition, ITT was expected to be in the driver's seat. In the 1970s it was, after all, the second largest supplier of telecommunications equipment in the world. But the company that had written the book on international telecommunications took a stumble that proved fatal to its decades-old telecommunications business. Targeting high-tech switching systems as its core telecommunications product, ITT sank over $1 billion in developing its System 12 telephone switch, through a complicated international network of nationally focused research, development, and production units which resisted coordination of their efforts. Yet the company promised shareholders, lenders, and even the U.S. government big paybacks in the form of lucrative national telephone system contracts.

As competitors from Canada, Sweden, Japan, France, and Germany began to make life difficult, ITT suddenly couldn't take the pressure. It called off its plans to enter the U.S. switching market. Not long afterwards, as one offshore opportunity after another slipped through its fingers, ITT called it quits. In 1986, the company whose name had been synonymous with international telecommunications since many telegraph wires were first strung, sold control of that business to the French Com-

---

[1]M. Wilkins, *The Maturing of Multinational Enterprise* (Harvard University Press, 1974).

pagnie Generale d'Electricite (GCE) for $600 million—a sum which, ironically, matched the amount the company a few years earlier had reportedly lost in another international venture, its Rayonier pulp business in Canada. ITT management, turning its attention to its hotel and other conglomerate holdings, proclaimed a major victory in having obtained so much cash for what was obviously, and irreversibly, a financial sinkhole.

In less than 18 months, the French turned the same telecommunications business around. GCE's Alcatel unit studied the System 12 problems and, primarily by reorganizing its design and production programs, quickly worked out the bugs that had disheartened ITT, and began booking orders worth hundreds of millions of dollars. Even West Germany, which ITT had largely considered the preserve of Siemens, gave large orders to the formerly American operation.

American "Global" Telephones, Part Two

When the monolithic once domestic counterpart to ITT announced it was going global in 1980, competitors around the world anxiously began to consider defensive strategies. With its immense economic and technical powers, AT&T was widely expected to be a threat in the world telecommunications markets. Their anxiety eased, however, when the American firm first began to show its international colors.

As the rest of the industry carefully observed, AT&T took its first step in Europe by buying a small Irish electronics firm in 1982. Red ink mounted fast, and an embarrassed AT&T had to conduct major layoffs to cut the business down to a size it could manage. Asked about the U.S. firm's handling of its European beachhead, an official of the Irish Development Authority stated that "the bottom line is that they didn't do their homework."

By 1985 the company had spent more than $350 million dollars in Europe without securing any significant telecommunications business. The company then began to focus almost exclusively on joint ventures to shorten its learning curve, thus diluting its power in the European markets. Years later, despite glowing predictions by its management, the firm had still to crack any major public switching market, the core markets for its telecommunications business. The company announced frequently during this period that its primary target, which would provide a foundation for global efforts, was France. It overconfidently expected to buy a major French producer that would provide it an immediate 15 percent market share. The French government sold the company to the Swedish firm LM Ericsson.

In France, as elsewhere, the company assigned U.S. personnel without significant European experience. Many customers who were asked to explain why AT&T was stumbling so badly focused on AT&T's style. When AT&T sought a large Italian contract in 1985, the Italian government didn't give the company serious consideration. As one Italian businessman close to the decision making stated: "there was a great deal of animosity toward AT&T in Italy. The Americans were considered somewhat arrogant. They were flatly rebuffed." An industry analyst with CIT Research in London, Patrick Whitten, similarly observed that "[AT&T executives] were fairly arrogant when they first set up in Europe. They felt everything was going to fall into their lap. It's hard to see where the thrust of their strategy is." Without a clear international strategy, without an experienced international organization, AT&T was going nowhere.

Henry Ergas, a telecommunications expert with the Paris-based Organization for Economic Cooperation and Development, concluded that although the industry was shaken when AT&T charged into Europe: "Today AT&T has nothing unique. The company has very good engineering capabilities, but it doesn't have a good international focus. And that's the difference between being good and great. Of the major companies, all are technically very good. They have strength and depth. What really will tell them apart is management capability on a global scale." AT&T began the long process of turning its European operations around in 1989 with the announcement of a major new joint venture in Italy which, the company promised, would assure it of major sales in that country. Meanwhile in 1988 the company reported its first annual loss in its 103 year history.

At least it might be said that the American firms that have taken aim, but misfired, at the global telecommunications business have had plenty of company. IBM moved into that sector in one massive stroke by buying Rolm for $1.5 billion in 1984. Its move was ushered in with sweeping statements from IBM's Hudson Valley offices about the company's commitment to global telecommunications as an integral part of a new communications/computer linkage that would create the "office of the future." Despite major efforts by IBM to build a European presence for its Rolm unit, the company failed to obtain any significant business on the continent. Many experts estimated that IBM's telecommunications efforts were losing $100 to $200 million annually. In late 1988 IBM sold most of its Rolm interests to Siemens AG and took the humbling step of agreeing that future IBM telecommunications sales in Europe would consist of Siemens equipment.

Tooling Out of an Industry

U.S. machine tool producers once reigned supreme in the world marketplace, holding 90 percent of the U.S. market and enjoying the lion's share of foreign markets. A generation ago foreign competition was a concern in a few offshore markets where local producers had certain logistical advantages. Year after year, machine tools were one of the leading U.S. exports and one of the most successful of America's basic industries. Thirty years ago the U.S. industry employed 75,000 workers, and enjoyed the highest level of investment per worker and highest productivity rates in the world. When engine blocks, tractor frames, refrigerator doors, airplane wings, automobile bodies, and thousands of other components were made across the globe, it was with machine tools labeled "Made in the USA."

But the U.S. industry left itself irresistibly vulnerable to offshore producers by producing and operating almost totally in the United States. Important technology was made available by the U.S. government through public research. The government further encouraged development of offshore competitors by imposing repeated export controls which limited U.S. exporters and virtually guaranteed "base loads" for new foreign plants. When the U.S. dollar became overvalued, the U.S. producers were unable to compete in export markets and powerless to defend against imports. Today the industry structure has reversed itself. Not only have U.S. firms lost their export markets, foreign companies actually control at least half of the U.S. machine tool market. From 1982 to 1987 the number of domestic U.S. machine tool plants shrank by one third. From its former perch as top producer in the world, the U.S. industry is today a distant fourth, behind Japan, Germany, and the Soviet Union. During the 1980 to 1987 period, U.S. employment in the industry dropped by 28 percent. At a huge auto body plant outside Mansfield, Ohio, workers recently hung a lonely American flag over the sole U.S. machine press in the ranks of over a dozen other nearly football field-sized machines brought from Germany and Japan.

In Search of the Global Identity

These diverse tales are united not because they demonstrate a common element. Rather it is the aspect that their subjects uniformly lacked that is the key: the global perspective and the global skills that must accompany that perspective needed to forge the effective global enterprise. Whether it was in the context of a temporary tactical setback, the loss of a business unit, or the effective loss of an industry, it was that perspective and those skills that were at stake. Those examples are far from unique. Similar stories of global skills and global foul-ups, international ignorance and international alacrity, whether in short-term tactical decisions or a once-in-a-decade strategic move, can be found in every business sector. Unfortunately, those stories are by no means balanced. The stories of foul-ups and ignorance far outweigh those that could be characterized as global success stories.

For many enterprises the obvious question immediately becomes: "How do we become global?" For most, that is a premature query. Other questions even more basic must be addressed first: "What is the global mentality?" and "What is the global enterprise?"

"Global" Is Not a Business

The global mentality is not an end to itself. In many respects, being global may be a state of mind, but a state of mind by itself generates only ethereal dividends. A number of companies, and government officials, keep trying to prove otherwise.

In 1982, amid extraordinary fanfare, the U.S. Congress promulgated the Export Trading Company Act, designed to end the country's international business problems by authorizing the formation of U.S. trading companies which would suddenly be able to compete with the mighty Japanese trading firms, the *sogo shosha*. The law is far from the only example, but it is perhaps the classic example, of the quick fix mentality the United States tries to apply in the international business arena.

While the 1982 law was scant on substance, the enthusiastic hubbub that rose over the idea of U.S. companies beginning to behave like Japanese *sogo shosha* warmed the hearts of many managers and officials. In many respects it was one more example of the Tokyo-psychosis discussed in the preceding chapter. It was also a prime example of the periodic, and always failed, efforts of the Congress to legislate international business acumen. Congressmen across the nation scampered to take credit for the passage of the law, and conference and seminar promoters made huge profits by packing in standing room only crowds to hear accountants and lawyers wax eloquent on international opportunities for anyone who formed a trading company.

No one bothered to point out that the Japanese *sogo shosha* which were the inspiration for the new legislation had fallen on tough times, with plummeting earnings. At the time of the legislation, the average net profit on sales for the *sogo shosha* had not exceeded *0.1 percent* for several years.[2] Mitsui & Co., one of the most prominent, had just suffered its first loss in 35 years. As a result of the global economy, life was changing rapidly for these trading firms, which even in the best of times were high risk businesses operating on the thinnest of margins. Global companies began to appreciate the strategic value, and profitability, of going directly into international markets. The Japanese industrial structure was beginning to feel the disadvantages of its export obsession. The trading companies that U.S. businesses were trying to emulate were even then aggressively deemphasizing their trading activities and moving into general contracting and equity investments as manufacturers in their own right. As America's international gurus were raving about the vital and successful role of trading companies in the global economy, a book entitled *The Era of Winter* was a best seller in Tokyo. Its theme was the coming demise of the trading company due to changes in the patterns of international business.

Bad news, or careful analysis, didn't seem to fit into the global mentality of the newborn U.S. trading firms. Thousands of trading companies were formed, most of them in a manner that had been perfectly legal even before passage of the new law. A large number received significant bank financing and even loans from the U.S. taxpayers through agencies such as the Small Business Administration. The next two years produced staggering examples of America's global mentality and its readiness to take on the global economy. A few examples from the ranks of those new firms that were loudly advertised as the symbols of America's newfound international strength, those firms that would turn around U.S. trade woes, are offered in what follows here:

---

[2]"Sears' Humbled Trading Empire," *Fortune*, June 25, 1984.

• A New Jersey school teacher who left his job, applied for a passport and obtained commitments from three companies to sell machine screws, fresh produce, and office furniture to anyone he might identify as an offshore customer. He left for Asia with high hopes and a credit card. When, after 10 days of sitting in his Hong Kong hotel, he obtained his first appointment, he immediately called home and ordered several thousand dollars worth of telex, telecopy, and other equipment. When he arrived for his sole appointment, his host excused himself: *He had assumed the American wanted to buy products from him.*

• A Midwestern municipal employee obtained a low interest government loan to set up his trading company after attending a two hour seminar on "how to do international business." When he left for Europe he was asked what products he was representing. His response: "If they just give me orders, I'll worry about filling them later."

• A rural cable television operator paid his local real estate lawyer $20,000 to set up a new trading company subsidiary. His marketing plan: send out 1,000 letters overseas with a list of U.S. manufacturers.

• A real estate developer who had never traveled outside his native Southeast established a trading company with the owner of a local savings and loan. Their plan: to develop resort properties outside the United States, preferably on the Mediterranean.

These operations shared two fundamental characteristics (1) their principals had essentially concluded that being international was in essence a business in itself and (2) they all failed.

These failures were by no means limited to school teachers and real estate salesmen. Control Data Corporation set up an export trading company which utterly failed to identify a successful mission for itself and was folded in 1984. The most spectacular failure of all is discussed below.

Four years after the 1982 law's passage, Michael Czinkota, then chairman of the National Center for Export-Import Studies, analyzed performance of these American *sogo shosha* and concluded, "Almost none of the companies that went into export trading are making any money at it."

Going global never insulates an enterprise from the basic rule that first, and foremost, a firm must know what business it is in. Without a self identity, success will always be elusive.

The Bigger They Come . . .

The most dramatic of the international failures arising out of the U.S. trading company fad began with great hoopla in media and political circles when Sears Roebuck & Co. formed Sears World Trade in March 1982. The premise certainly seemed valid; Edward Telling, then chairman and CEO, launched the company with an eloquent speech about how Americans "can no longer ignore our shortcomings in world trade." Therefore, "we can no longer manufacture and sell exclusively for our own consumption. We can no longer lose competitive ground on a world scale." If the concept sounded vague, it at least had a superficial credibility. Certainly if anyone could do it, the free world's biggest retailer would have the expertise and contacts to establish an international business model for the U.S. business community. Indeed, as Telling promised, the new operation would be "a truly significant factor in world trade."

Sears selected a Washington-based securities lawyer to head its Sears World Trade unit. Most other senior managers were also former Washington officials, ranging from the personal secretary of President Carter to a former deputy assistant secretary of HEW. Now surprisingly, this management team announced that the company would be based in Washington, on the thesis that the capital city would eventually become the center for U.S. international business. Observers around the world puzzled over why any merchandise trading firm would not establish itself on the front lines of such trade, such as in New York, London, or Hong Kong.

In press releases and speeches Sears World Trade executives raved about the company's plans. The firm was going to be the "biggest and the best American trading company." Within five years of formation, its CEO boasted, the company would be contributing *$5 to $10 billion* in sales a year to its parent company, with fat profit margins. Its speciality was to be selling to Japan. "If we can't sell in Japan, no one can," he bragged.[3]

---

[3]The rise and fall of Sears World Trade was widely chronicled in the media. See "Sears to Close Part of World Trade Unit," *Wall Street Journal*, October 29, 1986; "Sears Trade Unit Shifts Focus," *New York Times*, December 2, 1985; footnote 2, *supra*.

A visitor to Sears World Trade—the company spent millions renovating a high profile building with a prominent Pennsylvania Avenue address—would encounter much proselytizing about the virtues of international business. The company's multibillion dollar projections were conspicuous in conversations at the offices, as were references to how its senior executives had just returned from visits with one head of state or another. When asked to discuss specific business issues many Sears World Trade staffers were apt to instead spout off about how their chairman just met with the President of Mexico. Not nearly so conspicuous among those comments was a knowledge of basic practical aspects of international trade or a focus on specific details of actual business.

Sears' international picnic ended quickly. The bold talk of fat profits soon collided with the reality of the razor-thin margins and high risks characteristic of trading operations. The trading company never turned a profit, losing $60 million in its first four years. It securities lawyer/chairman, who had promised billions, quietly left in 1983. Much of its trading revenues were the result of the acquisition of existing trading operations in Europe. Wall Street quickly became disenchanted with the drifting, uncertain management of the firm. An analyst with Morgan Stanley & Company who followed the firm concluded that "it doesn't have a *raison d'etre*."

In 1986 Sears Roebuck finally accepted its failure and salvaged what it could of Sears World Trade by closing its U.S. operations and folding its international operations into its merchandising group. Postmortems in the newspapers and magazines around the country pointed to a number of obvious causes of the unit's demise: bad planning, rigid organizational structure, and inexperienced management. But in final analysis, there was perhaps little difference between the Sears World Trade and the Midwestern city worker who left for Europe to take orders for unknown suppliers to sell unidentified products to nonexistent customers. Both seemed to act as though international business was a sufficient goal unto itself, as though flying on a 747 for 10 hours would excuse them from the responsibility of actually doing business.

The Global Industry

The global mentality cannot really be embraced without a clear understanding of the nature of the global enterprise. Philosophers might debate the "concept" of riding a horse, but they could never really fathom the experience until they first shared an image of what a horse was and eventually had their feet in the stirrups. As the above described trading companies cogently proved, being global in the abstract is never enough to create a global winner. There is no universal definition of a global enterprise, and no formula that permits an analyst to quickly perform a few tests and stamp a company with a global seal of approval. Global industries are simpler to define: If markets and/or production in one country are affected by markets and production elsewhere in the world, the industry is, in the most elementary sense, global. Critical aspects like minimum production scale, market demands, and competition generally are shaped by the global economy in the mature global industry.

In the global industry, production of relatively standardized products are manipulated, along with a flow of materials, components, research, and technology from country to country, continent to continent, for maximum strategic advantage. A producer interested in participating in another's home market may gain the opportunity by a competitive attack in a third country. Competitors may buy materials on one continent, ship them to another for primary processing, then send them for final processing into key market countries. They may invest in a new production facility not for anticipated profit but to spoil a competitor's market and to deny that competitor global cash flow. Such international choreography, of which these are only brief examples, happens constantly, its moves based on close monitoring of changes in factors as diverse as exchange rates, international tax treaties, shipping costs, and consumer palates.

Myriad factors may work to convert a nonglobal industry into a global one. It may be the action of one major company which shifts production ostensibly for economies of scale, but in a way which intersects international borders and international markets. After doing so, the world may appear very differently to such a producer. Perhaps a major distribution barrier falls, such as a tariff, creating a natural attraction for the most economically produced goods, wherever their source. In some industries, consumer tastes or simple fads may drive a popular product into global channels almost involuntarily. Perhaps innovation in transportation or handling causes costs to markedly drop, likewise attracting the most efficiently produced products from abroad.

Technical innovation in products often drives an industry into a global mode. The introduction of transistors and integrated circuits made possible the mass production of the electronic entertainment products that consumers find so irresistible, but the huge cost of such production could only be supported by global sales volumes. Sometimes global impetus comes from legal action, as when the English language publishing industry began to globalize after the U.S. Justice Department forced U.S. and British publishers to abandon arrangements which had the effect of dividing the world into noncompeting territories.

In some cases a producer—often government supported—may, in the interest of creating jobs or using surplus materials, simply begin to produce so much that the domestic market "bursts open," forcing an overflow into extraterritorial channels. Likewise governments, usually in developing countries, may begin to attract previously domestic producers with huge, irresistible tenders for infrastructure projects such as power, rail, or communications systems. In the early days of the 20th century, if companies like Singer, International Harvester, or Tabulating Machine Company (later IBM) hadn't sent out marketing representatives, many countries would have all but dragged them out of the United States in their eagerness for modernization.

Until the late 1970s the tire industry was essentially a nationally defined, multidomestic business with segmented markets in regions around the world. In the 1980s, however, low growth put pressure on companies to invade each other's turf. Automobile producers, the biggest customers, began to demand that their suppliers "travel with them" to supply offshore plants. And currency fluctuations began to highlight the advantage of having production in more than one currency base. By the end of the decade the industry had become global.

Dinosaurs versus the World

The global companies are those that are able to successfully function in this milieu. Those who function in global industries but do not integrate themselves into their context will eventually suffer the fate of the dinosaurs. The fact that many dinosaurs were huge was of little consequence when their changing planet demanded they adapt or perish.

One of these modern day giants has been Siemens, the $33 billion German electronics manufacturer. Lumbering along with a bureaucracy of 350,000 workers, the 141-year old company became fat and unresponsive from protection and bountiful state contracts. Government contracts, for example, permit the company to supply cordless phones in Germany at a $665 retail price, compared to $79 and less for many models in the

United States. Siemens gets triple the U.S. price for the phone switches it sells in Germany.

Despite its early international initiatives—the company installed the first telegraph lines in Leningrad and India—for many years, the company has evidenced an emphatically parochial view. In its indisputably global industries of telecommunications, medical electronics, factory automation, and related businesses, the company has in the past held only small market shares in the United States and other key markets, out of all proportion to its position as the fourth largest integrated electronics producer in the world. Over one half of all its sales traditionally came from German customers. It suffers from a bloated organization and a history of being slow to innovate. In 1988, for example, its market share in Britain was 1 percent. For its key telephone switch systems, only 2 percent of its sales were in the United States.

The company today has embarked on an aggressive program to depart from its history as only a regional power. Siemens's finance director, Karl-Herman Baumann, recognizes that recent world developments require the company to change, "Our business is becoming global, and we cannot stay in one region of the world market." Perhaps it is not recent history that should be of most concern to Siemens and similiar firms that could be identified in North America, Europe, Australia, and Asia. More instructive may be a look at prehistory, when the leviathans became extinct, while smaller, more resilient creatures survived by adapting to changing global conditions.

The Global Enterprise

The day will soon arrive in many industries when there will indeed be a simple litmus test for identifying the global company. If a company is successful, it will be global. Until then, many managers and their companies will struggle to find a crisp and simple definition for something that is by its nature an extremely complex phenomenon.

There is, however, another way to define a global firm, one which helps to focus the discussion of how to become a global winner. A definition will focus on global characteristics. There may be no easy formula to identify the corner gym's stripling as the next heavyweight king but certainly those who step into the ring know when they've been hit by a champion.

The global firm typically:

Is ruled by the long-term strategic view, not short term temptations (is able to subordinate short-term profit for long-term improvement of position).

Sees markets around the world as interdependent elements, not independent opportunities.

Sells products with standardized characteristics, often with adaptions for local markets.

Approaches nearly all manufacturing decisions as strategic in nature.

In planning, starts with the global and "builds down" to the local.

Establishes and manages production facilities as critical international leverage points, not as supply centers for national markets.

Typically maximizes production scale economies through large primary manufacturing units with final assembly or processing often performed in key markets.

Is able to be an "insider" in key markets without losing the global perspective.

Has identified the critical leverage points of its industry, including (in most cases) distribution, key cash flow sources, production, quality control, innovation, and marketing, and seeks to exercise maximum control over those points globally.

Does not abide "empire building" by one unit in one country or region; success of one unit accrues to the benefit of the global system.

Uses innovation globally as a means of controlling the industry.

Due to long-term strategic perspective, is not enslaved to conventional by-the-number analysis of investment.

Relies upon a planet-wide, quick response information gathering apparatus.

Has a strong, broadly based, globally oriented legal, financial and political counseling staff.

Creates and promotes global instincts in its personnel.

Has a strong and effective global communications system.

Performs research and development in all its key markets.

There are many ways to be global, and many ways to combine these elements. But few firms that are global successes will be without these characteristics.

Casting Off the MNC Burden

Valuable lessons can be obtained by scrutinizing each of these characteristics. However, for many enterprises and their managers, one final barrier remains which prevents an objective approach to the global perspective and chills the development of effective global skills. That barrier is linked to one of the most pervasive myths discussed in Chapter 3. The myth of infallibility of the entity traditionally known as the multinational corporation (MNC).

The core problem is not simply that of mistakenly believing that MNCs are the epitome of global business. It runs much deeper. In essence it is a corollary of the infallibility myth: the omnipresence of the MNC mentality. The problem lies with the broader tendency to approach all international problems through the traditional MNC mindset, to use MNC management and MNC behavior as the benchmark for assuring global success.

MNC Artifacts

The term *multinational corporation* or abbreviation *MNC* has never carried a scientific definition. Today it is so overused that in many contexts it has become almost meaningless. One can find the media using the word to describe any enterprise that ships products across a national border; one that has foreigners on its staff; or one that is passive investor in an offshore company. But if there is any strict sense in the way the word is used, or an attempt is made to use the term in its original historical context, it would be in reference to the mainstream Fortune 500 entity that typically claims tens of thousands of employees, significant international sales, and platoons of executives with frayed passports.

The archetypal multinational was a German, American, and British invention of the 19th century. When the term was introduced into the vernacular, it was in reference to such firms as the early ITT, the General Electric, with plants on four continents by 1919, or the early Firestone Company, with 1,000,000 acres of Liberia under lease by 1926 for rubber production. To the extent the term is meaningful to management and planners today, it is in the sense of those prototypical institutions. Specifically, in archetypal form the MNC is an international operation organized along country lines. The parent company, whether in New York, San Francisco, or London, operates subsidiaries with high autonomy in manufacturing and sales management. Decisions on broad product planning, key capital expenditures, and senior personnel are made at headquarters. Primary research and development are done in the headquarters country.

Great emphasis is placed in this MNC structure upon "being local." Managers of a foreign subsidiary, when given the chance to chat about their jobs with even perfect strangers—as not infrequently happens in airport lounges or over transoceanic meals at 40,000 feet—will almost invariably brag at some point about their autonomy. "Headquarters in the States has to sign off on the biggest capital decisions, that's all," boasted the manager of an Australian MNC subsidiary. "Otherwise I'm on my own. Once every three or four years they have a say in our management. As long as we send dividends back, there's no interference."

"In Lyon," brags the manager of the French subsidiary of another U.S. MNC, "we are a French company. No one is aware that we are a U.S. corporation."

MNC managers have taken great pride that their Brazilian subsidiary is Brazilian, their Spanish subsidiary Spanish, and each a good corporate citizen, run by respected local managers, in their respective countries. Many CEOs brag about how they are able to operate their Brazilian subsidiary successfully with only one American, or their German unit without any Americans at all, as if such hands-off structure was an end to itself.

For reasons which should be obvious, but which are discussed in more detail later, these attitudes and the structure that creates them are often antithetical to the concept of global enterprise. Being an insider in key markets is important to the global firm, but a multiheaded, fragmented structure is repugnant, even deadly to it. Perhaps a natural outgrowth of this attitude was the tendency of many MNCs to expand without direction, following only the "golden rule": any foreign unit that turned a steady stream of gold—profit—got the additional gold of growth capital.

In the age of the MNC conglomerate the MNC headquarters manager busied himself reviewing balance sheets for the firm's hotel chain in Europe, its mining business in Chile, its electrical connector subsidiary in Japan, and its apparel manufacturer in Brazil. In a world in which international travelers spent half their time in steamship cabins, overseas communication depended on hard-wire telegraph systems, and international managers might meet once every few years, the traditional MNC was the natural device for conducting foreign business. There was no such thing as global business. There was business that had foreign counterparts. These companies had successful businesses in more than one nation. They were *multi*-national.

The MNC Handicap

Today a network of subsidiaries with loose connections at the top, sharing a name but not sharing production, materials, strategies, and sales policies is going to be a global loser. The headquarters of a large European consumer electronics producer recently had to suffer the indignity of having its U.S. subsidiary actually refuse to sell the parent company's own videocassette recorder product in the United States. Instead the subsidiary contracted Japan's Matsushita to obtain VCRs for resale over the European brand name.

In another instance, the division of a large U.S. company that made a sale of equipment to an Asian customer lost all possibility for future sales when the equipment needed repair. Qualified technicians were located in Asia at a subsidiary of the U.S. company, but the division management refused to permit them to make the repairs since they bore no relevance to their profit center.

In one more incident, a Japanese buying delegation called on the New York headquarters of an MNC but were rebuffed with little more than a handshake. They were instructed that only the sales division in Asia could handle their inquiry.

Global organizations are not within the vision of such myopic operations.

As trade barriers began to erode in the postwar period, another natural response was for the MNC, and those aspiring to join their ranks, to place greater emphasis on export manufacturing. When many plants were built in the United States or other home countries, designs included a certain export base load. Export production made MNC manufacturing decisions easier and provided an escape valve or cushion in situations of under or over supply in the domestic market (which always comes first). Indeed, for many companies the need for insider foreign production plants subsided. Many MNCs discovered the most streamlined international structure was one that concentrated production in huge plants with vast economies of scale, pumping out product for new world markets.

To Japan's growing disadvantage, this structure essentially became a model for the country's entire economy. The Japanese are not alone, however, in the United States and Europe many of the biggest MNCs also concentrate on large export factories located in their home countries. Such traditional operations are insufficient to meet the challenges of the global economy. It breeds a narrow, segmented, not a global, perspective. It builds exporters and/or multiple, distinct islands of production and sales. *It no longer is an international winner.*

Slimming to a Global Core

A major influence nurturing such attitudes and operations is the conglomerate profile of many MNCs. By accumulating diverse, often unrelated businesses, the MNC finds itself unable to reconcile conflicting goals and industry trends as global pressures mount. Some companies and some managers have accepted this reality and moved ahead with the challenge of reducing their operations to carefully focused global enterprises.

It is perhaps ironic that a good example of such effort is that of Britain's Grand Metropolitan PLC (Grand Met), since that company was for many years criticized as being far too widely invested, cast far too heavily in the shape of the old-style MNC conglomerate. In 1987, however, the company began to divest holdings as diverse as a U.S. daycare center chain, soft drink bottlers, and the Intercontinental Hotel chain. A fundamental and deliberate goal of this campaign has been to shed the company's image as a conglomerate. Explains CEO Allen Sheppard: "Ten years ago, if anybody had asked what Grand Met's strategy was, the answer would have been, well, to be successful" at any business that could turn a profit. "That was a perfectly acceptable definition in the 1970s, but it's wrong in the 1980s. And in the 1990s it would be a disaster." Recognizing that investors had consistently cast negative votes by undervaluing the stocks of such conglomerates, Sheppard's answer was to turn the company into what he calls "a powerful global player" in three related sectors: food, drink, and restaurants. After a recent $8 billion series of acquisitions, the firm is now the leading producer of alcoholic beverages in the world and the eighth largest food processor, as a result of its acquisition of Pillsbury, the largest hostile takeover ever by a British firm.

A similar pattern can be found in the global efforts of Swedish Match AB, in the past another high profile MNC conglomerate. Indeed, a generation ago the company was revered as a model of the conglomerate style, having built a highly profitable portfolio that included not only matches (it claims that 2.5 million of the firm's matches are lit around the world every minute) but also cattle farms, furniture, skis, lumber, car components, tractors, and packaging. Today Swedish Match has recognized the handicap that a conglomerate structure brings to any global effort and is working hard to grow away from that structure. The company is aggressively "deconglomerating" into three strategic businesses: consumer products (such as matches and lighters), packaging, and home improvements. The company is either the world or European market leader in each of those sectors. In the United States, General Electric has followed a similar path of turning a select core of business units into global leaders and gradually divesting its remaining businesses.

Most companies and most managers have yet to recognize that the MNC ethos is obsolete. Hundreds of MNCs around the planet continue to grind along the path they have navigated for years, proving themselves correct to their own minds by pushing out more or less predictable profits. Meanwhile thousands of other companies do all within their power to emulate them, to become another "big guy."

The evidence of this fallacy is mounting fast. Proof of the lack of global understanding, the lack of global perspective among senior managers, the lack of global operating skills—and the injury such shortcomings cause—can be found everyday on the pages of America's media. Nowhere is this evidence more compelling than in the attitudes and skills of many senior managers.

The Nonglobal CEO

In early 1989 when *The Wall Street Journal* published an article underscoring the need for international skills among CEOs, it assembled a profile of the typical contemporary American CEO. One of his key characteristics: "The first time he traveled overseas on business was as CEO."

A recent survey showed that two thirds of the CEOs of America's largest companies had no specialized international training or international experience. As Chapter 8 further details, the basic skills and expertise of American managers generally have a distinctly nonglobal cast, which inevitably finds its way into the characters of their enterprises. *One cannot separate the fact that U.S. firms are "innocents abroad" from the reality that most American managers individually are "innocents abroad."*

In 1988 the marketing research firm of Yankelovich Clancy Shulman conducted detailed interviews with over 600 CEOs of large U.S. companies.[4] When asked if U.S. firms generally were adapting well to the new global economy, only 8 percent of the CEOs said that they were adjusting well. Any candor and perspicacity that seemed to have been reflected in that response was not necessarily repeated with respect to a followup question. When asked about the global role of their own firms, 40 percent of the CEOs stated that "understanding foreign markets" was not important to their companies.

When even those CEOs who seem to accept the need for global action are asked to articulate about the global challenge, the answers are revealing and disturbing. They typically reflect a poor factual understanding of the global economy, a poor grasp of global skills, or just plain ignorance of international matters.

"We must develop strong trading companies, as the Japanese have done. These trading companies would represent business in the international markets."

This reply came from one CEO when asked what U.S. firms must do to respond to the global challenge.

The failed American response to the Japanese *sogo shosha* has already been discussed above. Even when they are successful, trading companies are trading companies. They are not, nor do they make, industry leaders. A company's stake in the global economy can never be successfully proxied to an agent. The trading company fixation that persists in the U.S. business community is in final analysis only another way of saying that "the rest of the world" can be simply delegated to someone else. Ultimately, it is one more facet of the home country versus the rest of the world mentality which is so antithetical to the global view.

"The key to winning internationally is to be in Asia ahead of the competition and maintain a leadership position there. The world economy of the next generation will be driven by the Asian countries."

These words, or words to the same effect, have been articulated by many CEOs from Seattle to Boston. They have been made the basic premise of many international operating plans. One of the more conspicuous of these

---

[4]"American Redux," *Business Month*, January 1989.

was the plan of Merrill Lynch to go global in 1982 by acquiring an interest in a Hong Kong securities firm named Sun Hung Kai. In a move that was reportedly the brainchild of the firm's most senior managers, the largest American brokerage house obtained the interest by trading to the founder of the firm, a onetime fish salesman from Canton named Fung King Hey, the largest single block of stock (4 percent) in Merrill Lynch, valued at over $100 million. The U.S. brokerage firm said it entered the arrangement, which stunned many in the investment community, "because we want to be a major international services firm." The chairman of Merrill Lynch International boasted at the time that "the investment . . . represents an important milestone in Merrill Lynch's expansion."

Merrill Lynch's managers seemed unconcerned about the vast uncertainty facing Hong Kong over the expiration of the British leases with China for much of the colony's territory, despite the fact that this same uncertainty was causing many seasoned Asia hands to caution against any investment until that landmark issue was resolved. Instead those managers saw the spectacular fortunes made in prior years in Hong Kong's bull markets.

Within months after their investment the Hong Kong bubble burst. The bottom dropped out of the stock market. Fears over Beijing's takeover of Hong Kong began to drive hundreds of millions of dollars out of the colony. The value of the local currency plunged to record lows. As huge losses piled up in its new Hong Kong operation, Merrill Lynch had to send further cash from New York, in part to shore up a local property subsidiary that lost over $75 million. It was further compelled to provide indemnities for a related banking company.

In the original deal, the Chinese partner had obtained a commitment from Merrill Lynch not to compete directly in Hong Kong. Having put all its eggs in one basket and then having that basket go rotten, Merrill Lynch finally called it quits.

In 1987 the New York firm severed its ties with its Chinese partner by selling out to a Hong Kong businessman. The sales price was closely guarded but widely believed to be a fraction of the original purchase price. Merrill Lynch refused to acknowledge any mistake, only stating publicly that "we have determined that the financial markets have changed significantly since the time of our investment."[5]

---

[5]"Merrill Lynch and Sun Hung Kai Sever Their Five Year Partnership," *Asia Wall Street Journal*, February 16, 1987.

"We are committed irreversibly to maintain a major global presence."

This expression, found in various wordings in many American corporate speeches and annual reports, is not merely ironic to many foreign observers, it sometimes evokes virtual guffaws. For years foreign competitors have watched, usually with delight, as new managers, new consultants, new owners, or even new fads seem to whimsically shift the geographic focus of U.S. companies. They observe actions like those of the U.S. software company, Ultimate Corporation, which sponsored a gala opening of a Hong Kong branch in 1988, presided over by the U.S. Consul General, then abruptly closed the operation a bare 90 days later.

American firms, observed a seasoned Dutch Asian hand, "are like the wind-up toy soldiers that march along until they hit the slightest obstruction, then sharply change direction until they hit the next bump." It is impossible to be global for the short-term, or only intermittently, while senior managers play the "foreign option" like a yo-yo.

"All we have to do is to dominate the U.S. market in order to control the globe."

The CEO who said this is in an industry where over half of the top ten producers are foreign. His firm doesn't have a single plant offshore, and manages its international sales from an export office at U.S. headquarters. His foreign competitors control offshore markets, and their presence in the U.S. is forcing gradual, but steady price (and profit) reductions. His domestic cash flow, markets, and production facilities are fast becoming hostage to offshore competitors, literally behind his back. The words might have been appropriate in a 1959 interview in *Fortune*. Today they are not only anachronistic but treacherous.

"If we can succeed in the United States, we can succeed anywhere in the world."

This expression is an attitude closely aligned with that above. At best such a viewpoint is naive and parochial. At worst it betrays an utter failure to grasp the basic significance of the global economy. Success, especially success in the extreme, at home provides poor preparation for globalizing. Philadelphia's West Coast Video stores have been phenomenally successful in the United States, becoming the top U.S. video rental franchise chain. In 1987 it launched, with an extravagant and high profile reception at the American embassy in London, a massive campaign to open 500 new stores in the United Kingdom by 1990. At last report it had one unit in the country—and that one was company owned.

"Producing and selling in the developing countries are the key to the future of U.S. business."

Another CEO offered these words in explaining how U.S. firms will function globally. Global competitors would certainly like to see U.S. companies focus on developing countries as the key to their future. They are apparently more attuned to the critical economic data than many U.S. firms. Global companies have their financial, production, and sales roots in the industrial world because that is where those roots find nourishment. For some companies in some industries—Swedish Match in the match industry is an example—the developing world provides significant markets and significant cash flow. From a demographic perspective, the developing countries are certainly "where the action is." But that observation does not hold true in terms of finances, resources, innovation, and political and legal stability.

For the well-run global enterprise, production in some strategic developing countries makes sense, but is by no means the panacea often implied by American internationalists. Bitter lessons have been learned about production in developing countries by the automobile industry. The Romanian Oltcit, the Malaysian Proton, and the Taiwanese Feeling were neither rare animals nor new subatomic particles. At various times during the late 1980s these were all car models projected by some analysts to sweep America off its feet. Private investors and governments joined in the plan to catapult Romania, Malaysia and Taiwan into the ranks of the affluent by producing low-cost cars.

The myth of the low-wage advantage was discussed in Chapter 3. Despite the betting of hundreds of millions of dollars on that myth, nearly all such developing country car export industries have been derailed by quality, technology, or general production mismanagement problems that quickly offset any labor cost advantage. Even the Yugoslav Yugo, the VW Fox (Brazil), and the Ford Festiva (Brazil), which at least caught the momentary attention of the U.S. market, faded quickly as consumers and dealers lost interest. While cars from Korea, produced by Hyundai with support from Detroit, and Mexico, produced in Detroit-owned assembly plants, have captured more than a negligible market share, they are clear exceptions to the rule.

The primitive Yanonamo Indians have three numbers in their vocabulary: *one, two, and more than two*. In a similar fashion many U.S. executives' international knowledge may be reduced to a two word vocabulary: *U.S. and non-U.S.* They look at the world with a profound oversimplification, built on stereotypes, inexperience, and even misinformation. Many seasoned internationalists have learned the hard way that, just as you wouldn't ask the Yanonamo to tally inventory, you can't expect many contemporary American managers to deal with global issues.

Acquiring the Global Mentality

Some senior managers have begun to accept that their perspectives on doing business in Indiana and Oregon are not always going to serve them well in the global economy. Some have even begun to understand that going offshore involves much more than obtaining passports for high-achieving U.S. managers or opening foreign offices. John Hinds, president of AT&T International, is at least able to look candidly at his firm's problems in establishing a global beachhead in Europe. "There are no magical solutions," Hinds has noted. "The international market is going to take some grubbing out."

That grubbing out, which requires the development of the skills and instincts discussed in the following chapters, is still unattainable to many firms. For that process cannot begin until they accept the global mentality, beginning with a grasp of the global nature of their industry. As previously noted, firms that have never even exported are caught in a global war, sometimes without their knowledge. The foreign company which today produces and sells like goods only in Asia or Europe may not be identified as a competitor but that producer may be engaged in conduct that will eventually slam into the unsuspecting U.S. firm like a speeding locomotive.

The global mentality, however, remains elusive. In the 1988 CEO survey discussed above, only 4 percent of the 600 CEOs polled felt that U.S. firms were competing well in foreign markets. They apparently agreed that a primary problem in improving the situation was America's provincial mentality. One chairman stated: "The single most important issue facing us is a slow, unwilling attitude toward international business. As business people we have not yet decided that we want to be part of the international scene, whereas our competitors know they want to be part of the American scene." The words of another CEO perhaps best summarized the consequences of this nonglobal attitude, "By the time we decide to be part of the international scene, it may be too late."

CHAPTER 8

GROWING GLOBAL INSTINCTS

There is perhaps no more telling evidence of most companies' nonglobal perspective than the constitution of their board of directors. Certainly the character of a board reflects much about a company's character and priorities generally. It is no coincidence that many Silicon Valley firms have computer scientists on their boards or that large defense contractors have retired generals or admirals on theirs. Inevitably, a corporate board makes a strong statement, often unintentionally, about the company's global commitment and global perspective.

In 1987 *The Economist* studied the participation of foreigners on the boards of U.S. and British firms.[1] It found that of the world's 100 largest companies, only 21 had any citizen of a country other than that of the company domicile on its board. Only nine of these companies were American, although 46 U.S. firms appeared on the list. At the end of 1986, the last time comprehensive data was compiled, most of the largest U.S. companies had no representative of the non-U.S. world on their primary boards, despite their decades-long dependence on international operations. General Motors, with foreign sales representing 31 percent of its total, reached its board decisions without input from an offshore member. Ford, with 41 percent foreign sales, had no foreign director. Neither Mobil, with 63 percent foreign sales, nor IBM, with over 50 percent foreign sales, had a director from outside the United States.

The Economist concluded that with respect to U.S. and British firms, also included in the study, "the boards of their (and almost inevitably all multinational) corporations are about as parochial as a revivalist meeting in Little Rock." The exceptions to this finding were, not sur-

---

[1]"Foreigners Welcome on Board," *The Economist*, April 25, 1987.

prisingly, some of the few U.S. firms that have largely made the global transition, such as Xerox (three foreigners), Dow Chemical (three), United Technologies (two), and Exxon (two).

When the worldwide recruitment firm of Korn Ferry did a similar but more recent study, it actually found that despite the already low share of overseas participation on the boards of large U.S. companies, *that share was declining* from the early 1980s. Most globalizing of boards seemed to be on the part of non-U.S. firms, such as Nestle, who recently recruited former Federal Reserve chairman Paul Volcker to become the *fifth* non-Swiss member of its 15 member board. The move to obtain U.S. input no doubt seemed obvious, even a necessity, to Nestle, with 30 percent of its sales in the United States. Such Swiss firms are leading the way with global boards. ABB, the electrical engineering company formed by the merger of Switzerland's Brown Boveri and Sweden's ASEA, has four nationalities represented on its eight member board. The official board language of ABB is English. The Swiss home furnishing company Forbo conducts board meetings in English, French, or German. The board of the Dutch global electronics firm Philips includes Dutch, German, French, British, Belgian, and U.S. nationals.

While many U.S. firms have been quick to respond to external pressures to recruit minorities or women to their boards, they apparently lack the will or the insight, or both, to respond to internal needs to globalize management. Japan's international companies have done no better. In 1987 *none* of the Japanese members of the top 100 companies had foreigners on their boards, despite their virtual dependence on foreign operations. Most German firms are doing little better. Daimler Benz, the largest German company, derives 60 percent of its income from offshore but maintains a 100 percent German board.

Some offshore companies, on the other hand, recognizing the significance of the U.S. market to their global operations, have gone so far as to appoint U.S. CEOs. Robert Bauman, formerly vice chairman of Textron, was recruited to head the U.K. consumer products company Beecham and engineered that company's 1989 merger with Smithkline Beckman. Alexander Giacco, an American, is managing director of Italy's Montedison.

The Global Right Stuff

The parochial character of most U.S. boards of directors is only one of the many symptoms of the nonglobal nature of American management.

The homegrown nature of boards does not have to be an insurmountable handicap; for smaller global aspirants particularly, recruiting foreigners to the board just to be global could be counterproductive. In the large MNC operation with scores of millions, even hundreds of millions of dollars in non-U.S. source income, and thus high stakes in the operating environments of foreign lands, however, the homogenized U.S. board is a significant problem. And whether or not it is a problem that is recognized by those companies, it *is* a problem that will inevitably handicap their efforts to become global.

The more important point evidenced by America's one dimensional boards is the broader lack of institutional sensitivity to global issues. In Chapter 7 we talked about the nonglobal CEO and now, above, about the nonglobal board of directors. Of course many managers can cite examples of companies that succeed despite their CEOs or directors, that succeed on the strength of middle management and "corporate culture," on the strength of instincts bred into the company, or of what in astronautical pursuits has been labeled the "right stuff." But those situations only underscore the point that a concept, a perspective, or a mode of operation must be imbedded in corporate culture to be utilized with any meaningful longterm success.

In the global enterprise the manager of the Louisiana production plant must be no less a global manager than the sales director based in Geneva. No company becomes global simply by acquiring a few internationally experienced managers, no matter how adept or how senior they may be. The global mentality must be fully integrated. The global right stuff must be thoroughly assimilated. *Global perspectives, global analysis, and global response must become instinctive.*

Global managers are made, not born. The instincts that prompt them to pump money into Japan in order to halt a competitor in Europe, or to build a bridge between a research unit in Holland and another in Maryland are not genetic. Individuals acquire those instincts through openmindedness and hard work. When enough managers are imbued with the right stuff, the global synergy will start to spark.

Back to Basics

For many managers, their international problem began years ago in schools across the country which relegated international subjects to classroom footnotes. Perhaps it should be no surprise that U.S. companies cannot seem to tap global perspectives and global managers, considering what they have to work with.

When the National Geographic Society surveyed U.S. high school seniors in 1987 it unveiled a virtual "geographic illiteracy."[2] In Hartford, Connecticut, 48 percent could not give the names of any three of the 40-plus countries of Africa. In Texas, 25 percent could not name the country located across their southern border. In Boston, 39 percent could not name the states comprising New England.

When another geography IQ survey widened the sample to over 10,000 people in nine industrial countries, American youths aged 18 to 24 scored the lowest of all age groups in all the countries. Of American adults generally, only those in Italy and Mexico scored lower. One in ten of the Americans identified the United States as a member of the Warsaw Pact. The news gets worse. Although 70 percent of the Americans said that it was absolutely necessary to be able to read a map in contemporary society, over one third of them were unable to identify the westernmost city on a map.

Gilbert M. Grosvenor, president of the National Geographic Society, concluded of such studies, "Our adult population, especially our young adults, do not understand the world at a time in our history when we face a critical economic need to understand foreign consumers, markets, customs, foreign strengths and weaknesses."

These surveys were certainly no fluke. They simply corroborated, in one of the most comprehensive forms to date, the U.S. geographic illiteracy. The evidence has also come from many other sources through the years. In another study several years ago 40 percent of high school seniors stated that Israel was an Arab nation. In a UNESCO study of nine countries, Americans were next to the last in comprehension of foreign cultures.

Of course, being global involves more than a grasp of geography. But the manager who can't place the Netherlands on the right continent is not likely to win many stars when he tries to negotiate with the Dutch. Not long ago an executive from a U.S. company started a negotiation in Guayaquil, Ecuador, by exclaiming, "Gee, I always thought Ecuador was in Central America." His counterparts thought the comment neither funny nor appropriate, but rather a reflection of insincerity, lack of preparation,

[2]"Americans Falter on Geography Test," *New York Times*, July 28, 1988.

and general ignorance that gave the discussions a very sour start. Another senior executive was bragging at a reception with Brazilian business leaders in Washington about the extensive investments his company had in Brazil. "You'll not find any firm in the U.S.A. that knows more about Brazil—you know, several of my managers even speak Spanish." The native tongue in Brazil is not Spanish but Portuguese.

The Provincial MBA

Companies are not managed by high school seniors or even by the typical adult who might emerge in a statistical cross section of America. To evaluate the global IQ of American managers it is therefore helpful to look at the institutions dedicated to training those managers.

Over 60 percent of the business schools in the United States offer *no* international courses. When Professor Michael E. McGill of Southern Methodist University published the results of a systematic study of America's 650 different MBA programs in 1988, he identified the lack of international focus as one of the primary shortcomings of those programs.[3] As Professor McGill underscored, with "American manufacturing going abroad, foreign investment capital coming to America, and competition for worldwide markets on the rise, it makes sense that America's future business leaders would spend a fair amount of their academic preparation studying international business." Yet his survey revealed that the "dominant emphasis in virtually every one of the 650 MBA programs currently operating is on domestic companies and markets."

Those few schools that publicize an international emphasis may be guilty of misrepresentation. The McGill study found that when "a program does advertise itself as having an international focus, it means little more than that some of the courses use cases about multinational companies or that the student may take one course in international finance or international marketing." *Business Week* considered the problem in 1988 and concluded, "American business schools, for the most part, teach their students about a world that bears little resemblance to the reality of a global economy."

As one of these former MBA students, now a marketing manager for South America in a large U.S. company, explained in the McGill study:

---

[3]"Attack of the Biz Kids," *Business Month*, December 1988.

"I know I wanted to go international all along so I picked my courses carefully. It wasn't difficult, my school didn't have much to offer. What I did take ended up being pretty useless." Of course, some students do absorb international sensitivities from the foreign students attending their classes—a large number of whom are sent by overseas companies as part of programs aimed at globalizing younger managers. It would be a difficult search indeed to find a U.S. company which in like fashion financed its employees to study abroad.

Some cynics might point out that there appears to be an inverse relationship between the global success of a country and the number of MBAs it produces. Germany and Japan enjoy trade surpluses of $60 to $100 billion and produce no MBAs. America produces nearly 70,000 MBAs a year and has been suffering trade deficits well in excess of $100 billion.

Inevitably business schools reflect the focus and priorities of the American business community, and vice versa. As mentioned in Chapter 7, roughly two thirds of the chairmen and presidents of the biggest U.S. international companies have had no international training and no experience in their company's international divisions or offshore units. An appalling number of American business and political leaders even show disturbing symptoms of the geographic illiteracy afflicting the average American. Several months ago a member of the Senate Foreign Relations Committee listened pensively to a detailed presentation by two representatives of the government of Cyprus regarding that nation's regional security problems. At the end of the review, the Senator thoughtfully looked up and asked, "Isn't Cyprus an island in the Middle East somewhere?"

An important indicator of the level and quality of the American manager's international preparation is the success rate for Americans posted overseas. While companies are usually reluctant to release data of this nature, studies that have been made show that between 20 to 50 percent of international assignments of American managers end in premature return, amounting essentially to failure in the posting. The rate jumps up to 70 percent for assignments to developing countries. The director of the Washington International Center, Robert Kohls, who is involved in training programs for international assignees, has estimated that 10,000 Americans annually take premature leave of their international assignments and return home. The annual direct costs alone of such corporate returnees has been estimated at *$2 billion nationally*, incurred by their U.S. employers.

The Water Factor

Their lack of international training and international perspective is doubtlessly playing a big role in another malady that seems to strike many managers. This malady might be termed the *water factor*: Whenever they cross over an ocean they seem to lose their business judgment and sometimes even their simple common sense.

Dayco Products is a $330 million Ohio-based producer of plastic and rubber products such as hoses and belts. The company has been in business for many years, presumably staying in business because its management exercised sound business judgment. But when an Austrian trading agent dangled an order for $120 million for tractor belts and hoses from the Soviet Union, the water factor apparently took over.

If it had received such a large order, representing a major proportion of its annual sales, from within the United States, the company doubtlessly would have conducted exhaustive credit checks and verifications, and probably obtained some assurance of payment before production. Certainly at most companies the word of an agent would not have been a sufficient basis for making such a huge commitment. Someone might even have stopped to calculate the absurdly high number of tractors that would have to be produced to consume $120 million worth of belts and hoses. Yet Dayco's senior managers excitedly signed a contract with the trading company, not the Soviet customer, and proceeded with production. Had they bothered to check with a seasoned international businessman, they would have almost certainly been informed that there was a simple device for security in such situations, used by many doing business with the centrally controlled economies. This device is a confirmed irrevocable letter of credit, guaranteeing payment by a well-known U.S. or European bank so long as the supplier met its commitment.

If the company had also thought to check the integrity of the Austrian agents on whom they were betting $120 million, it would have found they were subject to an outstanding arrest warrant in Vienna for questionable trading practices. Instead, the company began to churn out hundreds of thousands of belts and hoses for Russia. Two hundred factory workers worked overtime, as the company pulled out all stops to meet the Soviet order. Even though only a tiny fraction of the early billings sent to the trading firm were paid, Dayco continued to produce products for 20 months to fill the order.

Not only did the company agree to pay a huge commission to trading agents, it agreed to make the payment in advance. Without payment, or even order verification, from the customer, the Dayco chairman, who personally negotiated the deal, *approved over $13 million in advance commission payments* to the agent. At least half of the goods were shipped to a warehouse in Germany before the truth began to unfold. The $120 million order had been a fiction. There had been an initial order from Soviet tractor plants for less than one percent of the total but never anything more substantial. More than a few observers appreciated the irony when the company, not long after the fiasco, changed its name to Day International (since then the company was acquired by Armtek Corporation).

A popular science fiction story published many years ago involved the visit to earth of highly advanced beings who explained that the sun was about to explode. They would therefore transport the population of earth to another world in their huge starships. They even presented a book in their own language that set forth the details of their mission. The earth's scientists listened to their complicated explanation of the sun's pending doom, based on principles with which they had no experience, and finally agreed that the aliens must be correct. As the last starship carrying off humankind departed, one of the few humans who stayed behind deciphered the aliens' book. It was a cookbook, with instructions on how to prepare dishes with the tender flesh of homo sapiens. A water factor of a catastrophic degree was the theme of the story. Faced with complexity beyond their experience, humans accepted what they heard rather than exercising sound judgment by confessing ignorance or confusion.

In 1975 the giant French steel company Creusot Loire targeted Phoenix Steel of the United States as a vehicle for international expansion. Phoenix was by then a marginal producer of specialty steel saddled with an obsolete plant. Creusot rushed executives to Phoenix for evaluation of its assets. Caught in the excitement of an overseas acquisition, the French were victims of the water factor. They apparently became blinded to the condition of the plant.[4] One consultant remembers: "They [Phoenix] tried sprucing up with spray paint but anyone could see it was cosmetic. You just had to lean on something and see it fall to find out." In what many observers characterized as a suspension of sound judgment, Creusot

[4]"The Tricky Business of Transatlantic Alliances," *International Management*, April 1987.

nonetheless paid a vastly inflated price and then soon realized it had to invest another $100 million to build a new facility. When steel prices dropped in the early 1980s the financial pressure was too great. First Phoenix, then Creusot Loire declared bankruptcy

Global Mind, Open Mind

A critical element of the global mentality provides the ability to overcome the water factor, and concomitantly the ability to achieve the subtle interplay of skills and knowledge that characterizes the global manager. A shorthand way of expressing that element is adaptability. Simply put, international executives must adapt to their surroundings, and international companies must adapt to different business and social environments. Yet that simplicity is deceiving. So too the word *adapting* is deceiving. The global manager must have an open mind of the first order to be able to absorb and understand the ethos, the cultural priorities, the economic framework, the mentality of a foreign person, foreign enterprise, or foreign society generally. Many would indeed call this the ability to adapt. But the process is more than adapting. It is assimilation, it is the ability to grow, to expand, to absorb and to respond without abandoning one's basic frame of reference.

In essence the global mentality requires *the ability to remain so objective that one can become truly subjective within another country's market or industry, or within a foreign competitor's own frame of reference.* It means thinking and behaving like an insider in any country of the world. The starting place, but only the starting place, is in assimilating physical cultures, and the vagaries of communication and expression, understanding that there may be many ways to say the same thing or that the same thing may not have the same meaning around the planet.

I'm OK, You're a Zero

Many American manufacturers, and nearly all American politicians, gave a warm reception to the campaign begun in 1984 to incorporate a "Made in America" logo on U.S. exports. The symbol was the U.S. OK sign, consisting of an open hand with a circle made by the thumb and first finger connecting at their tips. The logo would, its promoters zealously promised, build American pride in international marketplaces and enhance the reputation of American producers.

The symbol was received overseas as another emblem of American insensitivity and arrogance, or, by the more forgiving, simply more American ignorance. No one involved in the campaign had considered whether the sign used had the same connotations overseas. It would have required no more than a few overseas phone calls to reveal that the symbol which the U.S. business community wanted to stamp on its exports has a number of meanings abroad, none of them close to that in the United States. Nearly all of them are pejorative in nature. In Belgium and France the same circular symbol essentially means "You're a zero." In many parts of Italy the symbol of American quality is an insult with anal overtones. Elsewhere in the Mediterranean it often connotes a male homosexual. In Tunisia, it means "I will kill you." In Greece, Turkey, and parts of Africa it is a rather crass sexual invitation.

Business, Not Folklore

For the global enterprise, the cultural gap is not the only gap of understanding that must be overcome, but it is the most obvious. Culture is not just folklore and quaint eating instruments. It also determines the way people are motivated. It is, in broadest terms, the indigenous framework for thinking, reacting, and communicating, whether as an employer or employee, customer or seller, investor or regulator.

The more traditional focus of cultural comparison is on language, communications, dress, art, and religion. These may be the source of the greatest distinctions between a people. Often the cultural distinctions of this nature are the easiest to identify. They can also cause some of the most glaring *faux pas* in America's global efforts:

• Early during his tenure, President Ronald Reagan made a speech in Mexico City. After speaking he sat down to very sparse applause, disconcerted over the unenthusiastic response. He later good-naturedly explained: "It was worse when a gentleman followed me and started a speech in Spanish, which I didn't understand, but he was being applauded with every paragraph. So, to hide my embarrassment, I started clapping before everyone else until our ambassador leaned over to me and said, 'I wouldn't do that if I were you. He's interpreting your speech.'"
• When Pillsbury started selling its Jolly Green Giant brand foods in Saudi Arabia it discovered that its label had been translated into Arabic literally as "intimidating green ogre."
• A major customer in Europe called, furious, to the U.S. supplier of a

large piece of production equipment, asking why it had been delivered six months early to a plant site still under construction. The European order date had been clearly marked 2/8/87. Under European custom, any European firm would have understood the numbers to mean 2 August. The U.S. firm had simply assumed the date was February 8.

• In preparation for the visit of John F. Kennedy to meet with Prime Minister Nehru in 1962, the White House sent six dozen signed photographs of the President to India. All of them were framed in cowhide— the skin of one of India's most sacred creatures.

The most obvious of these culture gaps is language. But language skills can be deceiving. Understanding of the language of a society may be obtained without any real grasp of that society's ethos, breeding a false confidence based on the language skills alone. Again and again, individuals are identified within a corporate framework as international experts simply because they speak more than one language.

Nothing illustrates this problem better than the difficulties that frequently have arisen between U.S. managers and their counterparts in Great Britain or Australia, ranging from confusion over the term *billion* (a million million to the British, but only a thousand million to the American) to shock over a perceived rudeness in the sometimes too-friendly, "macho-cowboy" style of American managers.

Some of the classic examples of the language gap giving rise to global mistakes are made in using U.S. brand names overseas, such as the green ogre problem Pillsbury had in the Middle East. General Motors tried to sell its Nova model in South America despite the fact that the Spanish translation of the name meant "no go." A large food processing company introduced its popular cooking oil product in Latin America without realizing its brand name translated as "jackass oil." Coca-Cola's relentless drive for a global brand name in China very nearly left the company with a product translated as "bite the wax tadpole"; it prudently compromised its policy to change the name to ideographs meaning "pleasure in the mouth." Meanwhile Kentucky Fried Chicken stuck by its well-known motto for its PRC units, leaving it with ads reading in Chinese "it makes you want to suck your fingers."

Thumbs Up, Thumbs Down

The spoken and written word is only the primary form of expression in a culture. A great deal of communication is accomplished by gestures, posture, and body language generally. In some countries people signify yes by shaking their heads from side to side in a fashion that would be considered as a definite no elsewhere. Pointing your toe over crossed legs at your host in Thailand is considered offensive. In many countries, a thumbs up signal is a vulgar gesture.

The Color of Understanding

In many countries colors may have a far greater significance than they do in the United States. They can be as much a part of a local culture as chopsticks or raw fish. The wrong color can defeat the effectiveness of an ad or product packaging, even going so far as to destroy the reputation of a product. The mourning color in many Asian countries is white, not the black familiar in the West. In the Ivory Coast dark red is often used to signify mourning. Pink is often not a feminine color outside the U.S. In many countries red is viewed as a more masculine color than blue and yellow more feminine than pink. In China red generally is a symbol of good luck, but in Turkey it is a symbol of death.

Colors are not the only cultural symbols that the global perspective must embrace. In the U.S. a bird that is primarily of European origin, the stork, represents the happy news of a birth. But in Singapore the stork is not nearly so pleasant a symbol; it is associated with maternal death. Foxes may conjure up slyness in the West, but in Japan they are associated with witches.

Religious symbols may vary widely and misunderstanding them can be disastrous. Many companies are surprised to discover that their factories in Thailand or certain other Asian countries have "spirit houses" at a strategic corner of the property to appease local spirits. In many instances at foreign investment projects, local Buddhist priests have been called to bless machinery. In one major joint venture involving a large Western textile firm, priests had to be brought in to exorcise bad spirits which workers insisted were causing machinery to malfunction and other mischief. Nearly always such rituals are simply accepted by prudent and tolerant local managers. In at least one case mass confusion was caused when a request arrived at the U.S. headquarters of a company for senior management approval of such a Buddhist exorcism ceremony on the floor of its Thai factory.

The global manager isn't charged with knowing the details of esoteric rituals in Asia or the meaning of colors in Kuala Lumpur. But the global manager recognizes that such aspects can have an impact on business, and if he has a plant staffed by workers who subscribe to such rituals, he makes it his business to assimilate them. He may not have to subscribe to the rituals, but he must be able to act in harmony with those who do.

Your Time or Mine?

To many observers outside the United States the primary characteristic of Americans is "go, go, go". In the words of one Swiss executive, "You Americans are gears in a fast moving machine, desperate not to stop in one place too long." More than a few non-Americans around the world watch in silent bemusement as Americans in hotels and restaurants compulsively study their watches and check plane tickets. London-based consultant Richard van den Bergh has studied the lack of communication and mutual misunderstanding in U.S. foreign operations and often ascribes them to such attitudes: "It's a typically American problem. The executive shows up at an eight o'clock board meeting and has to catch a plane for New York at noon."

Treatment of time is a cultural trait itself, as anyone who's ever heard *mañana* from someone south of the U.S. border could testify. Punctuality is a respected trait in most industrial countries, but it is not particularly so in South America, the Middle East, or many Asian countries.

Adjusting to the likelihood of a Saudi showing up one hour late for an appointment may seem facile. The challenge, however, is assimilating the mentality behind such action. It doesn't mean that locals cannot read watches; it means that they live in a milieu that emphasizes the social contact that derives from sitting around and "doing nothing" more than "getting down to business."

Tourist Managers

This time-set mind-set also plays a big role in creating what may be labeled the *tourist manager* image of American executives. A Dutch businessman was complaining about an unsuccessful round of negotiations with an American company. The U.S. firm had arrived in Amsterdam for a three day stay. They spent a half day touring the canals, a half day negotiating, a half day shopping, a half day negotiation, and a final half day negotiating before leaving. Each night they dutifully checked off one more four star restaurant off their list. They departed with only a fraction of the issues on their negotiation list resolved. "They weren't business-men. They were tourists," the Dutch manager groused.

Part of the problem, not uncommon among many of those who travel only infrequently, is the often irresistible urge to "see the sights." This impulse, and the not infrequent enslavement to the clock, can greatly distort global perceptions, and handicap efforts to build genuine global instincts.

• The president of a large West Coast corporation was asked to approve a project in Thailand involving an investment of over $20 million. He had a reputation of resisting overseas projects generally because they were too risky. After listening to the first half of a detailed political and financial risk assessment he stopped the presentation. "I've always felt good about Thailand. I know from personal experience that it is the kind of place we should invest in." A pleased but puzzled project manager quizzed the vice president/international over drinks that night. The vice president finally mentioned that he had been totally surprised by the approval. He confes-sed to knowing, however, that the CEO's sole experience in Thailand was a few days in a luxury resort on an island to which he had flown from Hong Kong without any exposure to the rest of the country. His sole experience with Thailand had been in a resort catering to Westerners. He had met no business leaders, no political leaders, and not experienced the country in any meaningful sense—but he had genuinely enjoyed his golf and tennis in Thailand.
• The CEO of a large Southeastern producer of industrial supplies an-nounced a five day tour of operations in four South American countries. When the new regional manager sent a list of plants, offices, and cus-tomers proposed for visits, the international division manager did not respond but instead asked for a summary of the best restaurants and golf courses in each of the cities to be visited.
• After a letter of intent had been signed, two teams of negotiators, one American and one Swedish, arrived in the neutral territory of London to negotiate a manufacturing joint venture for Sweden. The Americans an-nounced at the outset that they had four days to "do the deal"; senior management expected them to return in time for one of their monthly management meetings. The Swedes had made no return reservations and had planned on a week to ten days of meetings to hammer out the details

of the complex deal. After two days of slow progress the Americans began to voice almost hourly reminders that they were leaving soon, increasingly alienating their Swedish counterparts. When the group did indeed break up on the Americans' departure date, the Swedes returned home with the report that the U.S. firm was not seriously interested in doing the project.

• An international negotiator/consultant who works with many U.S. companies in China lists U.S. impatience as the single biggest impediment to successful negotiations in the Middle Kingdom. "It takes a week to accomplish in Beijing what you can do in New York in two hours, but many Americans seem unable to accept this," he points out.

Such reports could be repeated in the same general fact patterns, with varying details, for scores of companies in their activities around the globe. In essence the tourist manager syndrome is just another characteristic of the nonglobal manager. Implicit in such behavior is a perception that international business is not to be taken seriously. To many such individuals it becomes a form of entertainment, a pleasant change of pace from the real work to be done at home.

The Business of Adapting

Of course, interfacing with offshore cultures doesn't have to be without fun—and a sense of humor usually is an important global asset. When French managers of the ambitious Eurotunnel, or Chunnel, project landed at Folkestone in England for meetings in 1988, they were greeted by an enormous green inflatable frog. Humor can often smooth the rough edges around a culture gap.

But the global enterprise doesn't assimilate local culture because it is fun; it does so to be successful. Being able to profitably function in countries as varied as the Soviet Union, China, Brazil, Belgium, and Australia presents a challenge that goes far beyond learning how to use chopsticks, digest borscht, or acquiring the right inflection for intoning "g'day mate." Body language, religious symbols, local cuisine, and similar traditional cultural attributes may evidence the most obvious examples of the culture gap that must be bridged in global operations. But they represent only the surface of a deep body of more intangible differences. As in many aspects of global enterprise, the most important features are often the subtle ones.

The global enterprise and its managers understand that the way an individual buys, sells, responds to instructions, and functions in the workplace is defined in large part by the individual's culture.

In Indonesia the supervisor of an American offshore oil rig lost his temper with an Indonesian worker. In front of the employee and other workers he yelled for one of his staff to instruct the man to pack up and leave in the next boat off the rig. A mob of Indonesians grabbed fire axes and chased the supervisor into an office. They were chopping away the door when more level heads finally intervened. The supervisor's sharp words for the worker were totally inappropriate for an operation in the country, shaming the man in front of his peers in a culture that emphasizes self-restraint, nonconfrontation, and harmony in all interpersonal relations.

In the interior of China, also a culture that puts emotional restraint at a premium, U.S. supervisors at the site of a large factory construction project reportedly lost their patience so often in working with the Chinese that worker relations heated to the boiling point on several occasions, resulting in fistfights between Chinese and Americans. When the U.S. manager was giving a speech during ceremonies commemorating the conclusion of the project, firecrackers were lit as part of the festivity. Based on the history of soured relations he concluded that the Chinese were shooting at him, and to his great subsequent embarrassment he frantically threw himself down behind the podium.

Fortunately a breakdown of cultural relations seldom reaches the stage of physical violence. Yet less dramatic cultural breakdowns often occur, and can do violence to international business relations.

Adapting May Be the Law

Adapting to some local customs can often be a matter of law. Around the world, local labor laws establish a wide variety of standards for workers' roles in management, plant closings, and for worker benefits. The size or type of packaging is stipulated by law in countries such as Kenya, Singapore, and Malaysia. Soft drink bottlers in Ecuador were forced to spend millions of dollars on new equipment when the government required drinks to be in four stipulated sizes. Labeling laws similarly required careful adaption of packaging. The words *giant, jumbo* or *king* size are prohibited in India, as is the use of foreign trademarks. Chile prohibits manufacturers to print prices on product labels. In Venezuela, on the other hand, prices are required to be printed on labels. Since Islamic law prohibits use of animal fat, producers like Pillsbury must use vegetable shortening in their Middle East products.

France prohibits the use of foreign words in advertising. Fines have been levied for using hamburger instead of *bifteck hache* or show biz instead of *industrie de spectacle*. Finland bars ads for weight reducers, intimate products, alcohol, politics, or religion. Many countries prohibit the use of children in advertising. Australia enforces an often confusing statute against ads featuring images that may appeal to children if the product is not suitable for children; an ad using a Robin Hood image to advertise cigarettes had to be altered for this reason.

Prior to a 1986 visit to West Germany by General Motors chairman Roger Smith, lawyers for the company had to pose an awkward question to a German criminal prosecutor: Would Smith be arrested when he entered the country? The company and a flamboyant German entrepreneur were accused of violating German financial laws by arranging the sale of GM's Terex unit to a company of few, if any, assets. GM had wanted to be rid of the unit at almost any price. The down payment for the deal was $23 million which GM simultaneously invested in the purchasing company. Such a practice, called "round-tripping," is illegal in many countries and was, according to press accounts, directed by the CEO over the objections of his own international lawyers. Indeed, he apparently continued to pump round-tripping funds into the company even after becoming aware of its questionable status under German law.

Whether local laws forbid hamburger or round-tripping, the global company must be able to understand them and integrate compliance into its operations. The global impact of the inability to assimilate to laws in key operating countries has been felt by a number of foreign companies who have attempted a global move through the acquisition of minority interests in U.S. firms. In several instances, they have discovered that due to antitrust laws they are restrained from a broad range of joint activity with their U.S. partners. They have in some cases created the worst of all worlds for themselves through such lack of preparation, having tied their own hands in an affiliate relationship which they cannot control or even tap for sensitive business information. In some of these situations the foreign acquirers would have had more freedom to cooperate, and exchange information, with totally unrelated firms in the United States. A similar problem has arisen for U.S. firms seeking offshore takeovers when they have stumbled over national securities and financial laws imposing poison pills or other shareholder restraints totally unfamiliar in the United States.

Local custom also may require a number of obvious adaptions. Measurement units may vary considerably. The Betty Crocker cake recipe calling for one half cup of oil would bring confusion in the kitchens of most countries, where a cup is alien to local measurement systems. Limited consumer pocketbooks may require smaller packaging. In many South American countries Chiclets chewing gum are sold in two piece packages, not the 12 piece boxes known in the United States. Shampoos are sold in many developing countries in one-use-only bubble packages. One reason why Mr. Donut is said to have fared better in Japan than its archrival Dunkin'Donuts is its use of smaller coffee cups designed to fit Japanese hands. Mattel flopped when it tried to sell its U.S. version of the Barbie Doll in Japan; the doll became a huge success, however, when a Japanese licensee made its eyes dark, its legs shorter, and its breasts smaller.

Technical standards, whether embodied in law or custom, also pose major challenges in global assimilation. One of the primary aims of European market unification has been the elimination of the disparate technical standards which apply within the European Community (EC). N.V. Philips, the global Dutch-based electronics firm, has in the past made 29 different types of electrical outlets, 12 types of electrical cords, 12 technically different irons, 15 technically different cake mixers, 10 types of electric plugs, and 3 types of televisions just to be able to sell throughout the European Community. Electric plugs, for example, may have two prongs or three prongs. The prongs may be straight or angled, fat, sheathed, thin, round, flat, or rectangular; their faces may be round, square, pentagonal, or hexagonal. Some, for Britain, have fuses built in, others, for France, have small niches like keyholes.

Adapting to Failure?

An interesting dichotomy, and a compelling lesson in the global adapting of the kind elaborated above, was found for years in the Japanese operations of Warner-Lambert, the $3.5 billion consumer products company. The company's Schick division became a dominant seller, effectively controlling the wet shaving market, by adapting to Japanese practices and tapping into the country's traditional distribution system. At the same time the company's division selling candy products such as Dentyne and

Certs tried for years to go it alone with direct sales to retailers. Ignoring the lesson provided by its sister division, the unit lost millions. By refusing to adapt locally, the otherwise successful division was having to adapt to failure. Finally in the late 1970s the unit accepted the need to work with, not against, the local custom; before long it was earning a strong profit.

One of the best examples of failure induced by failure to adapt lies in the U.S. franchise industry. Multitudes of U.S. franchisors have tried to overlay their U.S. "package" onto foreign markets. The franchise, by its nature, can be defined as a system that resists adapting The fact that the same structure is used again and again, with unified standards for workers, production, store appearance, management, materials, and marketing, is often the key to franchise success.

There have been only two U.S. franchisors with reported long-term international success, McDonalds and Pepsico's Kentucky Fried Chicken. Even McDonalds has had its share of problems, as evidenced by its troubles in Paris described previously. And KFC has had many bumpy years but persevered overseas. Consumer habits vary widely offshore. Many resist the "rush, rush" style of the service that is the hallmark of many food and service franchises. "You have to learn the mores and the values" of a nation's consumers, notes Mark Battisello, vice president of Postal Instant Press Inc., which stumbled badly in Britain after investing several million dollars. "We have learned that every country isn't the same."

Lured into a false confidence by the similarity of language, many U.S. franchisors have considered the easiest overseas expansion market to be Great Britain. Their record there is revealing. Perkits Yogurt Inc. announced grandiose plans to open 200 to 250 British units; most British consumers presented with frozen yogurt wouldn't know if they were supposed to lick it, patch their walls with it, or use it to fertilize their flowers.

Computerland Corporation planned 60 units for Britain by 1987 but had to settle for only 20. Its rival Entre Computer struggled to open 15 units but gave up and closed the few units it had managed to open by early 1987. Burger King bought out all its UK franchises in 1983 after years of effort—all three. Tippy Tacos House of Texas enthusiastically announced its offer of a master franchise for Britain in 1986 but had no takers; tacos are as well known as frozen yogurt in England. The history of West Coast Video has already been mentioned. Its efforts to open 500 units in the UK by 1990 had netted a grand total of one, company owned, store by 1989. Some franchise companies that fell flat on their face in the UK, like Dunkin' Donuts, Burger King, and Thrifty Rent-a-Car have returned with a more realistic plan to build slowly with company owned units to acquire the necessary expertise and learn how to adapt to the British market.

Commenting on the offshore performance of U.S. franchisors, the president of the International Franchise Association, William B. Cherkasky, noted that his own studies demonstrated that "nearly two thirds of U.S. franchise executives felt there was no need to adapt their product, marketing, or business plans to a specific foreign market." Such attitudes explain in large part the high failure rates of U.S. franchises overseas.

The Common Sense Gap

The global perspective understands that adapting is more than accommodating consumers. It means that people can differ in basic ways of thinking or even what may be termed *common sense*.

In a nuclear reactor under construction in Brazil alarms began to scream as foreign experts were working with their local counterparts in the control room. According to the instruments the reactor's primary feed water was leaking heavily through a main valve. Although the system had not yet been fueled, they were terrified of what the leak might signify. They arrived at the site of the valve to find that workers had opened the valve to take showers with the reactor water.

Adapting at Home

Perhaps the problems of the culture gap are best evidenced to Americans by stories from their own country. Many foreign companies have stumbled badly in the United States, in the same way that multitudes of U.S. firms have stumbled offshore. A major Swiss global firm had so many difficulties between its U.S. and Swiss managers on operational and marketing issues in the United States that it finally engaged a special team of consultants to identify and resolve the problems behind the discord. One consultant involved in advising foreign firms in such situations has been Rodman Drake of the consulting firm of Cresap, McCormick & Paget. "There's more of a macho, cowboy, I'm in charge style of operating in the U.S.," he explains, in contrast to a more consensus building style overseas.

A transferee from the Dominican Republic to the New Jersey headquarters of a U.S. animal health products firm found that his American counterparts resisted the informal conversations or chitchat that would start meetings or workdays in Latin cultures. He felt that the Americans treated such efforts at collegiality as a waste of time. "It strikes us as cold-blooded," he reported when interviewed about the problem.

Nowhere are such problems more apparent than in Japanese/American joint ventures, where two distinctively different styles must coexist. Japanese managers perennially have problems in dealing with the directness of Americans; Americans have great difficulty with the opposite trait in Japanese. One U.S. manufacturing firm staged role playing among its Japanese and American employees, arranged by an international consulting firm. When a Japanese manager was asked to criticise an American in these simulations, "it took five runs of the same situation until he was direct enough that the American could realize he was being criticized," explained Gary Wederspahn, one of the consultants who arranged the exercise.[5]

By the Numbers

A critically important element of this global adaption is the ability to embrace different economic priorities. No manager will ever be able to truly succeed in the global economy until he or she appreciates that economic and business decisions are not approached from one universal framework around the world.

For many American companies there is no greater handicap in facing the global economy than the dichotomy in the economic priorities observed by American and offshore firms. As evidenced almost daily in the global economy, many, if not most, U.S. firms advance short-term quick return analysis to the centerpiece of decision making. The non-U.S. participants in the global economy largely approach decisions from the long

---

[5]"American Culture Is Often a Puzzle for Foreign Managers in the United States," *The Wall Street Journal*, February 12, 1986.

view, emphasizing long-term growth, long-term market share, and long-term return.

When Honda made a decision many years ago to enter the motorcycle market in Europe, it went forward with the strength of a long-term commitment, drawing from the cash flow of successful U.S. operations. It invested for seven years before attaining profitability in Europe. U.S. machine tool companies have been handicapped in their struggle to stay afloat by conglomerate parent companies which have denied them long-term capital commitments, often due to a pattern of frequent ownership transfers. James L. Koontz, CEO of the $100 million Kingsbury Machine Tool Corporation has been fighting a frustrating battle with global competitors for years. He left such a conglomerate owned operation to escape the problems caused by such mentalities as "employment is pared to the bone, research and development is cut, and horizons shortened to maximize short-term profit." Under such conditions, he complains, "You can never be a world leader."

Surveys conducted in Japan and the United States by James Abegglen, international consultant and professor of business at Tokyo's Sophia University, asked businessmen to list the principal purpose of their company. U.S. executives not surprisingly stated their primary purpose was maximizing return on investment. For Japanese executives the primary corporate goal was maximizing the market share. An earlier 1985 survey by Booz Allen & Hamilton of Japanese and U.S. managers, likewise found that Americans were most concerned with increasing return to stockholders. In that survey, the Japanese goal was expressed as becoming global leaders in their industry.

Although this dichotomy may be seen in this light as a variation in corporate culture, it amounts to far more than simply another cultural difference. It amounts to a constitutional difference. Companies dedicated to their markets focus on investment, competitive pricing, and other measures to expand market shares. The company obsessed with immediate profit may sell market share with price increases and scrutinize investment with suspicion for its effect on profit.

Increasingly it appears that the American high technology decline even may be suffering from this mentality. Nobel Laureate Arno Penzias of Bell Labs was asked in a 1989 interview about the U.S. technology posture. "It doesn't matter if we have the world's best superconductors," he complained, "because if people demand a 20 percent return a year, we will never invest enough in implementing the superconductors." Quality guru Dr. Edwards Deming often compares the United States and Japan in this respect: "The emphasis [in the U.S.] is on the quarterly dividend and the quick buck, while the emphasis in Japan is to plan decades ahead. The next quarterly dividend is not as important as the existence of the company 5, 10, or 20 years from now. One requirement for innovation is faith that there will be a future."

The world of the company in search of long-term growth and the company searching for ready cash look very different indeed. Observing from the record of losses and strategic defeats suffered due to this difference, it may ultimately be viewed as a flaw in the global efforts of U.S. firms. Many managers insist it is not their fault, but simply a response to insatiable investors. As one CEO in a 1988 nationwide poll noted, "American companies behave shortsightedly because of what they think the expectations of their investors are." Wall Street may indeed provide evidence of the unreasonable demands of investors, but so do corporate compensation systems which provide large rewards for managers who secure quick profits and concurrent disincentives for those who might otherwise foresake profits to gain a long-term strategic advantage.

"I am not convinced that the management goals and investment analysis perspective of American firms really reflect the demands of shareholders," noted an European manager who was returning home after a stint at the head of a U.S. subsidiary. "Rather I believe those structures vastly magnify those demands far out of proportion to reality." Wherever the fault lies, there are certainly steps managers can begin to take to deemphasize the short-term and to sensitize themselves and shareholders to the severe handicap the short-term mentality places on U.S. firms in succeeding in the global economy. U.S. firms don't necessarily have to embrace *in toto* the economic motives of their competitors. But until they learn how to at least look at the world through their competitors' eyes, they will consistently misjudge those competitors, and commit missteps as a consequence.

Until such perspectives are developed, and until U.S. firms are able to instinctively ask themselves what their competitors will be doing five and ten years hence, those firms will continue to play a perpetual game of catch-up around the world, a game in which they gradually slip further and further behind those who are able to manage with a global view. American Gary Hamel, lecturing at the London Business School, complains of U.S. firms, "We've been caught in a perpetual follower position because we've never understood the long-term strategic intentions of competitors."

U.S. CEOs are gradually growing into the global perspective and slowly beginning to show this sensitivity. In a 1988 survey of over 600 CEOs, 86 percent expressed the belief that U.S. business is generally too short-term oriented. But only 40 percent of those admitted that their own companies suffered from such orientation. (It's always someone else's firm that is afflicted with the malady.) Asked to comment generally on the American corporation and its problems, one CEO noted, "Bureaucracy is our main problem—short-term bureaucratic thinking." Another reflected the gradual reconciliation that is happening at some firms, and must happen at many more, "We have changed our executive compensation plan to emphasize long-term results rather than one year performance."

The Hidden Asset Scramble

How quickly are U.S. firms learning the lesson? In 1988 and 1989 a steady stream of U.S. firms were alerted by investment bankers of the hidden assets they had in Japan. Based primarily on the increased value of real estate holdings in Tokyo, U.S. companies began to yield to the temptation of liquidation. In 1988 when RJR Nabisco discovered its interest in a Japanese baking company joint venture was worth $92 million, it quickly sold out. McGraw-Hill Inc. surrendered its Japanese operations, representing equity in a publishing company, for a lump sum exceeding $200 million in 1988. A number of other U.S. firms rushed to sell all or part of their Japanese operations.

This onslaught of Japanese liquidations by U.S. firms provided an inadvertent baring of corporate souls. In some cases, the investment bankers who made scores of millions arranging such sales were in effect capitalizing on their client's lack of global perspective. The effectively operated global enterprise does not suddenly discover that a subsidiary, however minor a unit, is worth 50 or 100 times its previously estimated value. If it does, something has gone terribly wrong with its global intelligence and financial management system. When a lackluster unit that has quietly been sending back $5 million or less in dividends is indeed found to be worth $200 million or more in market value, the effective global corporation does not go running breathlessly to the auction block. It queries the significance of the strategic implications and the unit's overall global role. The increase of assets represents an important opportunity, but one which may be capitalized best by action less drastic than immediate liquidation. Sale of only a partial interest in the local stock market, collateralizing the interest to address cash flows needs elsewhere, sale of high value real estate while maintaining basic operations, or many other options may prove of greater global value.

The failure to effectively deal with the Japanese asset problem as a global issue shook some firms to their roots. As early as August 1986, Salomon Brothers Inc. released a report demonstrating that due to the value which had accumulated to Shaklee Corporation's Japanese subsidiary a takeover of the entire company could easily be financed by the subsequent sale of the Japanese unit. As the U.S. investment community began to awake, stirring a hostile bid for the company, the Yamanouchi Pharmaceutical Company of Japan first snapped-up the Japanese subsidiary, then the whole U.S. company by early 1989.

The WPP Group Plc. of the United Kingdom successfully stalked the New York's J. Walter Thompson with a deliberate eye on the company's Tokyo real estate. Not long after it finally acquired J. Walter Thompson, WPP sold that real estate for approximately $200 million. Likewise not long after its acquisition of Max Factor & Co., Revlon Inc. liquidated the company's Tokyo office building for $150 million cash. A number of such acquisitions of U.S. firms during this period were directly linked to such hidden assets in the Land of the Rising Sun, an aspect which many of the acquired firms treated as though they were powerless to affect or control.

Cashing Out the Future

The firms who decided to abandon Japan in favor of a one-time payoff evidence the short-term/quick fix mentality that handicaps many global aspirants. In reviewing such moves, Sidney Kock, senior vice president of Daiwa Securities Co.'s U.S. unit, reflected the doubt that many global companies felt over them, "Japan is a great market; a company should think twice about leaving for short-term gains." Referring to a company that has shown great global perseverance through the years—and that has often resisted the temptation of cashing out many of its international assets—Koch noted, "No matter what you offer Coca-Cola Co., they're not going to leave Japan. They tend to think long term."

It is not just Japanese asset troves that have reflected this orientation. The sharply ascending yen of recent years has produced a unique litmus test for the international strategies of many companies. In every sector where U.S. producers have an opportunity to sell in Japan, the high yen allowed those firms to price their products below those of Japanese producers, thereby expanding sales and market share, and expanding the U.S. participation in the Japanese economy generally.

The popular tactic, however, has proven to be increasing prices to match Japanese competitors' prices, thereby gaining much higher profits, as U.S. car producers did when the choice of short-term profit versus long-term market share was offered to them by the U.S./Japanese auto import restraints. American microchip makers were under particular scrutiny since they have been embroiled in a bitter trade dispute complaining that they were denied market share. When the yen soared during the period August 1986 through May 1987, providing an unprecedented opportunity to make share gains that would have had major global benefits for their business, the American producers were found to have responded by increasing prices by 66 percent. Meanwhile, they maintained their political barrage to complain of unfair market denial in Japan.

By contrast, the managing director of Campbell Soup's Japanese operations, interviewed during that same period, took the global strategic perspective, "We have a great opportunity to make Campbell's part of the Japanese consciousness" as a result of the surging yen. After years of grueling effort, having gained important control over its distribution by, among other things, leaving an overly restrictive joint venture, adapting special packaging, creating new soup formulations, and hammering away at the country's huge ranks of small shopkeepers, the yen/dollar adjustments catalyzed Campbell's operations. Short-term profit wasn't an option for a company that had dedicated itself to adding one of the world's largest markets to its global base. As other U.S. producers effectively raised their dollar prices, Campbell lowered the yen price for a can of soup by over 15 percent but maintained shopkeeper's profit margins. Two major grocery chains soon became customers. Even with lower prices, Campbells was making a strong profit, which it plowed right back into increasing its Japanese sales force and retail incentives.

Dupont converted the yen rise to strategic advantage as well, but not in pricing. The company determined that its Japanese sales were not heavily price sensitive, unlike Campbell's cans of soup. In a country where customers often confused it with S. T. Dupont, the French manufacturer of upscale cigarette lighters, the company turned its added exchange profits into investment to build its image and corporate infrastructure in Japan. A 20 story national headquarters was built, as well as a 200,000 square foot research and development center. It began trading its stock on the Tokyo exchange and conducted the kind of image-building, rather than product-specific, advertising that Japanese companies had pioneered around the world. Today Dupont has built strong new relationships as an insider with key industrial customers in Japan. It is consistently rated as one of the most sought after employers in Japan by college graduates.

The yen/dollar shift of the 1980s provided global opportunity on both sides of the Pacific. In 1986 when the strong yen forced Caterpillar Inc.'s primary competitor Komatsu to hike U.S. prices by 18 percent, Caterpillar did not follow the example of U.S. automakers. Resisting the obvious temptation, it sat back and watched Komatsu's market share sink, all the while fine-tuning its successful global production network, discussed in the next chapter. It was not an unfamiliar posture for Caterpillar, which has been blessed with farsighted management even during the worst of times. When recession-driven losses piled up in the early 1980s, the company made the painful decision to cut prices sharply whenever Komatsu did. As explained by Larry Hollis, an analyst who follows the firm for broker Robert W. Baird & Co., Caterpillar "had the choice of losing money or losing markets, and they chose to lose money." The pain didn't last for long. Today the company is in high gear, back on the track that brought it 50 years of consecutive profits prior to 1982.

A company operating solely out of North Platte, Nebraska, staffed by employees who have never left the state, may have more chance to succeed globally than many of those who are enslaved to the quick fix, quick return mentality. The short-term mentality afflicts U.S. firms in every industry and in countless ways. Three examples:

• A New York–based company in an emerging global industry negotiated a joint-venture factory project that would be the first production facility for any major U.S. or European competitor to be located in Asia, where sales have been soaring. The company that took this first step would deny global competitors vital new growth regions and vital sources of potential cash flow for years to come. The contract was signed but the headquarters staff would not approve the investment because all calculations by the corporate MBAs showed an investment payback of 4.5 years, not the 3 years that company policy required. Six weeks after the contract was signed, and while the investment analysis continued, a German competitor announced it had a similar Asian project, signed, approved, and slated for immediate construction. The U.S. headquarters staff sighed with relief that their headache had gone away, and closed the books on the project.

• A U.S. regional manager on his own initiative lined up a commitment from a top industry organization in the People's Republic of China for a joint venture that would be able to sell for the first time in China a low-priced consumer product with a proven track record in developing countries. The manager had located a factory in a special economic zone ready to convert to production, with experienced workers operating under one of the country's few wage incentive programs. The manager proudly sent the news home and received the following telex: "Do not proceed further unless you can assure 14 percent return by end of first year." For China, the project was an extremely good deal, but the seasoned Asia hand knew better than to guarantee quick profit in the PRC.

• A prime candidate to replace a retiring CEO had been identified. He was the head of a smaller but globally adept European competitor. He was brought across the Atlantic from his home country and spent three days studying the corporate culture of the U.S. firm. The personnel chief bragged about the executive compensation system. It had large bonuses pegged to meeting quarterly and annual profit hurdles and improvement over historic profit performance, and large bonus pools based on boosting annual net return on investment. The candidate left with chagrin, saying essentially that: "What interested me was the challenge of turning your company into a global contender, maybe the global leader. I can't imagine that is possible so long as your management is driven to do otherwise by your compensation system."

Although these are actual isolated incidents, the important point is that they are part of patterns which are widely dispersed among would-be American global contenders.

A number of acquisitions of U.S. companies and assets by offshore interests have raised cries of foul precisely because of this short-term/long-term dichotomy. When the owners of CBS Records were able to negotiate a price of over 20 times earnings in the sale of the company to Sony; when Shuwa Corporation blew U.S. bidders out of the water with bids of $620 million for the Arco Plaza or $175 million for the ABC/

Capital Cities offices; and when Bertelsmann AG took over Doubleday for 40 times earnings; many in the United States who would have preferred to make the purchases let loose a familiar cry "unlevel playing field!" They insisted the deals, and others like them, were further evidence of unfair trade.

The sales were freely negotiated at arms length, without the involvement of foreign governments. The difference was not one of fairness. The issue was of world view, of the ordering of economic priorities. To the Japanese and European purchasers the large prices made perfect sense. The return on properties like the Arco Plaza or ABC building may have appeared to be a low 7 to 8 percent to American parties; but to Shuwa, used to returns of even 3 or 4 percent, it was high. To Bertelsmann, dedicated to building a global publishing empire, the price for Doubleday appeared to be a bargain. It wasn't buying the company to appease U.S. bankers, and it didn't plan to turn around and sell it the next year. When he was asked by reporters and audiences around the United States why he could justify paying 20 times earnings for CBS Records, Chairman Akio Morita of Sony had a simple answer. In Tokyo, shares of Sony were bringing 50 times earnings.

The managers who fail to fathom that global competitors may look at an opportunity quite differently than they do, and who cannot assimilate that global competitors may act with very different priorities to pounce on an acquisition, a market, or an investment that their traditional analysis would reject, are not global managers. They may stand like the 18th century British commander who couldn't comprehend why Americans wouldn't stand and fight in rigid formation like British soldiers were trained to do. If attitudes don't change, the same fate awaits.

Growing Global Instincts

The U.S. Department of Commerce once estimated that for every 25 negotiations between Japanese and American companies, only one succeeds. The primary reasons for failure are lack of listening, lack of communication, and lack of a coinciding business culture.

Adapting to overseas business is vastly more than adapting to travel in 747s. While some aviators may disagree, jet travel is not a state of mind. Global management is. It is an integrated way of looking at competitors, customers, factories, markets, finance, and employees. It is a mentality built on a core of intercultural sensitivity and business skills sophisticated enough to recognize the variations of economic bias around the globe, a mentality that is instinctive and not turned on or off as international problems arise.

Ultimately the instincts that drive the global manager and, through him, the global enterprise, may be no less difficult to explain than the instincts that send an Arctic tern from the Antarctic to Canadian tundra each spring. Yet there is a big distinction between those natural instincts and those of the global manager. The global instincts can be, and are acquired. They are built through experience, through objectivity, and through the kind of aggressive but flexible, ambitious but not self-centered, thinking that has perhaps become alien to many molded in the lock-step American MBA fashion.

CHAPTER 9

LEVERAGING GLOBAL SUCCESS

A global enterprise is a living thing. It has a pulse that quickens or ebbs based on supply, market, and other stimuli. It has a variety of internal organs or elements, all very different in character and function but all critical to survival. It has a circulatory system that courses through complex routes to maintain those vital organs. For nourishment it relies on external factors such as material supplies, consumers, and financial institutions.

Throughout this complex interdependent system there are pressure points, points at which extra pressure or leverage applied in a knowing fashion can dramatically alter the health of the enterprise. In the East practitioners of the ancient art of acupressure use such leverage along "key meridians" or at vital points to manipulate human bodies. With adroit but subtle changes in emphasis on one part of the body they reportedly cure another part, leveraging pressure at one point to achieve health at another.

The adept global enterprise likewise utilizes its own pressure points, as well as those of competitors and the industry at large, for strategic advantage. As those enterprises learn, in the global economy battles are often not waged in all-out frontal attacks. They are fought quietly, often in faraway places, sometimes without any conspicuous hint of struggle—but always at these global leverage points.

Video Leverage

In 1946 two entrepreneurs opened a tiny manufacturing firm by the name of Tokyo Tsushin Kogyo Co. in a leaky unpainted shack on the southern side of Tokyo. The firm struggled to make unorthodox products of a type previously unknown on the planet. After several difficult years the company capitalized on a new American invention, the transistor, to make a tiny radio that it hoped to sell to Americans. Many retailers in the United States laughed at the idea that consumers would want anything other than bigger and bigger cabinet radios of the type then found in most homes. But one company, Bulova, perhaps glimpsed the future and ordered over 100,000 units. Although the huge order was several times the Japanese firm's total capital, it turned the order down. The reason: it would not, as the U.S. firm required, put Bulova's name on the radios. The Japanese salesman explained: "I am now taking the first step for the next 50 years of my company. Fifty years from now, I promise you that our name will be just as famous as your company name is today."

It took far less than 50 years for the company to achieve that popularity. By the late 1970s the firm started as Tokyo Tsushin Kogyo was sitting at the top of a lucrative consumer electronics empire that dominated many markets throughout the world. By then the company was better known by the new name the company chose to be more appealing to its American customers: Sony Corporation.

Frequently within Japan complaints were made about Sony's style. It was a renegade and liked going it alone. Because it didn't produce wholly within Japan, and because it aggressively adapted to the marketing techniques of its key markets, it was accused of being a foreigner within the Japanese economy. To a self-confident chairman Akio Morita, and informed observers around the world, the description had little of the pejorative sense that was intended. It emphasized that Sony had chosen to go its own way globally, to avoid the chains of the traditional "us versus them, export or die" Japanese way of business.

For all its success, by the mid-1980s Sony began to suffer an erosion of its dominance. Its massive investment in Betamax VCR technology began to turn sour as producers of competing machines and more importantly, producers of movie cassettes began to line up behind the VHS format. Sony engaged in some harsh soul-searching of the kind that many firms wouldn't be strong enough to endure. The company's basic premise of developing innovative consumer-based technology and selling the resulting products to the West began to look outdated as the consumer electronic competition overheated, the technical capabilities of lower-cost competitors in Taiwan and Korea improved sharply, consumers grew more and more demanding, and trade frictions added instability to key Western markets. Sony could no longer follow its solo course of developing high technology, novel technical products that consumers suddenly couldn't live without.

New leverage points had emerged for competitors that were dramatically affecting Sony's existence. The producers of the entertainment software, like records or cassettes, upon which Sony products depended found leverage in that dependence. Sony's competitors developed important economies of scale from sales to the hundreds of purchasers of semiconducters and other electronic components. Sony had always remained fiercely independent, refusing to sell components to third parties and instead manufacturing them solely for its own internal consumption. Despite Sony's global production strategies, the company had substantial production still based in Japan. As the yen climbed steadily in value, this caused competitive problems for such yen-denominated production. Competitors were also leveraging teams of suppliers, sellers, and major customers to develop critical mass in new product development.

Sony was undoubtedly a global player, but it had capitulated control of critical global leverage points. It faced the greatest challenge of its history and responded with global alacrity. The company was smart enough to recognize the way in which its world had changed and strong enough to take the drastic actions necessary to adapt to those changes. In a major strategic shift the company shattered precedent with its $2 billion acquisition of a key software producer, CBS Records. It began a campaign to acquire a major film studio. It created a division dedicated to supplying components to industrial users. It gained major new operating flexibility with new and expanded production facilities in France, Austria, Singapore, Malaysia, Italy, the United Kingdom, and the United States.

The company then reversed its go-it-alone style for generating new technology. The process behind the release of a major new family of products, the 8mm camcorder, the Video Walkman, and accompanying VHS-C compact videotapes, was the opposite of that for its independently developed Betamax technology. From the outset, Sony worked with over 100 companies who agreed to work on supporting technology. It threw away another tradition by agreeing to supply its camcorders for sale under other brand names.

A new, stronger global Sony again has competitors green with envy. Its new strategy will leave it with control over major sources of the software used in its products, right down to the recording contracts with stars such as Billy Joel and Bruce Springsteen. This is accompanied by major distribution channels which will lend themselves to sales of Sony's audio and video hardware. By the end of 1988, Sony's innovative camcorder, symbol of the new Sony, had 50 percent of the European, 30 percent of the Japanese, and 20 percent of the U.S. markets. Its new component supply division already claimed 11 percent of company total sales by the end of 1988. The company's net earnings rose 47 percent in 1988, and its stock reached record highs.

Losing the Geographic Mind-Set

For most companies the strategic leverage points that are critical to global survival and success include manufacturing plants, quality control, marketing and distribution channels, research and development, key markets and other important sources of cash flow, and key personnel. For many they also include organizational structure, information systems, personnel training and development, and transportation systems.

The global corporation understands that none of these leverage points is defined geographically *per se*. A market to such a firm is not Europe or the United States as such. It consists of groupings of industrial users of certain characteristics or consumers filling a certain demographic profile. Of course many of those profiles logically coincide with geographic borders. For such firms plants are built in 20 countries not due to a strategy to invest under 20 flags of the world, but because critical customer groupings, or materials, or other elements were found in 20 locations, which happened to be in 20 separate countries. In accessing those critical locations, national laws or trade barriers may play a role in the decision, but only one role. The global company does not build a plant in a country because it collects national flags or desires symmetrical maps of operations. It builds because it must economically serve a customer base within a country, or has a clear opportunity to develop a strategic export base. It builds to achieve a strategic stake.

The typical American firm does have key strategic operating regions where it recognizes a fundamental strategic stake. If sales in one of the regions go flat, it doesn't shut down. It shifts resources, refocuses marketing, or takes other measures. If a unit in that region doesn't turn a profit over the short-term then the company moves in assets to support it while it does whatever necessary to accomplish a turnaround. In the broadest sense this is consistent with strategic global behavior. Unfortunately, the regions accorded such emphasis by U.S. firms have names like Texas, Ohio, and North Carolina. Should an otherwise important but troubled region happen to fall outside the borders of the United States of America, the parent company's attitude is usually strikingly different.

The global company moves assets and other resources into troubled areas without pausing over national borders. If the area was important enough to invest in, it is usually important enough to save. But many U.S. companies have practiced a double standard. If the electronic widget plant in Germany doesn't report a profit for two years, it has become too troublesome for the double standard company who might sell it off and buy a resort hotel in Florida. There will be plenty of European or Japanese widget producers to buy the German plant, and Tampa feels a lot more comfortable than Stuttgart. The global company, on the other hand, understands that it can ill afford to treat California any differently than France, or Illinois differently than Korea, simply on the basis of geographic location.

The Global Fight at Home

Some of the most dramatic examples of global battles over leverage points can be found in the many global battlefields of North America. In almost any industry that could be considered global, or potentially global, the vast numbers and huge demands of U.S. customers, whether they be purchasers of ball bearings, televisions, razors, or any of thousands of other goods or services, make those customers of great strategic value. For many industries the United States alone represents 40 percent or more of the total global market. The United States represents a huge wellspring of cash flow, a major source for technology development, and a critical base for building factories to achieve scale economies.

It is for this reason that many of the fiercest battles between global competitors occur within the United States. One of the most obvious, and longest running of these battles, has been that of the consumer electronics war. The United States is the biggest single component of the vast global market for televisions, radios, VCRs, Walkmans, and myriad other audiovideo equipment. In 1969 U.S. producers held 82 percent of the U.S. television market.[1] Today that share is almost negligible, as is the U.S. share of its own consumer electronics market generally. The battle in-

---

[1]"U.S. Manufacturers Face Big Changes in Years Ahead," *The Wall Street Journal*, May 2, 1989.

stead pits Japanese firms against European firms. Sony and Matsushita (Panasonic, Quasar, Technics, JVC) represent the Japanese. The Europeans are represented by Thomson SA (which acquired General Electric's consumer electronics business in 1987) and Philips N.V. (Philco, Sylvania, Norelco, Magnavox in the United States), which dominates the European markets and many others with a network of over 400 factories worldwide. Thomson and Philips fight an uphill battle to chip away at cash flow, distribution, marketing, and other U.S. leverage points largely controlled by the Japanese.

At least there are still U.S. players in the global fight over the tire industry, which has also largely centered in the United States, although U.S. producers led the way for decades, dating back to the days of vast rubber plantations in Sumatra, the Philippines, Brazil, and Liberia controlled by U.S. producers. When currency swings, the globalization of the auto industry, and other factors put pressure on world's tire producers to globalize, it was the Japanese and European producers who most aggressively reacted. Their strategy was to acquire significant U.S. players who could provide both an instant share of the huge U.S. market (45 percent of the Western world's total) and international production capacity. Beginning in 1986, Pirelli of Italy, Continental of Germany, Michelin of France, and Bridgestone, controlled by the Ishibashi family of Japan, launched major campaigns to acquire firms like General Tire, Armstrong Tire, and Firestone. By mid-1988 the Germans had acquired General Tire, and Bridgestone, in the largest-ever Japanese acquisition in America ($2.6 billion), had snared Firestone. These moves in the United States have set the stage for a continued global fight of vast dimensions as world-based producers Goodyear, Michelin, and Bridgestone, each now with 15 to 20 percent of the global market, tangle with each other and aggressive contenders like Continental and Pirelli.

For the same reason that the United States is a major global battlefield, major battles also arise in other home countries of primary competitors. The strongest contenders often have been built upon a large home market, which continues to be an important source of cash flow for global operations. One of the classic global battles, which has seemed like a veritable roller coaster ride to anyone following it through the years, has been that in the heavy construction equipment industry. The sheer physical size of equipment and varying regional construction conditions promoted the evolution of domestic producers within key markets prior to any globalization effort. The Caterpillar tractors left by Navy Seabees around the world after World War II gave the then-Caterpillar Tractor Company a major headstart at globalization. It put this to good advantage. The company turned the abandoned Seabee vehicles into a business base for a worldwide network of dealers. Today's Caterpillar Inc. has endured major trials from cutbacks in major infrastructure projects around the world, sharp drops in commodity prices, and foreign exchange shifts. The company lost $1 billion from 1982 to 1983, but today, with sales $10 billion strong, it is a savvy global player.

One of the few competitors that has been able to seriously threaten Caterpillar across the board has been Komatsu, Japan's primary builder of construction equipment. Unlike Japan's typical international firm, the bulk of Komatsu's sales were inside Japan; at least 80 percent of the firm's cash flow originated from those Japanese sales. Although over 25 years ago Japan certainly did not rank as one of the world's biggest markets for construction equipment, Caterpillar adroitly moved into the country by means of a joint venture with one of Komatsu's few domestic competitors, Mitsubishi. Public financial records in Japan show that joint venture historically to have been a very minor source of income for Caterpillar. But the venture has played a vital strategic role for the U.S. firm. Through the venture, Caterpillar is able to force continued price competition on Komatsu in its home market, thereby not only chilling the cash flow that is available for Komatsu's forays elsewhere in the world but also greatly complicating decisions by the rival to expand capacity.

During the 1970s as Japan audio equipment exports were expanding meteorically, the world's largest producer of automatic record changers, BSR of Great Britain, took a similar global blocking action. Foreseeing a loss of market share in the United States and Europe to Japanese competitors, BSR committed major resources to entering a Japanese market already crowded with audio equipment makers. The company introduced new products designed to Japanese specifications and sold products with major price discounts and other dealer incentives. Competing Japanese producers had to face a whole new battle in their home market and could find little justification for the expanded capacity that BSR had initially feared.

In an earlier skirmish during the tire wars mentioned above, Goodyear made a winning global move in response to Michelin's initial entry into the U.S. market. Goodyear, already a player in Europe, dropped its European tire prices to such an extent that Michelin's investment capital for expansion began to dry up. The formerly family-owned French company eventually was forced to break with tradition and issue outside equity.

At least some U.S. firms grasped at an early date the need to take aim at the critical leverage points of foreign competitors in their own home countries before they arrived on U.S. shores. As noted above, Caterpillar, BSR, and Goodyear took blocking actions of this nature that provided handsome global payoffs. IBM, in many respects a strong global prototype, moved early into Japan before its two biggest Japanese threats, Hitachi and Fujitsu, could build unassailable positions in their country from which to level a global attack in the mainframe computer industry. Gaining 25 percent of the Japanese market at an early date, IBM slowed Japanese competition around the world by holding down their cash flow and production capacity. The action was only a stalling action—the Japanese today are aggressive players in the global market, and IBM's market share in Japan has slipped recently, but the years gained were invaluable to IBM in establishing its global empire.

In many U.S. industries awareness of the global economy doesn't begin to take hold until offshore competitors are selling in Missouri or soaking up market share in California. The mighty U.S. producers of consumer electronic goods whose ads filled the pages of *Life* and *Saturday Evening Post* a generation ago ignored the risk of producers overseas, hardly troubling to notice their efficient, low cost production capacity or the way they clearly built export markets. They laughed at even the prospect of competition from unknown foreign companies, much as jokes were made in Detroit about the efforts of a strange company named Toyota to sell tiny un-American cars in the United States 25 years ago. Those companies rolled into the United States like steamrollers flattening the globally insensitive, overconfident U.S. producers. Most of those U.S. firms are out of business. The lucky ones survive as subsidiaries of European or Japanese firms.

James Abegglen, international business consultant and Tokyo professor, has made something of a career out of comparing U.S. and Japanese firms. He is firmly convinced that U.S. businesses threatened from the Land of the Rising Sun must take the competition to the Japanese, not wait for it at home: "If a U.S. company is driven to fight the Japanese competition in the United States, the odds are very, very long against the U.S. company. . . If you wait until you're fighting the battle here, it's probably too late."

The Insider Leverage Points

To most global firms, becoming an insider in major markets is such an obvious requirement that it is a basic assumption of any strategic planning. IBM knew that if it was going to counter the Japanese effectively, it would have to do so as an insider player in the Japanese market.

If they were able to formulate an international plan at all, many companies would indeed state that it is to become an insider in as many key markets as possible. In effect, however, the insider strategy is an oversimplified approach to control of competitive leverage points, an approach which vaguely underscores the need to be overseas without articulating the interplay of the leverage points that underlie that need. In the most generalized of discussions, the insider approach may be helpful in understanding the need for global action. But the global firm must go far beyond that simplistic approach when it addresses the strategies that will shape its destiny.

A global firm ventures inside a key market in a number of ways for a number of strategic reasons, including one or a combination of the following:

Destabilizing a competitor's plans for production expansion.

Avoiding high duties or other protectionist political measures that local firms try to use as leverage points to shield themselves (e.g. as Japanese automakers have done in the United States, but failed to do in Europe,[2] or as Thomas Edison attempted in his ambitious but failed efforts to establish an international network of electric lamp factories in the 1880s.

Tapping into a core of technical expertise or research efforts uniquely available in the region (e.g. the Silicon Valley "magnet").

Creating local price competition to constrict competitors' cash flow that otherwise would support global expansion (e.g. Caterpillar versus Komatsu in Japan).

---

[2]The 11 percent market share Japanese automakers enjoy in Europe was achieved almost entirely through exports. Only 7 percent of the 1.5 million Japanese cars sold in Europe in 1988 were made in Europe, leaving them extremely vulnerable to protectionism. See "Japanese Automakers Jostling Past EC's Import Curbs," *The Wall Street Journal*, March 17, 1989.

Avoiding high international transportation costs that prevent effective competition in the market.

Becoming an ally or constituent of a local government that otherwise might be pressured to restrict a foreign role in the industry.

Tapping a pool of local production labor and/or materials to gain cost advantages over competitors or neutralize such an advantage already enjoyed by a competitor.

Cementing relationships with customers (as has been going on internationally since at least 1882, when Western Electric built a telephone factory near European customers in Belgium[3]).

Mitigating currency risks by establishing a base in a low or soft currency environment or, more importantly, obtaining the ability to manipulate multiple operations based on currency fluctuations.

To be able to successfully understand and satisfy consumer tastes and needs in a local market (e.g., the investment of many food and cosmetic companies).

Most often companies seek an insider position for a combination of such factors, and a position to attack a combination of leverage points. In 1987 and 1988 when Fuji Photo and Konica Corporation raised the stakes in their global war with Kodak by announcing new manufacturing facilities in the United States, the decisions were hailed as the natural way for them to go, meaning that there were so many reasons to take the steps that their logic could not be denied. The Japanese companies would find lower production costs in the United States, would be able to undermine Kodak's carefully developed image as the only U.S. film company, would cast monkey wrenches into Kodak's own pricing and production planning, and would gain an important currency hedge by diversifying away from a yen-only production base.

The Global Manufacturing Edge

The Uniden Group is a pariah in its home country. The highly successful Tokyo-based producer of cordless telephones, satellite television receivers, and citizens band radios has been the subject of books, speeches,

---

[3]M. Wilkins, *The Emergence of Multinational Enterprise* 51 (Harvard University Press 1970).

government debate, and other forms of criticism of its symbolic threat to the Land of the Rising Sun. The reason is that not one of the popular products that it sells in the United States, Europe (where it enjoys a 70 percent share in cordless telephone sales), and elsewhere bears the label "Made in Japan."

Uniden's management, focused on global operations since the start of the company in 1966, astonished onlookers by shutting the company's last Japanese factory in the late 1970s while it was still at the peak of its profit, making the then-largest labor severance payment in Japanese history. The company established subsidiaries in Europe and the United States and moved production into venues that offered the lowest cost while still maintaining quality. Sales units around the globe are able to order products directly from these far-flung plants. Only in 1987 when the Japanese government liberalized product standards for satellite receivers and cordless phones did Uniden begin selling those products in Japan. The company takes its criticism for being un-Japanese stoically but no doubt watches with some degree of satisfaction as more and more Japanese firms begin to grasp the difference between being global and being just a mega-exporter.

Of all the strategic decisions it must make, none have higher stakes for the global firm than those surrounding manufacturing. Few firms would disagree with this point, but often for the wrong reason. To all too many who have taken their first international step, the process is as follows: we are in the business of selling three-handled self-correcting electronic widgets. Since we are going to be an international company, where on the globe can we most cheaply make three-handled self-correcting electronic widgets?

When Lionel Trains decided that production in Mexico was cheaper, it locked up its U.S. plant and headed south. We have already seen the disaster that decision caused. Rawlings Sporting Goods expected it could save costs by sourcing baseball gloves in Asia; certainly all the projections prepared by its manufacturing personnel looked attractive. What nobody remembered to factor into the equation were the $200,000 to $300,000 in annual carrying costs the company had to pay for the next 10 years on its former U.S. plant building. "First you say—Gee whiz. It's cheaper to make it over there," admitted Robert Burrows, president of the company. But when the company later reviewed the possibility of sourcing sports clothes offshore, its analysis was much broader in nature. The costs for the clothing were sharply lower, but inventory, transportation, and duty costs added up fast. The "nail in the coffin," according to Burrows, was the quotas that caused base prices to wildly fluctuate, adding up to $5 per shirt when demand would be heavy. Rawlings decided to rely on U.S. production for the clothing.

After careful analysis many producers will indeed find large hidden costs in their offshore manufacturing plans. But such analysis is only one of the many steps of the global firm. Even before such cost analysis, fundamental strategic questions should be asked: Do all markets around the world demand a three-handled self-correcting electronic model of widget? Will some need a four-handled model? Will some not be willing to pay extra for self-correction features and want a manually adjusted widget? Would some markets be willing to pay more for added features like self-correcting and self-cleaning? What happens if some countries impose a technical standard of double insulation, or others a requirement for special safety fuses?

As further discussed in the marketing context in Chapter 10, in most industries it is a virtual certainty that products require some adaption to meet the myriad variations of market tastes and technical standards. But if such local adaption meant that the global producer must set up integrated production in every major market, most companies would find the global path one to certain bankruptcy.

Adapting a product is only one concern in globalizing production. Transportation costs, tariffs, customer relations, intellectual property protection, and financing sources all may be significant factors, as may any of the other factors listed as insider advantages above.

As discussed above, Caterpillar took a blocking action to make life difficult for its biggest competitor. But the company's greatest leverage came from its production network. Two thirds of the production cost in the heavy equipment industry is in the heavy components such as engines, axles, or transmissions that can only be efficiently produced in very large scale, very expensive plants. Yet local markets in regions such as Europe, Australia, Brazil, and Japan required a number of variations in the final product. Caterpillar reconciled these points with a global production network consisting of central large scale production facilities that ship high value components—avoiding the high cost of transporting large vehicles—to local plants which assemble the components and add distinct features for the local market. Such a flexible global production strategy has provided the company with a major leverage over its competition. Such systems make some products look like a veritable United Nations with respect to their "country of origin." Canada-based Massey Ferguson for many years assembled British engines, Mexican axles, U.S. sheet metal parts, and French transmissions to make many of its tractors. Singer sewing machines today are assembled in Taiwan from plastic shells made in Ohio, motors made in Brazil, and drive shafts made in Italy.

Although their company continues to have trouble becoming an effective global operator, managers of Siemens AG's circuit breaker business were able to establish a similar structure in South America, at a time when the company's German production capacity needed expansion and markets in South America were opening rapidly, Brazilian officials launched a campaign to lure foreign investment for the electrical equipment industry. Siemens accepted the offer of incentives and a degree of protection by building one key component factory in Brazil that both eliminated the need for more capacity in Germany and gained vital cost and political leverage in South America. The company was able to swap Brazilian components for other components from Germany needed to assemble a complete circuit breaker and became the largest supplier in Brazil.

The successful global company never reaches a manufacturing investment decision in a given country on the basis of that country's market alone. Most companies that construct a chain of self-contained plants, each operating independently, will find that chain fast becoming a noose in today's global economy.

The Global "Standard"

The geographically diverse, interdependent production network that is the foundation of most global enterprises thrives on standardization. For most industries the global product remains a myth, as discussed in Chapter 10, but standardization is a relative concept. Caterpillar has standardized by developing critical high value components that can be used on a number of vehicles. Control systems, processes, materials and material sources, and many other product aspects can be standardized. The effort to achieve standard end products from market to market is never ending for most global manufacturers. Nestle, with plants in 60 countries, is well aware of the fine-tuned local tastes that require it, for example, to sell 200 different formulations of instant coffee around the world. Yet the company engages in a constant struggle to push successful brands from one country to another and maximize the sale of similar products worldwide.

IBM has been a star player in this game. Its worldwide product line succeeds because it is is standardized—"IBM compatible" is emphasized by sellers of components from Augusta to Abidjan—but also because it is simultaneously able to be different according to the needs of local markets. The company sells over 20 different language keyboards in Europe alone and dozens of keyboards around the world. "What is important," emphasizes Swiss-born IBM vice chairman Kaspar Cassani, who has supervised IBM's international business for many years, "is that the concept of adaptability is built into the product." Adaptability itself becomes a standard feature.

At Becton Dickinson, the producer of hypodermic syringes, a farsighted management team began to convert its multinational businesses into a global enterprise by integrating all of its scattered regional operations in 1979. Over the next decade the company developed a finely tuned production organization with capital intensive syringe-only production dedicated in two plants and two other plants producing only labor-intensive needles in relatively low labor cost venues. A major step permitting such measures was the standardization of needle production that previously in the industry had been based on varying regional standards. A second important step for Becton was standardizing suppliers. It began utilizing a reduced number of proven suppliers for whom Becton was a customer of critical importance.

The Floating Factory

Such a flexible global production base permits a company to effectively use its production system as an evolving competitive weapon, instead of having to constantly defend it as a fixed-site vulnerability. When the Mexican peso dropped sharply against the dollar, Becton Dickinson used its Mexican plant as a major leverage point against its primary Japanese competitor, who had to depend on U.S. production for much of its international sales. By converting the Mexican plant from domestic production to export production, Becton gained a major cost advantage. Without such flexibility, on the other hand, Komatsu's heavily yen-based production has been a major handicap to effective competition with Caterpillar during the years of the strong yen. It was primarily this problem that pushed the company into a joint venture with U.S.-based Dresser Industries in 1988. The Japanese company was ready to overlook the reportedly rundown condition of the Dresser facilities in order to obtain a desperately needed dollar-based production site.

Goodyear didn't have to search for a new joint venture in 1986 when low-cost Korean producers suddenly began selling tires on the West Coast of the United States at 15 percent below the market price. Goodyear's U.S. plants couldn't match the price, but the company quickly turned to its Brazilian plant. The company was soon selling Brazilian-produced tires that matched the price of the Korean products. Goodyear's chairman has emphasized this incident in describing his company's strength against foreign producers, "We couldn't have done that if we were not a global company." General Motors, on the other hand, suffered heavily during the 1980s from its lack of flexibility in producing products for the European market. Wedded to parts factories in West Germany, the high German labor costs and strong German mark contributed significantly to GM's $2.2 billion loss outside the United States during that period.

The global production network of Philips N.V. allows the company to shift production in quick response to currency exchange swings or market demands. Over a recent five year period the company's primary production of 14 inch television sets was moved from the United States to Taiwan, then, as new currency swings developed, to Juarez, Mexico. Some Philips products have even recently been shifted from Singapore to Belgium for cost advantages.

The fantasy of many global manufacturing managers is to have a factory aboard a ship equipped with computer assisted design and manufacturing capabilities. The ship could then be steered to whatever country offered the best leverage from currency exchange and other cost advantages at a given moment. With the proper mix of strategically sited production facilities, some global companies have almost achieved the same floating effect.

The Challenge of Global Controls

The floating factory effect, however, relies upon sophisticated production control systems which transcend the experience of most contemporary factory managers. SKF, the Swedish bearing producer, pioneered an integrated system for fine-tuned coordination of production and sourcing over 15 years ago. Facing increased pressure from non-European producers, the company suffered from inefficiencies in running five separate, independently operated offshore subsidiaries. In 1973, after establishing a consolidated international research center in the Netherlands, the company launched its "Global Forecasting and Supply System". That system introduced a central office for production forecasting, increased automation in manufacturing, streamlined inventory procedures, and consolidated production according to product lines for economies of scale. In Europe alone, the system was so successful that by the end of the decade the company was able to increase production capacity while actually cutting the number of manufacturing centers from 22 to 16.

Such controls have been the key to global success in many firms. When U.S. auto companies tried to pinpoint the source of the huge cost advantage enjoyed by their Japanese competitors in the early 1980s, they discovered to their surprise that the primary element of that advantage was not labor related. Two thirds of the Japanese cost edge derived from better management, consisting essentially of better systems for control of inventory and quality.[4]

Dow Chemical has developed one of the more sophisticated production systems of any U.S.-based global firm. With a detailed computer program that was years in development, the company analyzes which of its many plants around the globe would be the most effective producer of any given product. The program integrates not merely labor, material, and other factory overhead costs, but also such elements as transportation expenses, exchange rates, and tax rates. Caterpillar Inc., concluding a billion dollar global modernization program which will cut production costs by 15 percent, operates a sophisticated computerized control network integrating suppliers and production facilities to assure the lowest cost sourcing and minimal global inventory costs.

The Italian megasuccess in the apparel industry, the family-owned Benetton Group, has turned global production control into a new art form. The company operates factories in Italy, France, Spain, Scotland, Brazil and the United States, as well as an extensive network of hundreds of subcontractors. Benetton designers style clothes on computer terminals that are linked to knitting and cutting machines that can produce a new sweater design within hours after it has first appeared on a computer screen. In a warehouse staffed by only 16 computer operators, 20,000 boxes of garments are handled in one day, each with a computer label that directs it to trucks bound for the hundreds of Benetton shops. Its system permits Benetton to make no garment before it is actually ordered by a store. Orders are relayed by computer link from over 75 agents around the world. The control system also allows the company to do the previously

[4]"Rising Tide of Imports Continue to Frustrate U.S. Managers," *The Wall Street Journal*, September 23, 1983.

unthinkable in the apparel industry: Stores can order hot items in the middle of a season and receive them within two to three weeks.

Ultimately, the global firm understands that there is virtually no aspect of production, short of day to day operating issues, that is not strategic in nature. This attitude stands in sharp contrast to the traditional practice of many U.S. firms who might identify only a few aspects such as production technology, location, and capacity as strategic in nature. For the global firm strategic elements may also include labor, quality, material supply, control systems, manufacturing inventories, and other aspects as defined by the particular industry. None of these has more vital strategic importance than quality.

The Quality of Global Survival

Several years ago an IBM factory in the Great Lakes region ordered components from a supplier in Japan. Its order stipulated a defect rate of 1.5 percent, a very extreme rate at that time which had eliminated many American firms from IBM's list of suppliers. When the order arrived from Japan, a separate pouch was enclosed with several of the components inside. A courteous cover letter explained, "We don't know why you want 1.5 percent defective parts, but for your convenience, we've packed them separately."

The quality issue is not a new one to American producers. Volume after volume has been written on the subject of manufacturing quality in the past three decades. Consulting firms have been launched, millions of dollars have been spent on seminars, and entire careers have been based solely on the basis of spreading the quality gospel. But seldom do these efforts put the issue in its global context that quality is not a problem for factory managers. It is a global survival and success issue.

Although most Japanese companies share many problems with their U.S. counterparts in trying to become global, the Japanese have largely mastered this critical attribute—although usually as manufacturing geniuses, not as global operators. Defects in a number of Japanese factories are measured in *parts per million*.

More than a decade ago, the management of Volkswagen AG in Germany justified the massive investment for a new plant in the United States as "paying the dues" for becoming global. While VW's step in opening a Pennsylvania plant in 1978 attracted considerable criticism—it was opened too late to preempt Japanese competitors, it was located in a hostile union environment, it was hampered by the manipulations of a resentful union in Germany, it was not properly supported by senior management in Germany—the ultimate problem for the United States operation was quality. U.S. consumers quickly found the Pennsylvania-built VW was not the same as the reliable old Beetle imported from Germany. As Khaled Majeed, a Wall Street analyst who followed the VW operations, noted in a 1987 analysis, many consumers believed that "the quality of the cars built in Pennsylvania wasn't up to the quality of the cars built in Germany."

When the company moved to improve its quality image by emphasizing its more upscale Audi cars, it took one of the greatest stumbles in automotive history. Alarmingly frequent reports of accidents allegedly caused by defects in the Audis sent sales plunging. Instead of the expanding sales projected in the VW/Audi plan for the United States, the company's sales dropped from a high of 600,000 cars (imports only) in 1970 to 169,000 in 1988. Sales of the U.S.-made cars slid from over 177,000 in 1980 to less than 75,000 by 1986.[5]

Desperately trying to salvage its U.S. presence, in 1983 VW called off plans to open a second U.S. plant in Michigan, already 80 percent built, and in 1985 closed its stamping plant in West Virginia. The defection of buyers, and heavy competition from Japanese producers who maintained exemplary quality standards finally proved too much. In 1988 the Pennsylvania plant was shut down, with a loss of almost 3,000 jobs.

The Volkswagen of America story is all the more striking because it has been German firms, along with the Japanese, who have shown the world the importance of quality in international operations. Germany has taken over the lead from the United States as the planet's top exporter not by selling boatloads of commodities, but primarily by selling specialized, top-of-the-market high-quality machines—medical electronics, machine tools, and similar products. The comparison of VW's products with those of BMW and Mercedes only exacerbated its problems.

Stihl, the German chainsaw manufacturer, makes every one of its own components, from plastic grips to fuel caps, to assure total quality in production. Customers around the world are willing to pay sharply higher prices because they know that if a chainsaw bears the Stihl label it will be of high quality and high reliability.

Many American companies have discovered the quality problem is not due to global perspectives but comes out of the drive for cost-effective

---

[5]"Can Volkswagen Stop Its U.S. Decline?," *Forbes*, April 3, 1989.

production. In approaching the problem, however, many are handicapped by a manufacturing tradition built on the "acceptable quality level" concept taught by production consultants for many years. This concept is based on a scientific manufacturing approach based on the inevitability of defects.

A catalyst for a new perspective on quality has been heavy competition from offshore, usually Japanese producers, who poured low-priced products of disturbingly uniform quality into U.S. markets. Many companies only then began to recognize that 20 to 25 percent of their factory budgets was devoted to identifying and correcting defects. Today many firms recognize the wisdom of Myron Tribus, head of the American Quality and Productivity Institute: "Quality is never your problem. It is the solution to your problem." Many of them wished they had paid more attention to quality "gurus" W. Edwards Deming and J. M. Juran who, finding little interest among U.S. firms, took their crusade for quality and productivity to Japan 30 years ago. Many Japanese companies attribute their success today to the teachings of those two Americans.

In 1976 when Hewlett Packard Co. groped for an answer to its severe quality problems at its plant in Japan, it turned to J. M. Juran's "total quality control" system. By making quality control and quality improvement part of every business plan and every managers performance review, the Japanese unit moved from the bottom of HP's profitability list to the very top. Between 1975 and 1982, the unit's product defect rate dropped 79 percent, manufacturing costs dropped 42 percent, revenues per employee increased 120 percent, and market share soared over 190 percent.

Today's global firms understand that quality must be a fact of life. Rockwell International captured 70 percent of Japan's market for high-speed modem boards by selling products from a factory in Dallas where quality is so integrated that the company does not need to inspect the final product for quality. Caterpillar's total quality control system certifies not only external but *internal* suppliers to its assembly lines.

For many years Motorola was mired in quality problems that almost buried the company. When Matsushita bought the company's television plant several years ago, it found a defect rate of *150 per 100 sets*. Matsushita applied methods that had propelled it to global success and soon lowered that rate to 4 per 100, while simultaneously improving productivity. Today a new quality-conscious Motorola is consistently beating out Japanese suppliers for sales of high-quality pagers to Japan's own Nippon Telegraph and Telephone. Renault, plagued by losses of over $4 billion from 1981 to 1986, focused on quality as a key to turning the company around; today the French car producer is earning its first profits in years. Over Renault production lines hang signs reading: "Quality Is Not an Option."

Becton Dickinson was not driven by the pressure of higher quality from competitors but rather by its own global insight in adopting world-wide quality standards for its hypodermic syringes, even though others still observed country-by-country standards. By basing worldwide production on its highest quality products, as sold in the United States, Becton Dickinson obtained major economies of scale and firmly implanted its posture as a high quality supplier.

Quality the Biggu Makku Way

Despite an infrequent *faux pas*, McDonald's Corporation has raised maintenance of global quality to an art form. Although the company's markets are highly variable, or multidomestic in nature, the secret to the company's international success is its global systems, all of which ultimately are focused on the preservation of quality. Certainly there are few industries where an anomaly in quality is more life threatening than in the fast food franchise business. The instillation of quality as a characteristic of service, moreover, is a great challenge anywhere on the globe. But whether the hungry customer wants a *biggu makku* in Osaka or a *chocolate tejturmix* (shake) in Budapest, he or she anticipates, and gets, the same value for their money, prepared in the same clean, efficient fashion from Hong Kong to Mexico City.

Across the planet enough filet of fish sandwiches and quarter pounders slide down the same stainless steel ramps under the same overseas golden arches to generate a fifth of the company's $11 billion-plus annual sales. Units operate in over 40 countries, and are spreading fast. Over 40 percent of the company's new stores are outside the United States, and overseas growth for the Illinois company is exceeding that in the United States. With the same phonebook-style operating manuals, stringent training, and painstaking inspections, the company is able to achieve a uniform temperature of oil for frying potatoes, the same squeaky clean bathrooms, and the same quality of food materials—despite occasional problems in finding U.S.-style potatoes—around the world.

That commitment to its standards has caused the company to resist some big temptations. Asked about introducing McDonald's to the billion-plus consumers of the People's Republic of China, the company's managing director in Hong Kong, Daniel Ng, expressed the company's quality concerns: "We don't have any plans to open anything on the mainland over the next few years. We need to be certain we can have the same quality of product, service, and cleanliness that we do anywhere else in the world."

The McDonald's story, and to some extent that of Pepsico's Kentucky Fried Chicken unit, stands as testimony to the difficulty of establishing franchise quality and a tribute to how determined efforts pay off globally, in sharp contrast to the previously discussed international failures of other U.S. franchise systems.

Massaging the Leverage Points

The global company understands instinctively that a market share decline in Europe is not just a problem for its European managers, any more than an efficiency improvement in its Wisconsin plant is a benefit only for the U.S. Midwest market. Identification of such markets and such production sites as global leverage points and commensurate skill in balancing those points brings the global firm creative solutions to such problems or creative leverage from such new advantages, perhaps by focusing the Wisconsin plant on production for the European market.

The company with a steady grip on its global future understands that a factory or a sales area which fails to turn a profit one year is not an instant liability, that support from the global system is justified. It may provide vital leverage even when not turning a short-term profit, or might offer the potential of vital leverage when currencies, markets, or production costs turn around. Such an organization understands that global business is by its nature one of arbitraging differences between varying locations, of using operations in one hemisphere as a lever to reach into another.

Chinese masters of the "key meridians" and "vital points" reportedly were able to raise patients from their deathbeds with the touch of their hands, lift away a pain in the skull by subtle manipulation of the patient's foot, and heal crippled legs by massaging a palm. The effective global enterprise has the power to perform analogous miracles in the global economy.

CHAPTER 10

THE STRATEGIC RESPONSE: GLOBAL MARKETING AND RESEARCH

Global Success, Copy by Copy

During the 1960s the photocopier business was an American business, and that American business was Xerox Corporation. With its first plain paper copier, the 914, the company revolutionized office life and marked up what was once a familiar phenomenon: another American high-tech victory. One of the most successful new products in commercial history, the 914 is today enshrined in the Smithsonian Institution. A confident and highly profitable Xerox barely blinked in the early 1970s when it first became evident that a handful of Japanese companies had targeted the industry. Even with the launch by Eastman Kodak and IBM of competing products during the mid-1970s Xerox still held 75 percent of the market.

By the end of that decade, however, Xerox's world had radically changed. Names like Ricoh, Canon, and Sharp were becoming familiar, as were their inexpensive but high-quality copiers that were ravenously consumed by office managers across the globe. Xerox's market share began to plummet, dropping to 35 percent by 1983. When the giant from Stamford, Connecticut, finally began to study its markets around the world and the way its new global competitors were being welcomed in those markets its self-confidence took a big blow.

Customers were enamored by the convenient, reliable machines made by the competitors, the small machines Xerox once had considered a minor market niche. What's more, the company discovered that the Japanese were selling the machines *for what it would cost Xerox to make the same units*. Further self-scrutiny, in comparison to its competitors, revealed a surprising number of quality problems, inefficiencies in production, and a lumbering bureaucracy that handicapped new product development.

In a flurry of reorganization, cost cutting, and refocus on its markets during the 1980s, a new Xerox emerged which could squarely meet the competition. A new line of copiers designed to compete with the Japanese models sold 600,000 units in three years. New streamlined product development teams, crisis teams, and problem solving teams replaced, in many respects, the previously bloated bureaucracy. Defects were cut by two thirds in just two years. Listening to customers around the globe, it redesigned certain user features like paper trays. Managers rediscovered the global context of the words of one of Xerox's founders, Joseph C. Wilson: The job of Xerox workers was "to satisfy the customer. Period."

Xerox understood that the key to the success of its competitors was low cost, high-quality production. Moving research centers into its key markets as well as the backyards of its competitors, it today conducts research in Japan, Canada, and Great Britain as well as the United States. Using a Japanese subsidiary to search for lessons among its key competitors that might apply to Xerox's worldwide operations, the company slashed its number of outside suppliers from 5,000 to 300. Total manufacturing costs were cut in half. Its total rethinking of its operations paid off big: The company's photocopy market share began to recover. With a framework of 23 factories in 15 countries and marketing operations in 130 countries, the company today can claim that one third of the approximately 1 trillion copies made on photocopiers and printers around the world annually are made on Xerox machines.

Losing the Global Tennis Racquet

Several years ago Donnay Sporting Goods S.A. was on top of the tennis world. The Belgian company enjoyed fat profits from its global sales while Bjorn Borg represented its tennis racquet, traditionally high quality wooden models. The company's inability to evolve its products, however, led it straight to bankruptcy proceedings in 1988.

Donnay acted as though it could produce its old style wooden racquets forever. As competitors, and customers, turned to lower cost Asian factories for their racquets, Donnay refused to move from its home in Couvin, Belgium. Its assembly line was 10 times longer than those of competitors. As the world's tennis players turned to graphite, Donnay slowly changed—to metal, which fit its production facility easier than graphite. When Bjorn Borg retired, the company made the desperate move of selling cheaper racquets to discount retailers; the move hurt its already deteriorating image. In 1987 the company finally got around to creating a marketing manager position. But in a tennis world addicted to graphite products, 80 percent of which originate in Taiwan and South Korea, Donnay had done too little too late.

Strategic Marketing, Strategic Response

These examples from two very different companies highlight a set of leverage points distinct from those discussed in Chapter 9. In simplest terms these points are directly anchored in markets and market responsiveness. More specifically, they deal with customer relationships and product innovation and adaption, and with the way the global organization perceives itself and functions in international markets. In the global economy key customers are obvious leverage points for global strength and advantage. But no less so are products themselves and elements of product design, as well as product innovation and the system that creates it.

In the global economy the most efficient producer in the world will not stand a chance unless it knows its international markets and how to use those markets to its advantage (also, hopefully, to its competitor's disadvantage). The most effective of global operators is able to artfully shape its markets, even create its own markets.

To the quick-fix manager, international marketing is simple: The aspiring global firm only needs to find packaging that can withstand international shipping and handling, slip in the product, and the customers of the global village will deluge it with orders. Indeed, books have been written and some consultant's careers launched on the premise that the world is homogenized. Once products are standardized, such global marketeers assert, they quickly can be sold on every continent in the same fashion.

Even Marshall McLuhan would likely reject the notion that his global village is such a homogenized, one-dimensional entity. The effective global enterprise understands, with few exceptions, that in marketing globalize does not mean standardize in the strictest sense. Such enterprises understand that marketing is a function of complex cultural, physical, and legal aspects.

Sentenced to the Global Pen

One company that listened to the "one-product/one-world" gurus was Parker Pen. Its senior management was converted to those gurus' thinking in a mid-1980s global marketing fad fueled by a book on the subject written by a Harvard University professor, who preached that "the world's needs and desires have been irrevocably homogenized."

Struggling with an international operation that produced 500 styles of pens in 18 plants and utilized separate marketing and packaging in 150 different countries, the company zealously embraced global marketing. Parker hired one advertising agency to create one marketing campaign for use around the world. It then standardized its products by dropping hundreds of its styles and consolidating production to only eight factories.

Parker's dramatic efforts produced dramatic results. Local managers rebelled, resentful of being forced into a marketing straitjacket. Like most one-product/one-world advertising, the Parker ads were criticized as dull and ineffective. Gary Stibel, a principal in the New England Consulting Group, condemned such efforts, "It's marketing reduced to the lowest common denominator . . . vanilla marketing." Parker's sales plummeted, profits disappeared, and the company suffered a $12 million loss in 1985. A year later the struggling pen business was purchased by a British management team, who quickly ousted those executives who had pushed the global marketing program. Local managers soon once more were able to adapt marketing to their local custom.

The Coke Syndrome

The banner most frequently waved by those who espouse simplistic, homogenized global marketing, is that of Coca-Cola. That soft drink, enjoying what many surveys have shown to be the most widely known trademark on the planet (followed by IBM, Sony, Porsche, McDonalds, and Disney), may be the closest thing to an homogenous global product found anywhere in the world. The one-product/one-world proponents emphasize that one finds the same bottle, the same logo, the same bottlecap affiliated with the product around the world. They suggest that a bottling plant and local marketing plan could be lifted from Nigeria and dropped in Topeka or taken from Munich to Montevideo without any consumers knowing the difference.

But how many U.S. consumers have recently seen local shelves stocked with the once familiar blue-green Coke bottles that are still familiar sights in many other countries? And the consumers in those developing countries certainly would be nonplussed—and some offended—if they suddenly were confronted with low calorie, low caffeine, cherry, combination diet and low caffeine, and other permutations of the basic coke product that have become fixtures on U.S. shelves.

The soft drink industry is indeed a good example of the manner in which markets must be accommodated and products adapted for varying market requirements around the globe. A popular Pepsico soft drink in the Moslem countries is a thick currant and blackberry soda called Shani, sold heavily during the holy month of Ramadan. A Coca-Cola produced coffee drink, Georgia Coffee, is a big success in Japan, but efforts to export it failed. A major soft drink seller in Asia is Hi-C Soy Milk, which understandably isn't a big seller in the United States. Suntory, owner of one of the major soft drinks in Japan (much of which is actually bottled in California and shipped across the Pacific) fell flat on its face when it tried to introduce its product in the United States. The problem may have been connected to the name of the drink: Calpis.

A number of cocoa malt drinks are popular around the world, but in different market niches. In Scandinavia, Britain, and Australia, cocoa malt is believed to be a soporific and advertising focuses on the drink as a wholesome nightcap. In other countries, like India, the cocoa drinks are viewed as stimulants, and advertising focuses on the drink as an energy source.

Diet Coke may be big in the United States, but, as Ira C. Herbert, Coca-Cola's marketing director has noted, it "clearly in many ways isn't appropriate for some undeveloped worlds." There the thought of unwanted or surplus calories seems like a cruel joke. As previously mentioned, Coke's quest for a global brand was stymied in China, where Coca-Cola was found to translate as "bite the wax tadpole."

Indeed, the varying cultural perceptions of brands presents a major, sometimes insurmountable, problem for the would-be one-product/one-world proponent. We have seen how one of GM's popular compact models was sent to South America with a name that translated as "no go" in Spanish. Japanese purchasers of Exxon's gasoline puzzle over a brand name, Esso, which to them means "stalled car." Even venerable Rolls Royce had to retreat from the use of Silver Mist as a global brand name when it discovered that "mist" was the linguistic equivalent of "manure" in German.

Products perceived as global typically are varying products sharing a common name. Nescafe is a label affixed to over 200 different formulations of coffee around the world. They are blended to local tastes. Few could argue with 3-M's marketing record; that innovative company learned long ago that the global product is often a fiction. Says CEO Allan Jacobson, "Don't think you can retail everywhere in the world, especially with products that have been developed for the U.S. market."

To many, one of the more obvious products for globalizing has seemed to be household appliances. Not so. Companies like Maytag, Whirlpool, and Philips continue global efforts but have been frustrated by marked differences in local markets. With respect to washing machines, for example, France is fiercely loyal to top loading machines while Great Britain is big on front loaders. Although the same name is used, the different models make for higher production costs. Xerox did its best to find a universal photocopy machine for its world efforts but had to settle for a U.S./Europe design and an Asian design, adapted for different paper, higher resolution for discerning ideograph languages, and widely varying electrical power standards.

The need for such physical adaption of a global product is sometimes as subtle as a dump truck. When Winnebago Industries began to market its recreational vehicles in Japan, it quickly discovered that most of its vehicles would not even fit on Japan's system of narrow roads and tunnels. Furniture maker Richardson Industries had to rethink its Japanese plans when it found that its 82 inch cabinets would not even fit into many of Japan's low-ceiling homes.

The sauce on the Big Mac in France has more mustard and less sugar than Americans find at U.S. McDonald's. The standardized McDonald's menu reflects the need to adapt: The menu includes beer in Germany, wine in France, and McSpaghetti in some pasta-oriented countries. To match local preferences, Betty Crocker cake mixes in Britain require more eggs than in the United States. Colgate Palmolive toothpaste sold in the Middle East is spicier than that sold elsewhere. Campbell produces many formulations of soups offshore that are not found in the United States. Indeed, consumer palates vary so much that Campbell has even carved the United States into 22 pieces that address discrete regional tastes with special products and special advertising. Likewise in the

United States, Thomas Lipton finds that Midwesterners want their instant tea unsweetened, but New Englanders like it presweetened.

New York's Ogilvy & Mather ad agency utilizes consumer profiles based on eight different U.S. regions, each with distinctive buying habits. In 1988, McDonalds used 74 different ad agencies in the U.S. alone. Any American, Canadian, or Englishman who thinks that common tongues or common cultures engender the same tastes in food has but to take a bite of that Australian staple, Vegemite, to be convinced otherwise.

Even when the product is the same, the market may be very different from one country to the next. In the United States, Heineken has always been sold as a premium label. Not so in Great Britain, where it is positioned as a more basic blue-collar brew. California's Blue Diamond almond growers cooperative sells 70 percent of the world's almonds by shrewd use of differing markets. The cooperative's chief executive, Roger Baccigaluppi, has been an indefatigable world traveler in recent years, capturing the Japanese market by developing such products as almond tofu, almond soysauce, and almond miso soup. In the Soviet Union he cornered sales by using almonds' high-protein and lack of cholesterol to sell them as a healthy snack food. They have now been officially endorsed as part of the massive Soviet antialcoholism campaign. West Germany is Blue Diamond's largest market outside the United States. There Baccigaluppi was able to displace Spanish imports by pursuing a variety of tactics. He demonstrated the higher quality of his product; established uses previously unfamiliar in Germany, such as almond butter and baked goods with slivered almonds; and offered annual contracts as opposed to spot orders. Such innovative marketing played a major role in boosting Blue Diamond production from 80 million pounds in 1968 to 460 million by 1985.[1]

A Global Leg Up in Denmark

There *is* perhaps one true prototype of the one-product/one-world operation, an exceptional one missed in the writings of the global marketeers. A quiet company based in a remote hamlet in Denmark sells $500 million of the same product annually to consumers in over 125 countries. The product is Lego building blocks, made by Interlego A.S. In Europe these

[1]"Mother of Invention," *Forbes,* March 10, 1986.

blocks are found in 80 percent of all households with children; in the United States the figure is 65 percent.[2]

With a closely integrated complex of factories in six countries and 5,800 employees, the company routinely turns one of the highest profits in the toy industry. The Kristiansen family which owns the company is often cited as proof of the wisdom of Mark Twain, who advised "put all your eggs in one basket—and watch that basket."

Global Market Synergies

A number of observers have cited the fallacies of global marketing as proof that the concept of the global company itself is a fallacy, that since there can be no global product—except perhaps in the toy industry—in the strictest sense, there is no *raison d'etre* for the global company. Such comments ignore a number of critical facts.

First, the problems of brand names and multifaceted consumer tastes have little effect on the vast number of global or potentially global companies who are not involved with consumer products; the suppliers of plastics, metals, minerals, chemicals, electrical components, machine tools, and thousands of other raw materials or industrial equipment meeting similiar, or identical, demands around the world.

Furthermore, the essence of the global company is never *per se* the *single* global product in its strictest meaning. That essence is the use of global systems, of global networks, and diverse global building blocks to create global synergies. It is adding two on one continent, one on the other, and one on another to create five.

Those who zealously pursue the one-product/one-world approach are just as wrong in thinking that mere technological advances, lowering of official trade barriers, or McLuhanesque images of a global village can give life to the global product. As mentioned in Chapter 1, in many respects the world has not gotten smaller; those advances and openings have only highlighted the rich diversity of the planet's population.

The global manager understands that truth lies elsewhere: Neither the orthodox global marketeers à la Parker Pen's erstwhile management

---

[2]"How Lego Software, Lego Toys Connect with Fifth Graders," *The Wall Street Journal*, March 7, 1989.

nor the global naysayers who would take a segmented, localized view of the world have grasped the reality of the global enterprise.

To such an enterprise neither production nor marketing is an all-or-nothing, stand-alone proposition. They thrive on synergy, on critical mass, which by no means require homogeneity to exist. In that worldview, standardization is always a relative concept. Caterpillar wouldn't succeed if it had tried to sell one product as the panacea for all earthmoving problems anywhere on the planet; much of its success, however, can be attributed to the standardization and interchangeability of parts and components discussed in Chapter 9. When Black & Decker decided it had to become global to fight its primary competitor, Makita of Japan, its first step was to standardize its products in a relative sense, creating streamlined families of products which could be moved with ease in multiple markets. "We have been working very hard to globalize the range of our products so we can compete," noted Alan Larson, Black & Decker's executive vice president for Western hemisphere operations, while discussing the company's new global perspectives.

Global players understand that the world's consumers are not a single one-dimensional mass but they do perceive the synergies that are available when marketing is approached globally. Many large consumer product companies package a few ads for worldwide distribution; local managers then choose the ad best suited for local markets. Millions of dollars can thus be saved in advertising, often in a single country alone. When Colgate Palmolive introduced its Colgate tartar control toothpaste in more than 40 nations, managers in each of those countries could choose one of two ads. The company estimated that savings could exceed $1 million in each country utilizing one of the global ads. Such global marketing moves have been highly successful for Colgate Palmolive. Reuben Mark, chairman and CEO, emphasized in 1988 that "Colgate's global marketing thrust . . . has been a key element in the company's recent increase in profitability."

Yet never does the global company lose sight of the ideal of standardization. A number of strong global operators have been successful in achieving what might have been impossible a generation ago: *adapting markets to their products.* A number of examples can be found in consumer foods where adept companies have stood by standard products in which they have large investments and have been able to turn around the cultural tastes of a reluctant population and make them avid customers. It is not an exercise for global novices.

The Global Breakfast and the "Black Food" Challenge

Kellogg Co. took up this challenge when it began introducing cold cereals into societies which had never experienced such products. When the company made a commitment to change traditional eating habits in France years ago, led by its flagship brand of Cornflakes, it was greeted with great skepticism. Market research showed that 30 percent of the French totally skipped breakfast and the rest typically had a *café au lait* and a slice of bread or a croissant in the morning. The population was adverse, moreover, to eating products made of corn, a grain traditionally viewed as a food for livestock. When packages of corn on the cob were introduced during the 1980s in France, they had to be sold as exotic vegetables with instructions on how to boil and eat the product.

With the formation of a new French subsidiary in 1968, the company began its long siege of the French market. A major problem arose when the French tried to eat their cornflakes immersed in the hot milk that typically sat on the French breakfast table. The company patiently printed instructions on the box: "Pour into bowl. Add cold milk and sugar to taste. Eat." Other brands were introduced by faces familiar in the United States, such as Tony le Tigre. By 1985 the country was up to 10 ounces of cold cereal per capita (compared to 9 pounds in the U.S., and 13 pounds in Australia) and Kellogg was selling 13 brands, with 55 percent of a market worth $42 million. The long years of effort had paid off and promised much greater rewards in the future for a market at last attuned to Kellogg's global plans.

Such uphill battles represent some of the greatest challenges for the global company. Those challenges are multiplying as more companies and industries globalize. U.S. petfood makers are trying to persuade Europeans that their dogs can safely, and willingly, eat dry dogfood. A battle has been waged in recent years by Nestle to convert British consumers to its low-calorie, high-margin frozen entrees sold as Lean Cuisine. From 1985 to 1989 by these efforts the Swiss company developed a $100 million market for itself in Britain where none had existed before.[3] Heinz has joined that fray now with its own Weight Watcher meals, another product line with global aspirations. The two firms are facing off in Germany, where a new campaign of market conversion is beginning.

---

[3]"Nestle Shows How to Gobble Markets," *Fortune*, January 16, 1989.

When Nabisco began to push its U.S. lines of cookies in Japan in the mid-1980s, local managers were pessimistic about one particular product, Oreos. Managing director of the firm's Japanese subsidiary, Eiji Irino, recalls how many felt: "Black food? No one in Japan would eat it." After a few short years of skillful marketing, Oreos are today the number one cookie in Japan.

Gillette has achieved similiar victories in converting consumers to the use of many personal care products. When it found that only a tiny percentage of men in many developing countries used anything other than water to soften their beards before shaving, the company understood it couldn't simply start stocking local stores with its shaving cream and expect it to sell. It commenced an ambitious campaign of live shaving demonstration shows, traveling village to village, corner to corner, wherever it could find potential users. The program has been very successful; in one year in Guadalajara, Mexico, for example, Gillette almost doubled the number of men using shaving cream. Similiar efforts are made by the company with respect to hair care products, deodorant, and other consumer goods to achieve the market penetration long enjoyed by its original product, razor blades. (Fidel Castro once told a reporter that he first grew a beard because no Gillette blades were available when he was fighting in the mountains of Cuba).

Many companies who market with alacrity in their home markets, and readily recognize the vital nature of key customer relationships in that market, fail to translate that recognition into the global context. The global enterprise doesn't open its factory doors and sell off its truck docks. It lives with its critical customers around the globe, some of whom themselves may be global but many of whom may not be.

Staying "Down the Street" from Customers

In the central Ohio region surrounding Marysville, a number of small, freshly built factories can be found bearing unfamiliar but distinctly Oriental names. They are the facilities of auto parts producers, clustered about Honda's huge Marysville facility, who traveled from Japan with their customer. The move was a natural one for those who understood that their business wasn't simply producing auto parts but rather was supplying elements for the production of Honda vehicles. The global perspective of Honda itself, incorporating fundamental tenets of low-cost, reliability, and high-quality, requires closeknit, stable relationships with a select group of qualified suppliers. The existence of the Pacific Ocean was but a minor footnote in that perspective.

It was unthinkable for Honda to consider opening a new factory and start accepting parts from the cheapest supplier that walked through the door. Even small parts producers without international operations quickly grasped that they were strategically important to Honda, just as Honda was to them. Today at least 140 Japanese parts suppliers produce parts in the United States for Honda and other carmakers from the Land of the Rising Sun. Despite aggressive efforts by U.S. suppliers to replace them, many U.S. suppliers were unable to meet the Japanese quality standards.

Supplier relationships like most other aspects of production are strategic for the global company. The relationship is reciprocal, as reflected in the story of Japanese carmakers. The natural progression from this fact are moves by suppliers in tandem with key customers as those customers move around the world.

In early 1989 Wall Street had a flurry of interest in Ferro Corporation of Cleveland, a maker of ceramics, plastics, and pigments. A primary reason for this interest was the discovery by investors and analysts of Ferro's global position. For three decades the company had been quietly moving around the world in tandem with its customers. It has therefore been in a much stronger position than competitors who simply exported from home country plants. Commenting on this interest in Ferro, Paul Branstad, senior vice president and head of Booz Allen & Hamilton's global strategy practice, emphasized that in the coming years "all the forces in business will favor companies that are truly international in scope as opposed to exporters." Customer relationships are a critical aspect, Branstad noted, "Increasingly, the leverage in business today is gravitating toward more intimate relationships with the customer." Ferro has long understood that oceans and national borders can't get in the way of those relationships.

Low-profile, but highly successful AMP Inc., a $2.3 billion producer of electrical connectors, likewise started early with its global customer perspective, building its first factories overseas more than 35 years ago. In 1959 when its major Italian customer, Fiat, decided it would no longer import connectors, AMP quickly invested in a new Italian factory. AMP had little to complain about when the Japanese carmakers began bringing their Japanese suppliers with them in their ventures overseas. AMP had been a Japan-based supplier for Honda, Toyota, and Nissan for years.

E. I. Dupont also has long been an inside supplier to those auto-makers. Both AMP and Dupont even work alongside designers at their key customers to shape new products in which their respective products can be used. When Xerox had large customers expand from Japan to the United States and Europe, the company transferred account executives from Japan to accompany them and assure that Xerox would expand with them. Such moves were part of the company's "global arrangements for marketing effectiveness," or GAME, program.

In sharp contrast is Eastman Kodak, a company that did not pursue such an opportunity for nearly a century and paid for it dearly. Kodak first began supplying the Japanese market in the late 19th century, but despite its huge market and critical base for competition, until recently it simply treated Japan like one more export sales territory. Only in the late 1980s did Kodak assign a senior executive to Japan and begin aggressive marketing of its products with Japanese customers, long after strong Japanese competitors had developed and moved in on Kodak's U.S. market.

The Research and Development Link

Vitally linked to global marketing as another leverage point of response is the role of research and development in global operations. The global economy acts as a huge accelerator in the spread of technology and as an amplifier for customer interest in continually new or advanced products. Research and development may be driven from many global aspects—in some industries, such as aircraft or pharmaceuticals, research and development costs are so great that a global base has become necessary to sustain them. Thirty years ago a telecommunications switching system cost $10 to $20 million to develop and had a useful life of 25 years. Today's complex digital systems cost up to $1 billion to develop but may become obsolete in a decade or less. Nothing less than a significant share of the global markets can support such an effort. Around the world, competition in some sectors may be so fierce that a failure to match the step-by-step technical development of a competitor spells catastrophe.

It is no coincidence that one of the United States' most powerful global leaders, IBM, established an international network of research facilities many years ago. Through those facilities IBM stays at the front of markets, frustrating competitors again and again with its relentless pace in product development and release of new products. Many competitors around the world complain of the unfair advantage that IBM has through its global research base. When low cost offshore producers of bearings required Timken to become more globally competitive in the 1970s the company successfully adopted a similiar strategy, enhancing and diversifying its international research base, to gain an edge as the industry's technological leader.

Sony operates advanced video research centers in both Japan and California. Allentown, Pennsylvania based Air Products Co. spends over 20 percent of its research budget overseas. Even toymaker Lego is funding research at MIT to explore high-tech applications for its products. Family owned S. C. Johnson & Sons, today has research labs in Japan, Europe, the United States, and Argentina, as well as applications labs in each of its other major markets.[4]

The firm that is a technology follower cannot become a global leader. In its somnolent days before the advent of globally-focused manager Robert Bauman, the United Kingdom's Beecham Plc. suffered severely from a follower image. When competitors introduced tartar control formulations of toothpaste, a key Beecham product line, the company did not get an equivalent product into the marketplace for two years. More than a few observers noted with irony that when a restrengthened Beecham was able to take over (technically, a merger) Smithkline of the United States, it was due to the fact that Smithkline itself had become severely weakened by an inability to launch new products after its primary traditional products had matured.

Over the long-term, the global enterprise can successfully produce neither products nor technology from one fixed geographic base. Research and development must be in touch with key markets and key customers, wherever they may be. Caterpillar designs its equipment at multiple international locations; recently it introduced a new global product line of excavators developed at its design center in Japan.

Also in Japan, a market with the world's highest per capita consumption of pharmaceuticals, Upjohn Co. decided it couldn't afford to be without a research connection. The company opened a 100 scientist facility in 1988. The reciprocal lesson has long been lost by Upjohn's competitors within Japan. The Japanese pharmaceutical industry has been extremely weak internationally, owing in large part to the lack of effective international research efforts. For years, the important drugs on the Japa-

---

[4]"Managing When It's All in the Family," *New York Times*, April 9, 1989.

nese market were imports or produced under offshore license. In 1988 and 1989 this trend began to subside as large producers like Yamanouchi Pharmaceutical, Takeda Chemical, Otsuka Pharmaceutical, and Eisai Co. began to develop research facilities outside Japan.

It becomes easier to understand the problems that Germany's giant Siemens has had in going global when it is revealed that parts of the company are still involved in making telephone equipment that was first introduced in 1953. The company does have a huge research and development budget—it has spent several billion dollars on R&D in recent years—but it has been slow to translate that effort into new products. Ironically, one of Siemens biggest high-tech successes has been the CAT scanner, a product that, as previously discussed, was created by a British firm, Thorn EMI. Thorn itself proved unable to handle global development and marketing of its product. The problems of both Siemens and Thorn illustrate the further point that the R&D of the global firm must be based equally in business and science. Technological Ph.D. stars, and huge R&D budgets can be found at many firms—Hoffmann LaRoche joins Siemens in these ranks—that have been pointedly unsuccessful at launching major new products in recent years. Video cassette recorder technology was developed by technically-driven personnel in the United States. It required market-driven companies in Japan and Europe to turn that technology into a market worth scores of billions in sales. A similar observation could be made for the transistor, first developed by Bell Labs in 1947, in its promulgation of the consumer electronics industry. Opening the history books, one would find the same morale for the multiple high-tech ventures of Thomas Edison, most of which became extremely lucrative only after the technically-driven Edison was forced out of their management.

The successful global player learns the difficult task of integrating technology and market objectives and to include technical development as an element of product management. Part of the success of AMP, the Harrisburg-based global producer of connectors metioned above, can be attributed to the fact that it barely distinguishes between applied and basic research. The company's 2,000-plus scientists and engineers work at every stage of product development, focusing not only on their connector products but on the machines used by customers to install them. The company understands the strategic link between their products and such machines. The highest quality connectors in the world will be useless to a global producer of cars, trains, or televisions if it does not have an efficient, reliable method for installing them. The firm spends an average of 9 percent of sales on research and development—a level that would be considered quite high by many. AMP considers this to be simply in the proper course of business for a global leader. The company's record of success speaks for itself.

Technological leapfrog among competitors has been especially conspicuous in the consumer electronics industry. Audiophiles and videophiles from Syracuse to Sydney could easily compile a rough list of minor and major technology breakthroughs that temporarily have allowed one producer then another to take the lead in the ever-maneuvering electronics market. The basic VCR of 15 years ago was quickly followed by units with programmable memories that could record an event four days in the future and soon advanced to units handling four or more events up to 14 days in the future. Eight track players, cassette players, digital tapes, compact discs, stereophonic, quadraphonic, dozens of permutations in woofers and tweeters for speakers . . . the list is virtually an endless one and grows constantly.

Sony preempted competitors with its high-quality, compact camcorders in 1988. Matsushita, having shed the image of being a technology follower (the company was once nicknamed *maneshita denki,* for "electronics that are copied"), struck back with a global VCR that can automatically adapt to the many different television color and video line signals used in major markets around the world.[5]

Global Information Synapses

Implicit in the global enterprise response leverage points of marketing and R&D are fine-tuned systems for the collection and dissemination of information. As John Naisbitt, author of *Megatrends,* and others have pointed out, the information "float", or the delay in dispersal of information across the planet, has effectively disappeared in the global economy. Beijing and Boise are separated by but a momentary electronic signal. Continents are separated not by oceans in the information context, but mere electrical synapses. Market changes, technology developments, and

---

[5]"Matsushita Video Recorder Bridges Global TV Signals," *The Wall Street Journal,* March 27, 1989.

new government policies and laws can be reported almost immediately, allowing reaction of a speed which would have dizzied a prior generation.

The information float, however, has been replaced by the information flood. Companies who simply establish information networks without proper guidance and management, quickly find themselves swamped with confusing, redundant, and/or meaningless detail, a destiny easily as calamitous as having never penetrated the information float at all.

A vital aspect of the global information systems, and one which reflects why such systems cannot be divorced from either R&D or strategic marketing efforts, is the ability to gain insight into technical developments by key competitors. The global firm must keep all technological bases covered. This ability in Ferro Corporation played an important factor in Wall Street's discovery of the company in early 1989, when stock analysts publicly emphasized the firm's global strengths. As Paul Branstad of Booz Allen & Hamilton's international strategy unit stated in reviewing Ferro, "only a company with strong indigenous operations in a number of countries will be able to stay technologically current."

The history of consumer electronics over the past two decades could have been rewritten, along with that of the semiconductor and other high-tech industries which are heavily tied to that industry, if one American company had developed a stronger information and intelligence system. RCA Corporation was a major potential primary producer of VCRs. The company had to choose between making VCRs and videodisc players. It chose the latter, based in large part on a determination that it was technically not viable to mass produce the pickup heads for video recorders; U.S. production machines had a .5 mil tolerance, but a .2 mil tolerance was required. RCA therefore linked its consumer electronics destiny to videodisc players. Sony and Matsushita, with more confidence in their technology, within months had solved the pickup head production problem and were on the way to domination of the consumer electronics market.

No successful global strategy can be developed or implemented without a solid basis in real-time, accurate information. A number of surveys have shown that American managers typically are not as well informed about current industry events as their foreign competitors. Certainly information practices vary considerably. British executives have been found to read three times as many newspapers as their American counterparts. Japanese companies assign many overseas middle managers solely for the purpose of collecting information and studying foreign markets and technology. More than a few puzzled American managers have received an explanation from a newly arrived Japanese businessman in New York, Chicago, or Los Angeles that his job is to "study America."

An expeditious, but discriminating information network is not an end to itself. It is a tool of the global company, one which breeds global success when used well, whether in responding to market changes, technical advances, or identifying and securing investment opportunities. Inescapably, one element of global strategy must be the ability to respond quickly. A decade ago, major decisions such as the siting of a new offshore production facility often took a year or more to resolve and five years or more to implement. Retired Westinghouse chairman Douglas Danforth, speaking of this new time sensitivity in international operations, has noted that years ago, "We could plan where we wanted to be, what we wanted to manufacture, we could align and train a work force and take six or seven years to do the whole thing." Westinghouse has improved that time delay considerably, recently taking three years to open a new facility in South Korea, but as Danforth has noted, in the future "you want to be much quicker than that."

Observers have been nearly blinded with the speed with which some global enterprises are able to move. In 1987 when it heard that Heublein was for sale by its parent RJR Nabisco, the United Kingdom's Grand Metropolitan Plc. put together a $1.3 billion deal *in just four days*. Grand Met's CEO Allen Sheppard noted to duly impressed observers, "Operating within a strategy doesn't preclude being opportunistic and light-footed."

The Distribution Connection

Similar responsiveness must be built into another critical market leverage point for global enterprises: product distribution systems. Most successful global enterprises have found—some by costly lesson, some by initial insight—that the best distribution system for their global operations is one carefully customized to those operations. This does not mean rejecting traditional distribution systems in key markets; as previously discussed, many companies have been stung badly in countries like Japan by trying to repudiate local systems and "do their own thing" without regard to local tradition. The starting place usually must be a fit with local, national, or regional systems, adapting that disparate network into an efficient global pattern.

Global innovation in distribution systems often can become a key strategic leverage point. Even in that most rigid of frameworks, Japan, some degree of innovation can, and has, worked, as evidenced by previously mentioned success by Campbell Soup and Warner Lambert. Several years ago in Europe, Outboard Marine Corporation obtained major improvement in international customer service and credit arrangements, as well as concurrent savings in costs, when, despite complaints from local trade groups, it moved from a traditional three level distribution framework to a more efficient two tier system. A key part of Swedish Match AB's global strategy in pushing consumer products like its Wilkinson razors or Cricket lighters has been the innovative use of distribution techniques, especially the development of nontraditional point of sale distribution.

On the other side of the Pacific, Makita used such a strategy when it began its head-to-head competition with Black & Decker in power tools. Makita invaded Black & Decker's markets not through Black & Decker's traditional outlets but through large discount home centers. The remarkable Interlego AS eliminated many rivals by taking the innovative step of selling directly to retailers in its top markets around the world, creating almost irresistible appeal among buyers for its high-quality, high-margin global product. Years ago many Far Eastern producers of electronic timepieces got the jump on traditional makers of spring-activated watches by selling to nontraditional outlets like camera shops.

If careful attention to distribution can bring big global returns, then inattention or disorganization in distribution can bring commensurate penalties. When Revlon first tried to sell global cosmetics in Japan, it turned many retailers against it by refusing to deal with all but elite outlets. When that plan failed, the company made an 180 degree turn and tried to distribute its products on a broad mass market basis through low-priced channels. Customers and merchants both became alienated.

For many global companies the most critical aspect of distribution is simply the speed of delivery. Chapter 9 discussed Benetton's remarkable ability to move sweaters at lightning speed into the marketplace. Again the global operations of Caterpillar can be called upon as an example of what the effective global operator can achieve. Through its global system of nearly 200 dealers and over 1,100 branch stores, the company is able to deliver *99.5 percent* of all customer parts orders around the world *within 48 hours*. That global system is so highly respected that Caterpillar has been asked to handle distribution for a number of firms, including Navistar and the U.K.'s Rover Group.[6]

Global Response, Global Winning

When the Swedish firm L. M. Ericsson was threatened with losing out to much larger competitors in the fierce international telecommunications business, it turned to the smaller government telephone systems which had been its traditional strength. Ericsson didn't have the resources to produce the huge electronic switching systems which were rapidly replacing electromechanical systems. Working with its customers, tapping a small but highly effective research program, the company struck a winning global reponse. It introduced modular technology that the smaller phone systems could gradually phase into their existing systems without the expensive and often disruptive total replacement involved in the larger megasystems. Ericsson faced a global crisis, uncovered a previously unidentified global need, and produced an answer that assured its survival.

In the global enterprise such reactions must become second nature. The global winner understands that markets are never static, competition is never static, and technology is never static. It knows the strategic importance of selling not only today's products but also the promise of tomorrow's products. It has its eyes on the world but its feet are firmly planted with the customer down the street—whether that customer is in Augsburg or Atlanta, Milwaukee or Manila.

---

[6]"This Cat is Acting Like a Tiger," *Fortune*, December 19, 1988.

CHAPTER 11

STRATEGIC
GLOBAL ORGANIZING

One of the most severe handicaps that many enterprises face in their effort to win in the global economy is not a tariff, not a trade war, not an unstable currency, or a hemorrhage of technology. It is an aspect totally under their control, a problem of their making whose resolution must inexorably be of their own making. It is their organizational structure.

Many organizational structures have failed to keep pace with the global economy. The need for rapid response in the factory and laboratory, the demand for straddling multiple cultures with varying laws, customs, and business cultures, and the reality of white-hot competition in many emerging global industries, requires the need for maximum flexibility in an organization with miminum loss to core strategies. The global economy demands production coordination, information gathering, marketing, and research and development systems of unprecedented dimensions.

If this organizational problem does not receive the proper attention in many enterprises, it is not due to *lack* of attention. A tour through the corporate annals of any dozen large corporations with international operations could easily lead to the conclusion that for most companies international problems are organizational problems. Judging by the amount of activity and resources devoted to them, international organizational and related personnel problems would indeed seem to overshadow mere global strategic concerns at many companies.

Ask an international manager who was with Westinghouse during the 1970s and his main memory is likely to be that the company totally reorganized its international operations three times during that decade. Dozens of large international companies over the past two decades have leapt from one structure to another as if in a game of musical chairs coached by consultants and professors. To some of those involved, experimentation with the global matrix, the unitary international division, and the integrated world product division seemed to become an end unto itself. "I had the impression our main *raison d'etre* as international managers was to find the perfect symmetry for our organization chart," recently groused a veteran of frequent international reorganizing in two large multinationals over the past 15 years.

No enterprise is going to become a global winner until it beats its own organizational problems. Proper organization is an indispensable tool for global success. Lack of proper organization in a competitor, moreover, can be a vital weakness, and has decided the outcome of many global economic battles. It is in this sense that organizational aspects become a further major set of global leverage points.

The efficient, well-tuned global organization can be aimed and fired at competitive problems in the way the well-tuned crew, using wind, sail, cannon, and other of their own "leverage points," could bring an 18th century frigate to bear upon and conquer an enemy vessel on the high seas. Organizational weakness of a company, resulting in slow response, inept execution of strategies, and inefficient distribution or production can have no less an impact in the balance of a global industry.

Feeling the Organizational Squeeze

Anyone trying to understand how General Motors could have lost over $2 billion in Europe in a few short years during the early 1980s would ultimately find a trail leading to Russelsheim, West Germany. In that town near Frankfurt sat the offices of GM's largest European subsidiary, Adam Opel AG, as well as the company's European headquarters. As became painfully obvious in retrospect, all too often it seemed that the European headquarters *was* Adam Opel AG. Opel's CEO was GM's senior European manager. Heavy emphasis on the German operation strapped the European business with entrenched German suppliers even as their costs went sky-high with the rise of the mark. GM's top European managers often were found to be heavily involved not in regional issues but with problems in Opel's local factories and their very expensive 60,000 German workers. A former GM manager, looking back on frustrating years in Europe as losses accumulated in increments of *$100s of millions*, commented: "We often didn't seem like an American company or a European company. Instead we were a German company that had occasional out-side interference."

If one scrutinized the facts behind the heavy worldwide losses of Texas Instruments (TI) in the mid-1980s, one would find not only the downturn in semiconductors that affected the entire industry but also that TI's international organization sharply accentuated the effect of that downturn. Overseas managers ran individual fiefdoms, with control over the regional factories that sourced the products they sold. As a result many factories built up large capacity to meet local demand even when TI's factories elsewhere in the world needed business. When the bottom fell out of the semiconductor market in 1985, the excess capacity engen-dered by this structure dealt the company a severe blow.

While N.V. Philips casts a giant shadow over industries like con-sumer electronics, lighting, telecommunications, and data systems, a look behind the scenes at the company often gives solace to Philips's competitors. Although today the company is undertaking a difficult re-structuring, the organization that existed for many decades as the com-pany spread its influence around the world casts its own shadow over the company's global future.

Philips traditionally operated 60 highly independent national subsid-iaries, employing well over 300,000 workers worldwide. Managers in this organization lived a sheltered life with, typically, seven weeks vaca-tion, large annual bonuses, and a policy of no lateral recruitment of senior management. Many observers have complained that Philips managers were simply not profit oriented at all due to the soft life they enjoyed. When Philips announced that its planned merger of its medical electronics business with Britain's GEC had fallen through, GEC representatives publicly stated that it was because Philips was too disorganized to estab-lish its negotiating position. When Philips' European factories needed to market their video cassette recorders, the company's American unit re-fused to sell them. Such disorganization pays its own kind of dividends. In 1988 the company's net income amounted to 1.8 percent of sales; its net borrowing, compared to equity capital in 1987, was over 70 percent. Professor C. K. Prahalad of the University of Michigan noted after con-sulting with Philips on its need for change: "The real challenge for Philips is to create a sense of urgency for change, not just at the top, but down the entire organization."

That sense of urgency slowly began to sink into the organization of Reynolds Metals Co. during the late 1980s. Individual managers in foreign countries ran production and sales organizations as mini-empires. In Europe alone the company had independent operations in Italy, Germany, Spain, Holland, France, Austria, and Belgium. Managers in those countries, along with others across the globe—25 in all—were integrated only by the fact that they all reported to the president of Reynolds International in Richmond, Virginia. Reynolds's chairman, William Bourke, today engaged in a major restructuring of those operations, is realistic enough to admit the problems that framework caused. "You had salesmen from four or five different Reynolds companies calling on the same accounts—and selling the same product lines," commented Bourke in early 1989. Separate, often duplicate production facilities under independent country managers effectively prevented any integrated production plans for sourcing products at the lowest cost facility.

Many such firms might at least take relative comfort by looking at Germany's Siemens. The elephantine company has more than 350,000 employees in over 300 separately identified businesses. At a 1988 seminar for European executives the company's chief planner admitted that Siemens was doing well, or had a leadership position, in no more than one half of these businesses. With each business in its separate compartment, synergy between R&D and marketing has often been alien at Siemens. In the company's bloated bureaucracy new product approval often has taken many months. Such structural problems have taken their toll. As mentioned in Chapter 10, the company has chronic problems in trying to develop new products. In the United States in 1988, the company lost $212 million. Its global telecommunications business has been losing $100 million annually. The company has one of the lowest sales per worker ratios of any company in its related businesses.

Cadbury Schweppes has, by any objective standard, been an aggressively expanding participant in the global food and drink industry during the last decade. Yet if one studied the company during most of the 1980s and preceding decades, a marketing and research structure of surprising fragmentation would have been found. With a multinational structure of nearly autonomous country managers reporting to London headquarters and a marketing strategy that consisted of essentially selling products and sometimes brands that had succeeded in Great Britain, the company had a widely fluctuating record in the marketplace. A number of products nurtured in England, like the candy bars "Wispa" and "Ronda," were unmitigated flops when exported into this international system. Local country managers were so unpredictable and slow in introducing new products, moreover, that competitors were sometimes able to establish competing knockoff versions in foreign markets before the original Cadbury product ever appeared. Local management was so independent in establishing in-country promotion that ratios of advertising cost to sales varied dramatically, from 1.5 to 5 percent. Expensive research undertaken in England was disseminated to local units but not followed up; sometimes it was totally ignored. Without a steady flow of winning products from home, the company's U.S. factory was often operating at less than half capacity. When asked about the long-standing problem of finding products for the U.S. market and the structure that aggravated the problem, the company's CEO stated that he didn't want to move too quickly because "it would have brought about the danger of repercussions in the company."

Colonizing Failure

Each of the companies described above have at least today acknowledged the organizational barriers they face in finding global success and have undertaken initiatives, discussed below, to eliminate those barriers. While the answers they are finding are, inescapably, tailored to their discrete circumstances, the problems they face are far from unique.

Many of those problems, and those of countless other global aspirants, can be traced back to an outdated multinational organizational framework that might be described as colonial. As in administration of European colonies of a bygone era, the mother country headquarters, in the colonial multinational, is interested above all in receiving vessels laden with treasure. To accomplish this in a world of complex geography and disparate cultures, the easiest method seemed to be to establish a country manager, a viceroy, and a governor general, as it were, in major foreign outposts. Such managers were variously responsible for producing and selling products first developed back home, or otherwise subjecting populations to civilizing influence and collecting sales receipts in the form of taxes.

Individual viceroys in this multinational scheme had little interaction among themselves, reporting to the motherland without knowledge of events in neighboring lands. With reports traveling by sea, or the equally slow means found in a number of multinationals, senior ministers or managers at home often perceived their world based on stale information, sometimes leading to delusion. If local works—whether factories or civil engineering projects—were to be built, the local viceroys always found compelling reasons for them to be constructed in their territory—first and foremost, and sometimes only, because such works added to their power base.

One of the better known "private" enterprises of the colonial era was the Hudson Bay Company. That fur company reflected the epitome of absentee management in the colonial structure. Decisions made by managers far removed from local operations filtered down to the local level over a period of months or even years. No governor, or "CEO," of the Company actually visited the Hudson Bay until 1934, 264 years after the Company's founding. Some modern international firms still suffer from such absentee management syndrome.

Of course, administering a uniform colonial policy was always difficult due to the many differences in colonies, or local subsidiaries. Many companies who have awakened to the problems of such "colonial" structures, discovered that quality control, expense allocation, and other accounting practices varied widely between country units. The results were virtual different "languages" being spoken between units; in some operations, unknown to senior headquarters management, even product line definitions have varied from "colony" to "colony."

The Strategic Global Organization

The most important point in establishing the global organization, or remedying those of a colonial or other counterproductive bent, is that *organization is always a strategic element of the global firm.* Senior managers may worry about organization, but many personnel also feel that efforts to globalize an organization amount to simply a distraction from important efforts like keeping their local factories busy. When MIT's Sloan Management Review published the results of a study of 250 managers in some of the world's largest companies relating to organizational perspectives,[1] one of the basic conclusions was that in most such firms, "limited organizational capability . . . represents the most critical constraint in responding to new strategic demands."

Organization as the framework for execution of strategic global management *must* itself be considered as strategic. The enterprise that is

---

[1]C. Bartlett and S. Ghoshal, "Managing Across Borders, New Strategic Requirements," *Sloan Management Review*, (Summer 1987).

able to address the global economy successfully, moreover, understands that:

> Different elements of a global enterprise (R&D, sales, production, financial management) may need to have different organizational structures.
>
> Global organizations consist of personnel; an organization cannot be made global without attention to the globalization of its people.
>
> Organizational structures *always* must *evolve* as an enterprise, its industry, and/or its markets change. Flexibility is the primary hallmark of the global organization.

There is no single formula, no panacea, no mystical combination that can create a foolpoof organizational success in the global economy. Anyone who thinks they have one, or can find one, is already starting out with a handicap. Some companies *knew* in the 1970s that the matrix structure, with rigid division according to function and geography, usually with dual reporting channels on a functional and geographical basis, was the *only* viable international structure. The companies that championed the matrix cause—including Westinghouse, Citibank, and Dow Chemical—beat a retreat as they began to perceive the tension and conflict generated by the structure. Others insisted that the international division was the only way to go, with one unit responsible for *all* matters outside the home country; such frameworks have slowly become discredited as managers became sensitized to the profound problems arising when offshore operations are segregated from the rest of the business. It is perhaps no coincidence that while such international organization, reorganization, and re-reorganization activity was preoccupying many of America's largest firms, the country's participation in the world economy slipped substantially.

The global organization solution is never a simple one. Conflicting goals and pressures may arise at every turn. The need to adapt to local conditions and maximize local responsiveness demands a decentralized structure. The need for maximizing standardization across borders seems to demand a strong central organization. The need for centralized control over R&D efforts, while still tapping into local technology and local markets, may call for a hybrid central organization with a regionalized emphasis. Reporting lines for managers in various markets may need to vary to assure that senior managers are closely linked to subordinates in markets of global significance, but that their lives are not cluttered with data on markets that can be delegated to competent professionals working under global guidelines. Applying the same organizational structure to all operations and failing to evolve organizations with changing global exigencies have been fatal to many candidates for global success.

The failure of ITT to carry on its successful tradition in telecommunications has been discussed in Chapter 7. If any single reason could be ascribed to that failure—and to the success of the European firm that took over ITT's business—it would be organization. ITT's inability to develop a global switching system, despite an expenditure of over $1 billion, was primarily linked to the fact that national units around the world were steeped in a tradition of local autonomy, and corporate systems were set up to measure and encourage performance on an individual national basis. In many respects the structure represented the colonial MNC described above, despite the advanced, high-tech, forward thinking public image of ITT. Presented with the need for a product that by its nature had to be developed cooperatively, with common standards and joint research, those units seemed unable to meet that need. Without a properly integrated development structure, the new generation of equipment upon which ITT's telecommunications future depended was stillborn. As we have seen, the onetime flagship of American telecommunications was forced to divest its overseas business.

If a divorce of ITT from its international telecommunications roots would have seemed impossible a few years ago, so too would have seemed a separation of General Electric from its cherished consumer electronics business. Yet the company's colonial empire of mini-GEs in countries around the world was ill-equipped to meet the challenge of competitors in the Far East. Indeed, the GE organization might have been described as the perfect misfit. The company's nearly autonomous offshore units were delegated everything *but* research and development, which was kept in the United States in the traditional multinational corporate style of developing products at home for eventual dispersal around the world. The company thus denied itself viable access to critical research activity underway at locations elsewhere around the globe, activity that was being readily tapped by its competitors. In such a structure, an effort to globally integrate production, research, and market input is akin to turning a 1,000 foot tanker around once it is proceeding at full speed. When the company finally decided to begin to globalize its consumer electronics business by shifting production to Asian sources and undertaking to globally integrate product development, the effort was far too slow, and therefore too late to overcome the strong lead of its competitors. The GE business was eventually taken over by Thomson S.A. of France.

The Local Global Manager

Despite an apparent belief to the contrary by some corporate managers, organizations are not globalized by decree or memo from a headquarters office. Organizations, after all, are people. A number of organizations trying to become global lose sight of this fact; so long as they maintain that perspective, they will not become global winners.

The essence behind any enterprise with a global perspective and global skill is the existence of individual managers with global perspective and global skill. To what extent have American, and other, international firms acknowledged that reality? The global CEO was discussed in Chapter 7. Consider the following brief additional examples:

• When international projects such as the establishment of a new production operation or a new manufacturing joint venture must be negotiated, a surprising number of firms have been found to dispatch an engineer with no particular international experience to negotiate and conclude the arrangements. In such organizations such projects are viewed as simply "building a factory", meaning it is a job for an engineer. When one such engineer returned with an agreement to build a facility, it was discovered that the engineer had sought out the CEO of the joint venture partner and negotiated additional agreements for marketing, product line commitments, and performance guarantees, having hired a local interpreter from his hotel for advice on local business customs.

• A Midwest factory manager returned the day after departure for a critical negotiation in Europe. The manager had been turned back at the airport for not having a passport. The passport wasn't forgotten. *The manager didn't have one.*

• A company dispatched a financial manager to negotiate an offshore sourcing relationship. Three days later a phone call came requesting explanation of the terms CIF, FOB, and "confirmed letter of credit." The financial manager complained that such "little details" seemed overly important to the foreign firm's negotiators. After a week a telex arrived from the foreign firm, politely asking if the U.S. firm could send an experienced negotiator so the contract could be concluded.

The emphasis placed on international experience in senior management, and the role of international managers generally, are perhaps the best indicators of the global orientation, and global commitment, of many organizations. Many farsighted executives work to obtain offshore assignments so they can be "where the action is," where, often, the future of the company lies. But when they return, due to the organizational structure, they are frequently compartmentalized into an international office or simply shunted into a domestic assignment without any opportunity to utilize that international expertise.

When, as pointed out in Chapter 7, *The Wall Street Journal* compiled a profile of the typical CEO of the year 2000, it was of a markedly global operator. Yet current reality at many firms would give little hint of that future. International executives may tend to be well paid and to enjoy high profiles in their assignment location, but such assignments are often a poor route for advancement in many companies. When Korn Ferry, the international recruitment firm, surveyed advancement in large U.S. companies in 1979, only 2 percent of executives considered the international route to be a fast track to the CEO's office. In a similar survey in 1985 that number actually dropped to 0.5 percent. Likewise, when the international consulting firm of Moran, Stahl & Boyer recently conducted an analogous survey it found that only 4 percent of U.S. companies considered overseas assignments to "have a positive effect on career advancement." Indeed, for many firms with international operations, international personnel issues are viewed primarily as a reentry problem, not one of how best to train personnel and integrate international perspectives throughout the operation.

Many managers and corporations struggle with the fact that offshore managers often feel alienated from mainstream operations in the home country and, upon return, find that the offshore experience may amount to a handicap in the sense that it has kept them out of the attention of senior managers who control key advancement decisions. "I struggled to get an international position," complained a U.S. manager posted in Germany in 1987, "but now I know it was a mistake—out of sight, out of mind. Nobody that really counts in the home office has an inkling of what I'm doing." Despite the great demands for integration of offshore skills and the huge need for sensitizing entire organizations to global issues that arise in the global economy, many firms simply perceive their international personnel issues in terms of the "reentry problem."

That attitude is a highly revealing symptom of a much deeper problem at such companies. The concept of reentry is alien to the global enterprise. The reentry mentality is based on an implicit perception of a domestic us (U.S. operations) versus them (overseas operations). It involves a dichotomous worldview that is incompatible with global operations. In the global firm, the manager who arrives in Denver from Dusseldorf is viewed as an important competitive asset, not an outsider who has to relearn life in the "real world."

The problem is by no means confined to U.S. firms. It plagues many, if not most, Japanese "international" firms and a number of European companies. European firms, however, have led the way in globalizing personnel, as they have in globalizing boards of directors. A review of the chief executives in Germany's 25 largest companies shows that 15 spent a part of their careers outside Germany. Notes Klaus Evard, director of the European Business School, located near Frankfurt, "Young German managers know they won't advance without succeeding in a foreign post." In 1988 a global company based in Great Britain identified 240 candidates as successors for its top 190 management positions; almost 100 of them were not even British nationals; 37 percent had held jobs outside their native country.

One would like to think that U.S. firms are beginning to learn from such lessons in adapting their own organizations to the global economy. Yet, in addition to the ever-strong reentry mentality noted above, another trend can be identified. Many managers' primary view of offshore assignments is as a cost that must be contained; to them international personnel policy should consist of minimizing the use of Americans offshore. When Professor Stephen J. Korbin of Pennsylvania's Wharton School studied personnel practices in 126 large U.S. multinational companies, he found that over a 10 year period half of them had *reduced* the use of American managers overseas.[2] To green-visored MBAs such "cost containment" may be appealing. Unfortunately, at many firms such efforts amount to a containment of any meaningful globalization. Its effect, in final analysis,

---

[2]"Are Multinationals Better After the Yankees Go Home?" *The Wall Street Journal*, May 8, 1989.

is a reawakening, or reinforcing, of the colonial mentality that has handicapped so many global efforts.

Encouragement can at least be taken from a number of U.S. firms that *have* accepted the need for truly global organizations. Looking to the company's CEOs of the future, Dow Chemical chairman Paul Orrefice insists that experience in running a foreign unit will be a *sine qua non*. "About five years of international experience" should do, noted Orrefice in early 1989. Trying to more deliberately develop future CEOs in this mold, Dow has set up a global panel to address the need. In 1989 Merck & Co. ceased defining its senior executive training programs along national lines, assuring a strong degree of internationalization in future training. Douglas Danforth, former chairman of Westinghouse Electric Co. Inc. capsulizes advice for future CEOs in two words: "Travel overseas." Professor Noel Tichy of the University of Michigan's graduate school of business uses three words to characterize the future CEO: "Global, global, global."

Finding the Global Remedy

The lessons of strategic global organization are being learned at each of the companies mentioned at the start of this discussion. GM, Texas Instruments, Reynolds Metals, Philips, Siemens, and Cadbury Schweppes, after acknowledging the global penalties being paid due to their international organizations have each taken major remedial steps.

A large part of General Motors's answer to the devastating problems in Europe that were handicapping the rest of its global operations was the physical separation of its European headquarters from its German operations. In the late 1980s the company moved its European headquarters office to Zurich, and began a major deemphasis of high-cost German suppliers in its European operations as part of a long overdue program of production cost cutting. By setting up European headquarters in one of the few European countries where it has no production, the company lent added objectivity and credibility to its new European management team. Moreover, before the increasingly important European Community regulators in Brussels, the company is able to project the pan-European image it needs rather than the German profile it previously had. And the company finds that an international Zurich-based team, including Canadian,

British, American, and German managers, is much more effective in building consensus among its diverse European unit.[3]

Reynolds Metals found a very similiar solution to its wide ranging problems. The company established a Reynolds Europe headquarters office in Lausanne, Switzerland to coordinate marketing, distribution, and production for its previously disjointed operating companies on the continent. Directors of national subsidiaries report to a new president of Reynolds Europe and now are able to complement each other instead of competing with each other. Production has been consolidated and coordinated so that orders can be sourced at the lowest cost facility without causing territorial disputes among country managers.

CEO Jerry Junkins of Texas Instruments wrestled with international tradition at his company and finally hammered out a structure in which managers clearly serve to build global business, not protect local turf. Managers in key markets were given direct global responsibilities. When, for example, the manager of Japanese operations, who had previously pressed for expansion of capacity of Japanese-produced semiconductor products was also made head of TI's worldwide semiconductor chip business, the perspective changed radically: Why build new Japanese capacity when there were factories elsewhere around the world with capacity to spare? Junkins also required managers with such global responsibilities to meet with each other quarterly to review and formulate global strategies. The company is firmly in touch with customers, technology, and manufacturing throughout the world—in part through a network of over 40,000 computer terminals in 50 countries.

The European giants of Philips and Siemens have committed themselves to taking on their own counterproductive bureaucracies. Philips has moved management control for its 60 national organizations to four global product groups. It purchased the 42 percent of the stock in its North American unit that was previously held by the public. It determined that some large business segments where it is not a leader, such as appliances and medical electronics, should be sold or placed in joint ventures with existing leaders. It is even asking itself why it is in some businesses at all, such as the production of toothbrushes.

---

[3]"General Motors' Big European Overhaul," *Business Week*, February 10, 1986.

Siemens has tried to quicken its historically glacial pace of reform with the most severe management restructuring in the company's history. Three, and in some cases, four levels of management are being eliminated. Managers in production and research are being integrated, sometimes through physical relocation to the same site. Although Philips decided centralization of its farflung units was needed, Siemens needed to encourage innovation and independence. It is splitting its seven major groups into up to 30 new units. A major initiative, in which Siemens is not alone, lies in finding partners for support in strengthening its global organization.

GLOBAL JOINT VENTURES: STRATEGIC ALLIANCES, STRATEGIC PITFALLS

"Nothing has happened in the last 20 years that is more important to international companies than the discovery of the joint venture," commented a British manager during a February 1989 discussion of global competition in the computer industry. While one might debate whether joint ventures were discovered, invented, or just naturally grew out of preexisting concepts, one cannot deny that recently joint ventures have been making a heavy mark on the shape of global competition—and certainly not in the computer industry alone. If global problems can indeed be characterized as organizational problems for many enterprises, then it might also be said that in recent years some international managers often have seen many international organization problems as joint venture issues.

Carlo De Benedetti, the aggressive chairman of Olivetti who revitalized his company through joint ventures, is an unabashed apostle of such collaborative structures: unless a company enjoys world-scale production already, says De Benedetti, the "only way to be German in Germany, Canadian in Canada, Japanese in Japan is through alliances. In the high-tech market of the 1990s, we will see a shaking out of the isolated and a shaking in of the allied."

Such perspectives may sometimes exaggerate the role of joint ventures in international business, but they do reflect the great emphasis that has been placed on the cooperative business structures that attract various labels, including joint ventures, cooperative alliances, and cooperative ventures. Such structures have become a prevalent aspect of much inter-national business—sometimes good, sometimes bad, but prevalent none-theless.

Texaco's gas stations and supporting refineries east of the Missis-sippi are owned jointly by Saudi Arabia and Texaco. Komatsu answered its need for dollar-based production and Dresser its need to fill its produc-tion lines by forming a 50/50 joint venture. Nynex has a dozen relation-ships in Asia and Europe as a platform for its international business. Texas Instruments sued Hitachi over patent infringement in 1986; as the companies learned more about one another in their settlement negotia-tions, they grew so familiar, and mutually respectful, that they formed a joint venture two years later. The global auto industry is a tangled web of such alliances: Chrysler and Fiat jointly market Alfa Romeo cars in North America, GM and Toyota jointly make cars in California, Ford and Nissan make minivans in Ohio, Daewoo produces the Pontiac Lemans with GM in Korea, and Chrysler produces cars with Mitsubishi in Illi-nois. The entire Japanese car industry, often the target of vehemence from Detroit, bears a surprisingly red, white, and blue cast behind the scenes: Ford has a 25 percent in Mazda; GM shares 42 percent of Isuzu, and 5.3 percent of Suzuki; and Chrysler holds 24 percent of Mitsubishi. Likewise, the U.S. steel industry is today structured around strategic alli-ances with Asian producers, including alliances between USX and Kobe Steel, LTV Corporation and Sumitomo Metal Industries, Inland Steel and Nippon Steel, Wheeling-Pittsburgh Steel and Nisshin Steel, and Armco Inc. and Kawasaki Steel.

As discussed below, a number of costly mistakes have been commit-ted in the quest for joint ventures. Some companies have, as seen in the influence of the seemingly endless books, articles, speeches, seminars, and consulting memos on the subject, been caught in a joint venture fad, as it were, using them too often, and too easily, for their own good. Others do not appreciate the strategic global synergies available in the well-planned joint venture and forego them entirely.

Those possible synergies must be the focus of the international firm in its quest for such alliances. It is the joint venture as strategic alliance that justifies focus upon them by global managers. And it is the danger of strategic missteps in such alliances that requires extraordinary diligence in their preparation and execution.

The strategic needs that may be addressed in the strategic alliance, are myriad. They include:

Sharing the Risk and High Cost of
Research and Development

One of the most conspicuous of joint venture rationales shows us the need for a partner to share the huge R&D expenses required in some industries. Not even the largest of companies are immune from this need. In 1985 IBM's then vice chairman, Paul Rizzo, emphasized that the computer giant was keenly aware of the need for alliances in technology development: "We're looking at a set of technologies which is going to involve humanity in every dimension. There is no way any one organization all by itself, without cooperating, collaborating, and understanding others, can be successful." Sony and Philips have created a venture for development of technology related audiovideo compact discs. The Texas Instruments/Hitachi joint venture mentioned above is dedicated to developing an advanced 16 megabit RAM chip. The venture is utilizing the companies' tandem efforts with separate research but with access to each other's work. Explained TI's executive vice president, Wally Rhines, after the joint venture was announced, "If anything goes wrong with either company's design, we both have a fallback position." Motorola is likewise doing what once would have been anathema to some of its managers. After accusing the Japanese producers of dumping chips, the company has teamed up in semiconductor chip production with Toshiba. If you can't beat them, join them.

Penetrating an Otherwise Protected Market

In some countries where stiff protection is accorded domestic producers through high tariffs or strict limits on foreign investment, the only viable path into the market may be as a partner with such a local producer. Such an avenue has been followed frequently in countries like Brazil and most centrally controlled economies.

Penetrating a Heavily Concentrated Industry

In some industries with a small number of dominating companies, one of the few available paths for entering the industry may be as a partner of an existing participant. AT&T leapt into 28 separate alliances when it decided to go global, on the premise that it had to get inside the highly concentrated international telecommunications industry.

Sharing or Diluting Production Costs through
Combined Production
When Ford and Volkswagen merged their operations in Brazil and Argentina, a major reason was the need to gain desperately needed efficiencies by shared production.

Strategic Preemption
While most ventures cannot survive on this basis alone, an influential element in some ventures may be the role the venture plays in the prevention of an alliance with another competitor. Mitsubishi Motors reportedly considered this a major factor in its decision to join in a venture with Korea's Hyundai Motors for production of low-cost automobiles; Hyundai was being courted as a joint venture partner by Mitsubishi's competitors in Japan.

Obtaining or Maximizing Marketing/Distribution Channels
A joint venture partner may offer badly needed distribution and marketing assets. The British pharmaceutical firm Glaxo owes much of the huge success of its product Zantac to comarketing alliances—with Hoffman La Roche in the United States—which sold the product in markets where Glaxo had little or no marketing presence. Harris and 3M have taken a similar marketing step by jointly marketing photocopy machines. An important reason for Corning Glass Works's joint venture with Asahi Glass for making television tube glass was explained by the venture's CEO, John Loose, "A lot of Japanese tubemakers have moved to the United States and Asahi has good relationships with them that we want to take advantage of."

To Gain Strategic Leverage with an Important Supplier,
and Strategic Knowledge of the Supplier's Products
General Motors joined with Japanese robotmaker, Fanus Ltd., to form a venture to produce production line robots, many of which go into GM's own factories.

These factors most often work in combination. Honeywell recognized it simply couldn't obtain alone the necessary efficiency of scale in both marketing and production or allocate the vast sums required for research to effectively compete in the global computer business. It joined with Cie des Machines Bull of France and NEC Corporation of Japan in a master operating joint venture that overnight became the third largest computer company in the world. When LOF Glass of the United States and Nippon Glass joined in a venture to supply auto glass in Korea, technology and marketing cross-fertilization was the reason. LOF contributes both technology and its relationship with U.S. producers operating or sourcing autos in Korea, and Nippon brought its highly efficient production technologies and relationships with Japanese automakers.

Dreaming Different Dreams

As mentioned above, too many enterprises suffer from a "low joint venture threshold." They are too easy in accepting or soliciting joint ventures. They are so focused on the potential benefits that potential damage or losses are often overlooked.

Whether or not they like it, the strategic alliance is a fact of life for many firms in the global economy. Texas Instruments, like many U.S. firms, was once adamantly against *any* joint venture. But as development costs for individual chips soared past the $1 billion mark and customers demanded more and more variety in products, TI recognized that the world had changed. Explained TI's semiconductor group president Pat Weber, "We've become more realistic about what it takes to be successful in the complexities of global markets."

Olivetti's Carlo De Benedetti has been succeeding due to a careful regime of alliances. He understands the need to approach potential partners with the utmost scrutiny. A joint venture to De Benedetti is a marriage, and must rest on a high degree of commitment: "It's much easier to live with a girlfriend. But normally in that relationship you don't have any children; you don't create anything for the future. It's the same between companies engaged in joint ventures. It's much easier to have a simple arrangement by which you go to bed sometimes—say twice a week or twice a month—with an ally, let us say in a supplier relationship. But I believe an effective alliance must join the life of the two companies. That's the only way to create something for the future."

De Benedetti would no doubt appreciate an analogy often heard in China to describe troubled marriages and, today, joint venture partners who find themselves incompatible: The partners are "sleeping in the same bed but dreaming different dreams." Too many different dreams may lead to nightmares, and even divorce. The average success rate for joint venture is only 43 percent, and the average life span is only 3.5 years, according to a study done by Professor Kathryn Rudie Harrigan of Columbia University. Between 1972 and mid-1976, the Boston Consulting Group found that 40 Japanese/foreign joint ventures, often involving Fortune 500 firms, failed. A Harvard Business School study reviewed 1,100 U.S./foreign joint ventures entered into before 1967 and found a 30 percent failure rate.

Nearly two decades ago European newspapers were filled with bubbly reports of the new company that was going to wrestle away domination of the world computer industry from IBM. That new challenger was a high-profile joint venture between Dutch, German, and French computer producers named Unidata. Hundreds of technical experts and executives were assigned to the venture. If the venture had realized even one tenth of the accomplishments projected for it, Unidata would have been a huge success. Instead each partner seemed to spend much time alleging false motives by one or both of the others or trying to find machinery and systems that might be compatible among the widely diverse participating facilities. Unidata was dissolved in 1975 without ever having launched a single product.

No less spectacular a failure was that of the union between two European tiremakers, Pirelli & Co. of Italy and Dunlop Holdings Ltd. of Great Britain; the new global contender promised by the venture simply burst apart with what were reported as irreconcilable cultural differences. The marketing joint venture established by TRW and Fujitsu in the United States during the early 1980s simply collapsed under the weight of a double management system. Fujitsu eventually reorganized the unit as a wholly owned subsidiary.

By all appearances, Dow Chemical and Germany's BASF had a good thing going in their long-standing joint venture, Dow-Badische, which was formed in 1958 to make fibers and chemical materials. The unit built sales up to $300 million. But the parties' goals began to drift apart. Dow finally called it quits on the grounds that the venture was moving too far away from Dow's mainstream chemical business. The unit was dissolved in 1978.

A big boost in Siemens's struggle to build its global operations was expected from a joint venture with Westinghouse that was to sell at least $300 million annually of a wide range of industrial automation and control systems. The project never survived negotiations. The announced cause has long been a cliché for joint venture failure: "lack of common ground between the partners."

The seeming fad of joint venture consortium banks in the 1970s

(Nordic Banking Group, Midland and International Banks, Orion Bank, among others) came to a halt in the early 1980s as one venture after another was terminated. Orion Bank, with members Westdeutsche Landesbank, Credito Italiano, Mitsubishi, and Chase Manhattan, seemed to offer the whole catalog of joint venture problems in explaining the need to call off the venture: inadequate controls, lack of global strategy, conflicts of interest, political squabbling within the ranks, and lack of integrated systems.

The stakes were high in the joint venture formed in March 1988 between Plessey Plc. and General Electric Company of Britain when they combined their telecommunications business into a 50/50 $3.2 billion unit. Designed to create a new major global entity in the industry, the companies cooperation did not even survive a year before Plessey sent a formal letter demanding that GEC turn over its shares to Plessey. The reason was that GEC had joined with Siemens in a hostile takeover bid for Plessey.

Many press accounts of such joint venture endings downplay the consequences to the partners. One classic epitaph to a joint venture a few years ago: "We appear to have agreed that the best way to 'work' together is not to work together."

Making the Global Alliance Work

There is no generic global alliance, just as there exists no generic global winner. Therefore, there exists no simple formula for success in an alliance, just as there exists none for achieving general global success. Winners in alliances and in global competition are produced by development of perspectives and sensitivities, acquisition of skills and information, and careful application of all those attributes. Experience in past alliances, both winners and losers, does, however, point to a number of guidelines:

First, Know Your Goals

Philosophical, as well as strategic, questions may need to be asked. As Cornings' vice chairman, Thomas C. MacAvoy, noted several years ago when reviewing the impetus for his company's many joint ventures, "Would you rather have half of a large pie, or all of a small pie?" When AT&T charged overseas in the early 1980s, it did so under the influence of "alliance fever" and an unfocused appetite for foreign relationships.

The company quickly formed 28 joint ventures, which included a number of archrivals as partners in separate alliances; doubts rapidly spread about AT&T's loyalty and motives. Most notable among these tense relationships were those with bitter competitors Olivetti and Philips. From the outset Philips reportedly resented the Olivetti connection, uncertain of how far it should trust AT&T; eventually Philips saw the futility of continuing as an equal partner with the American firm and divested itself into a minority position. AT&T's 25 percent ownership in Olivetti (turning Olivetti itself into an Italian/American alliance) turned into a stormy clash of egos. AT&T announced to the world that the two companies would share production and sales of computers; sales were far below expectation, however, and the production activity was dropped. AT&T then announced the companies would share research; Olivetti announced it did not agree with AT&T's research agenda. Having gotten "all dressed up with nowhere to go" the parties finally ended the partnership in July 1989, with AT&T incurring a $100 million paper loss to divest its interest.

Within this context, is the need to integrate external standards such as local law. When GM and Toyota developed their California production venture, duration and capacity were not a negotiation issue. Those aspects were established by regulators at the Federal Trade Commission. Westinghouse Electric Corporation and ABB Asea Brown Boveri Ltd. had to likewise integrate regulators' views into their alliance strategy when the U.S. Justice Department prohibited them from joining their steam turbine generator businesses as part of a larger joint venture combination of their electrical transmission and distribution equipment units.

Be Flexible
For many, the global alliance is the ultimate test of the adaptability needed in global business. A joint venture in the United States between a U.S. and a German firm suffered chronically from the failure of U.S. workers to follow procedures which had been imported from Germany. The partners frequently discussed the problem, and the Americans often proposed loosening the standards in a manner appropriate to U.S. custom. The inevitable answer was, "No, we will operate the way we do in Germany." It is no coincidence that lists of international joint ventures have conspicuously few German names.

Protect the Crown Jewels

In 1986 California's LaPine Technology was cited frequently as an example of the type of international strategic alliance that U.S. firms should use as a model to develop global competitiveness. When engineer turned entrepreneur, Anthony LaPine, decided to apply innovative new technology for production of 3.5 inch hard disc drives, he persuaded Prudential Bache Trade Corporation to join him. Together they identified Japan's Kyocera Corporation, a low-cost producer of drives, as the third member of their new high-tech venture. A factory was built, and *Forbes* and other magazines published glowing reports of the alliance. When months later, the company needed capital, LaPine's partners insisted on a bigger slice of the pie. LaPine and his core group of entrepreneur/technologists were effectively pushed out. Kyocera, by then enjoying the use of the new LaPine technology in Japan, began to slow down shipments of drives to customers, who consequently began to defect. As sales plummeted wholesale layoffs at LaPine Technologies commenced. The U.S. company finally filed suit in California against Kyocera. The main charge was Kyocera "had fraudulently induced LaPine to enter agreements in order to gain access to LaPine's technology and proprietary information."

When Varian Associates of the United States joined with NEC to produce and sell Varian's semiconductor chips in Japan, the U.S. firm's high hopes were quickly dashed. The Japanese partner, strengthened by a majority position required by Japanese law, seemed to want to focus on production technology only, not sales. Varian walked away from the venture. When Texas Instruments entered its joint venture with Hitachi for development of a new semiconductor, TI insisted that the technology owned separately by the parties be separately cataloged at the outset for added protection.

In the late 1980s Matsushita's JVC unit had the technology tables turned on it by Thomson S.A. of France. The two firms had been building video cassette recorders in France on a modest scale. JVC had been willing to share its production technology with Thomson, many believed, because it gained insider status in a protected market and it never considered Thomson a serious contender with sales of only 800,000 units compared to JVC's own 5 million-plus. JVC would thus always enjoy an insurmountable advantage of scale in the world market. Thomson, however, soaked up Japanese VCR technology, even hiring laid-off Swiss watchmakers to analyze and improve its new precision manufacturing capabilities. Suddenly Thomson shocked JVC by swapping its medical equipment business to General Electric of the United States for GE's consumer electronics business. Overnight it had VCR sales of over 5 million units, and JVC had a very different perspective of the joint venture.

Obviously, the technology exchange in an alliance will often not be equal. A number of Western companies have readily, and reasonably, accepted joint venture frameworks in which they agree to a fair sharing of technology in exchange for capital or other benefits. But other ventures may amount to an extortion of technology. As Professor Robert Reich of Harvard University and others have charged, a number of ventures, poorly planned by their U.S. partners, may "give away our future" through technology transfer.

"All we seem to do as the U.S. partner in these ventures is to teach and design. It's like we were saying you in the Far East can handle the scutwork of manufacturing," groused one U.S. veteran of several joint venture negotiations between United States and Asian firms. In 1986 an Australian/Asia hand briefly met with a team of U.S. negotiators who were concluding an alliance contract with a competitor; he summarized his advice with an old axiom, "Mates, when you sup with the devil, use a bloody long spoon."

Know Your Partner
Not infrequently, joint venture partners have entered into commitments based on a misunderstanding of their partner's strengths. Cleveland-based Van Dorn Co. was more circumspect when it joined with Reifenhauser of Germany to sell German plastic extrusion systems in the United States; the two firms had been doing business with each other for more than 20 years prior to the joint venture.

Build Commitment and Loyalty
Too many ventures are an afterthought in the mind of the partners' management. Lack of commitment in following through with goals has perhaps condemned more ventures than any other cause. When Corning Glass, whose successful experiences are more fully discussed below, found in its joint venture with Genentech that the Genentech employees assigned to the venture, "on leave" from the home office, were not committed to the venture, Corning took a dramatic step: It convinced Genentech to obtain the resignation of those employees, so that their only

employer was the joint venture. Performance improved practically overnight.

Joint ventures between strong rivals may never completely solve the loyalty problem. In an alliance between ICL, the British computer firm, and Fujitsu, which was clearly looking for market development in Europe, Fujitsu once tried to fly ICL's 200 most important customers to Japan to show them its own facilities. One of the few ventures Corning has had to terminate was in Indonesia. Not long after signing documents for the venture, whose business was to be production and sale of dinnerware dishes, Corning's partner was found to be selling their own competing line of dishes in the country. In AT&T's disastrous joint venture with Olivetti, the American firm intended that Olivetti sell AT&T's minicomputers in Europe even though Olivetti continued to sell its own competing minicomputers in the same markets.

Identify and Agree to Basic Management Systems in Advance

Companies which grew up on opposite sides of an ocean often have bred very different management systems. One company may be used to informal management built on strong interpersonal relationships. Its partner may run its business strictly by the book, with frequent meetings, hierarchical committee structures, and detailed accounting systems. The six-year effort by German and American companies to engage in the joint production of a battle tank failed because of differences in basic systems related to procurement and management. A good rule of thumb: make the match between parties of comparable size, which means they are more likely to share the same appreciation for control systems.

Avoid Overmanagement or "Micromanagement"

The use of shared management, in which both parties try to actively participate in management is often disastrous. A 1982 study of such ventures found that at least one half of them were eventually liquidated or reorganized. A corollary problem is that of the partner who tries to manage "micro" details from afar.

Know What's Going On

Balanced against the need to avoid overmanagement is the need to maintain current knowledge of venture activity. In joint ventures, as in arms negotiations, a sound principle is "trust but verify." Partners who sign into a joint venture and then leave it behind, waiting for cash, may receive unpleasant surprises. In a joint venture with Mitsubishi Heavy Industries, Boeing was worried that its partner was trying to discover Boeing's aircraft wing production technology. Boeing established a monitoring system to cover all information flows to Japan. These "back bearings" revealed that Mitsubishi wasn't looking for wing technology, but it was looking for Boeing's expertise in project management. A frequent discovery by U.S. managers in many joint ventures is that visitors from its foreign partner outnumber reciprocal visits by its own staff, often by a factor of 10 or 20 to 1.

No American company has more experience with strategic alliances than Corning Glass Works. The $250 million venture it announced in 1988 to produce television tube glass with Asahi Glass was counted as number 38, in 12 countries, since 1924—although the company's first joint venture was in 1880 with Thomas Edison. Pittsburgh Corning, Dow Corning, Iwaki Glass, Samsung Corning, Siecon (Siemens/Corning), Genencor, Ciba Corning Diagnostics . . . the list of major operating alliances is extensive. In 1987 over half of the firm's operating income came from joint venture profits. Whether they are important to Corning because they are successful or successful because they are important is more than a rhetorical point. The company doesn't enter negotiations unless it has carefully weighed the strategic aspects of a proposed venture and after negotiations it continues to recognize the importance of commitment. The company's record is solid proof of its commitment: only six of its joint ventures have failed in 65 years.

Analysts have tried to ascertain Corning's secret. There is no secret. What they find is an approach imbued with diplomacy, willingness to listen, give and take (the company never argues about having its name placed second in the title of ventures), mutual respect, and trust. James Houghton, chairman and great-great-grandson of the company's founder, notes, "If the partners continually have to look over each other's shoulder, then the offspring venture will have little chance of surviving."

The Global Galapagos

It is no great surprise to those enterprises which have successfully globalized their personnel, and which have the rare strength of managers who see their jobs in global perspective, to find that global organizational problems often take care of themselves. But when the global machine begins to hum it *is* surprising how nebulous that machine seems, how difficult it is to place it into the carefully labeled niches of organizational texts and theories.

The global system by its nature cannot be a rigid structure. Increasingly, firms in the global track are finding that they cannot place people in a box with instructions not to cross its rigid parameters. Those enterprises find that the dominant factors in their organizations have far less to do with organizational charts than with informal interrelationships, with networks and multidimensional teams which flexibly work within global strategies according to changing global exigencies. It was in the Galapagos Islands that Charles Darwin found the most striking proof of his theories, where he was able to demonstrate that evolution is based on changing environments and successful, perpetual adaption thereto. Global firms understand above all the overriding need to be able to evolve, and the reality that the economy in which they function has become a Galapagos of planetary proportions.

CHAPTER 12

ACCEPTING THE GLOBAL CHALLENGE

The final years of the 20th century bring with them challenges and opportunities of a dimension never before experienced on the planet. They are ushering in an era for which there is no precedent in human history, no ready rules for guidance, no guarantees for the success of any enterprise, no matter how large or successful an enterprise may have been in the past. These years are introducing the age of the maturing global economy.

The closing months of the century's ninth decade brought stark evidence of this new age in the form of major new global initiatives. Fault lines in many industries cracked wide open and new global entities emerged. Both reflected the far-reaching and high-stakes intensity of competition on a global scale and underscored the linkage between success and the exercise of global perspectives and skills.

Delivering a Global Winner

During 1988 Federal Express, United Parcel Service, Australia's TNT Ltd, and Hong Kong-based DHL began a battle of historic proportions over the international air express business. With a global market estimated at over $15 billion, projected to grow by 20 percent annually due to greatly increasing demand for rapid dispatch of information and documents in international business, the air delivery service had been a global industry waiting to happen.

Launching their battles with fleets of jets and trucks, navigating a difficult course through international treaties, regional competitors, and customs bureaucracies, the contenders have been engaged in hot competition on each other's home turf—as well as Europe, where no major European-based competitor survived. First one player, then another, displayed adept use of joint ventures, acquisitions, electronic tracking systems, and fleet-footed couriers to gain an edge in the competition. UPS acquired a trucking system in Japan. DHL initiated a huge advertising campaign in its weakest market, the United States. Federal Express acquired Tiger International. UPS acquired seven European delivery firms. Federal Express acquired similar companies in France, Italy, and Great Britain. Having secured Europe, the top firms began to focus on Asia, where the battle is today being fiercely waged in the backyards of DHL and TNT. At last report, the U.S. Postal Service was playing a spoiler role by sharply reducing its international delivery charges, and European freight handlers were placing the battered pieces of their businesses into a consortium with an eye on new global markets. The sudden global focus of the industry has given it an entirely new face in a matter of months.

Home appliances have represented another emerging global industry, with realignments, divestitures, and market conquests creating new global players and eliminating possible contenders at a rapid pace. In late 1988, Whirlpool acquired control of the appliance business of N.V. Philips, adding $2 billion in sales to the Michigan-based company's international base. This followed closely the acquisition of White Consolidated Industries by Sweden's Electrolux and the merger of Maytag and Magic Chef Inc. In early 1989, General Electric became a 50 percent partner in the $1 billion European appliance business of Britain's General Electric Co. Plc. Commenting on such rapid changes in the industry, *Appliance Magazine* editor James Stevens noted, "if you're not a global winner, I wonder how you're going to survive."

The Time-Warner merger finalized in July 1989 only fanned the flames of frantic competition in the global media/entertainment industry. Asked to explain the move, Warner chairman Steven J. Ross emphasized that the object was to gain strengths for the global battle being waged at home and abroad, "We're competing with the multinationals of many, many countries." Meanwhile, smaller units in the industry continue to be acquired or dissolved, either directly or indirectly by the actions of media giants from the United States, France, Australia, Britain, Germany, and Japan. NBC retained consultants McKinsey & Co. to advise it on global expansion; not long afterwards it began negotiations to acquire an interest in a European broadcaster, partly in exchange for NBC programming. Even newspapers are reaching across the waters. *USA Today*, for example, is now being printed in the Netherlands and Switzerland. Worrell Enterprises, a newspaper chain based in Charlottesville, Virginia, is reportedly accumulating capital to buy papers in France and Spain.[1]

As part of the globalization of the media, even professional sports in its own way is going global. American baseball, football, and/or basketball games are already viewed on televisions in Britain, Hong Kong, Iceland, Australia, Japan, Italy, Mexico, Venezuela, Spain, and Zimbabwe. A spring satellite league of the National Football League is expected to start soon, including teams based in Europe.

The list of the new competitive battles underway as a result of global pressures is a long and exciting one. Once secure corporate giants in Europe are finding themselves subject to takeovers styled after U.S. campaigns. Huge government-backed companies like Japan's NTT are moving towards breakup and total privatization. Heavyweights Toyoseika (Japan), CMB Packaging (France/Britain), Continental Can (United States), Tetrapak (Sweden), Owens Illinois (United States), St. Gobain (France) and others, are slugging it out in the world packaging industry. Little known Pechiney of France turned the industry on its head in 1988, overnight becoming one of the largest producers in the world by a $1 billion acquisition of American National Can. Global battles are profoundly rocking the pharmaceutical industry, waged by leaders like Merck, Sandoz, newly combined Smithkline Beecham, Hoechst, Glaxo, Ciba-Geigy, Bayer, Lilly, Takeda and American Home Products.

A BOLD NEW WORLD

The global economy is not making itself felt solely through rumblings and heavings in specific industries. Many industries may be experiencing figurative global earthquakes, but the aftershocks and tremors underscore other aspects and trends of global life, which are the theme of this chapter.

Building the Global Infrastructure

One of the less subtle tremors of this nature was felt on the other side of the planet in April 1989. U.S. takeover specialist T. Boone Pickens sud-

---

[1]"News Companies Test Foreign Waters, But Only with a Toe," *New York Times*, May 8, 1989.

denly announced that he held over 20 percent of auto parts maker Koito Manufacturing. Japanese firms have steadfastly believed in controlled, usually slow growth from within; in their world, firms traditionally have not been acquired, but only occasionally combined by consensus. Visitors to Tokyo often have been told, with thinly veiled disdain, that acquisitions were "not the Japanese way."

With the opening of Tokyo to American investment bankers and brokerage firms, an increasingly global merger and acquisition (M&A) culture had already descended on Japan. Even before the Pickens raid on Koito, M&A books were popular reading among young Tokyo executives and full page ads by U.S. investment bankers were becoming familiar in Japanese business papers like *Nihon Keizai Shimbun*. But the spectre of a hostile bid, not to mention a hostile bid *by a foreigner* or a simple case of the greenmail that had become commonplace in the United States, hit some Japanese financial and management circles like a Pearl Harbor in reverse. Pickens introduced a new perspective on stockholder rights to a society that too often overlooks such rights. It was a healthy dose of global reality for insular Japan. Like its ally across the Pacific, Japanese society may not be totally comfortable with the realities of the global economy, but it can't live without them.

This fact was likewise evidenced when another major global thread surfaced in the fabric of Japanese life concurrently with Pickens' Koito campaign. In a melodrama interwoven with distinctly Japanese themes— even the *hari kari* of a loyal "samurai" lieutenant—and powerful global aspects, the tenure of Prime Minister Nobura Takeshita came to an abrupt end. The details of the accompanying scandal were well aired in the media. A cloud of insider trading, political gifts of stock, and conflict of interest became so heavy in world opinion that Japan's long-ruling Liberal Democratic Party could not withstand the pressure.

Many Japanese comments to Westerners about the affair were characterized by acrimony. They were often to the effect that "there's nothing wrong with what he did . . . it's traditional . . . what he did has always been done by leaders in Japan." Therein lay the global benchmark of the affair. No longer were political and business leaders able to stand behind the shield of local tradition to justify any action. A subtle standard of global practice and global acceptability with respect to government and corporate relations had insinuated itself into Tokyo's morality, with dramatic effect for Mr. Takeshita.

The Takeshita and Koito affairs were evidence of a highly significant phenomenon occurring within the global economy: the building of a global milieu or infrastructure for the conduct of the economy. That infrastructure is an amorphous mixture of law, morals, financial guidelines, technical standards, and myriad other elements of regularity in form and practice.

Gradually, and not always even deliberately or consciously, private and public institutions are creating that infrastructure as a natural adjunct to global business. Although some effort has been underway for decades, such as that behind the General Agreement for Tariffs and Trade, the infrastructure remains little more than embryonic. The General Agreement on Tariffs and Trade, which imposes a rational discipline for merchandise trade, still covers only a fraction of the goods moved around the world. Expansion of that framework remains an important task of national governments and multilateral bodies around the planet.

Global Apples, Global Oranges

Yet such multilateral trade structures represent but one wall of the house in which global enterprises will eventually live. Just as important to global enterprises are efforts to assure equal understanding and treatment of basic commercial and financial devices, to assure that a financial statement in one country means the same as one in another, to assure that the "apple" discussed by the banker in St. Louis is not really an "orange" to his or her counterpart in Frankfurt. While some quasi-public groups like the Paris-based International Chamber of Commerce have made great strides in regularizing some areas such as international arbitration and documentary credits, the task remains largely unfinished.

Many international investors, both individual and corporate, have stumbled severely due to lack of uniform financial guidelines. Companies organized under the laws of many European countries, for example, do not consolidate their earnings, so that foreign subsidiaries, including those incurring losses, may be deleted from stockholder information. BMW sells two thirds of its cars outside the Federal Republic of Germany but its reports disclose only its income within Germany. Most companies in Europe also report financial results only once a year, instead of quarterly as in the United States. Companies are also able to conceal costs and assets under catch-all categories which are meaningless to investors.

In 1986, Siemens AG listed as "other costs" in its balance sheet the lump sum of DM6.5 billion, a number four times the net profit of the company, without any explanation to its stockholders. Bad debts, holder reserves, foreign currency transactions, are likewise impossible to ascertain in many companies around the world. Companies in Italy are able to list assets at acquisition cost without regard to current value. German standards have been so lax that in one notorious case a major union-owned company, Heue Heimat, was found to have been reporting a profit to the public for many years during which it was in fact accumulating operating losses exceeding DM500 million.

Progress is being made. In 1987 the United States and Great Britain agreed to observe identical standards for capital ratios in banks. In July 1988 a group of 12 industrial nations agreed on minimum capital adequacy standards for banks, triggering the sale of assets by several large U.S. banks in order to meet those standards. In 1989 the Organization for Economic Cooperation and Development agreed to new guidelines to liberalize capital movements, facilitating international mergers and global underwritings. As part of the EC market unification effort, similar measures for uniform disclosure of at least minimal financial information have been adopted. European insurance companies in 1989 also introduced standards for global electronic communications to facilitate processing of insurance information.[2]

The International Organization of Securities Commissioners is attempting to build an international consensus for management and capital guidelines applicable to securities firms. In November 1988 the SEC chairman, David Ruder, proposed to that body a comprehensive blueprint for a global securities market, including as key elements, structures of dissemination of information, processing of orders, payment procedures, disclosure systems, and auditing standards. Ruder understood the problem well. "The challenge facing regulators is to assure efficiency and honesty," throughout such a global system, he noted at the time.

The infrastructure problem is further evidenced in countries like Switzerland, South Korea, Brazil, Singapore and Sweden which permit grossly disproportionate treatment between foreign and domestic shareholders. Sweden, for example, permits companies to sharply restrict voting rights of stock held by foreigners. SKF of Sweden restricts its stock so that foreign nationals may only own shares that carry one thousandth of a vote. A survey by the Washington-based Investor Responsibility Re-

[2]"European Insurers Testing Global Standards," *Journal of Commerce*, April 26, 1989.

search Center determined that Swiss company shares gave foreign investors less than one fifth the rights available under U.S. securities laws.[3]

Such countries must understand that such treatment is antithetical to the very global system upon which so many of their own enterprises vitally depend. Switzerland already is starting to loosen such restrictions after recognizing the negative impact they have on capital flows. The pace has not been quick enough for several Swiss firms—including Nestle, Sandoz, Alusuisse, and Hoffman LaRoche—which recently have restructured their own equity to ease such restrictions in order to make themselves more attractive to international sources of capital.

Global Diversification of Equity

It will also become inconsistent with the global economy for a global enterprise to be linked exclusively to the financial institutions, and shareholders, of only one country. Already, many of the financial advisers and bankers to large companies in the industrial countries operate in multiple international locations, in effect making global resources available on a local basis. Chapter 2 reviewed the close linkage in key financial markets around the globe. Yet these aspects represent but the embryonic form of what inevitably must become a truly global securities system.

From the perspective of the fund manager, banker, and broker, such international diversification spreads risk. From the perspective of the global enterprise access to capital through markets in multiple countries also provides a major new degree of flexibility, a new, and advantageous set, of financial leverage points. The future of global equity has arrived for a small number of companies who are already global leaders in other respects. Sony stock is listed on 18 stock exchanges around the planet. IBM is listed not only in the United States but in Austria, Belgium, Canada, England, France, Germany, Japan, Switzerland, and the Netherlands. United Technologies common stock is listed in New York, London, Paris, Frankfurt, Geneva, Lausanne, Basel, Zurich, Brussels, and Amsterdam. Xerox stock is traded in six nations.

Some countries, with more capital than they can absorb, like

---

[3]The IRRC, using American stockholder rights as a base of 100, assigned Switzerland a "shareholder rights" score of 18. Italy and Holland received scores of 40, Germany, France, and Japan scores of 48. The survey was reported in *The Economist*, April 29, 1989.

Switzerland and Japan, are natural venues for initial global listing. Indeed, firms insisting on keeping their equity linked to American markets may be denying themselves important opportunities. Over the past 20 years, the U.S. equity markets share of the world markets have plummeted from 66 percent to roughly 30 percent.

The Challenge to Government

A significant, but little publicized phenomenon of the late 1980s was the opening of offices for national industry groups and trade associations on foreign shores, to monitor and react to international events on the part of entire industries. Likewise, on a discrete company basis, corporations in many industrial countries are introducing internal trade policy units for a similar purpose. Merck & Co., for example, recently inaugurated such a unit with an emphasis in its charter on the complex political developments in a unifying Europe. When informed of such developments, a career employee of the U.S. State Department slightly bristled: "I don't understand what they think they're doing. Why do they think the U.S. government has embassies?"

It has not been the purpose of this book to focus upon such attitudes or upon political action, legislated industrial policy, or other governmental involvements, impediments, and incentives in the global economy. Extensive effort has been made in that respect by myriad economists, political scientists, speechwriters, legislators, editors, and others; some of that effort has been well-informed and well-reasoned, much of it has been otherwise. For many companies, it has also been a serious distraction from the vitally important issues of creating the global enterprise. Suffice it to say enterprises are never launched into the ranks of global winners by governments or solely on the strength of government action. Yet governments can play vital roles in helping to erect the infrastructure which will nurture global enterprises and in promoting the involvement of new entries onto the global plateau. Any U.S. company involved in international business—and those members of government who are able to engage in honest self-appraisal—will admit there is great room for improvement in such respects.

One major problem is the seemingly whimsical way in which legislated ground rules are so frequently altered. An American overseas manager, whose senior position often exposed him to lawmakers in Europe and the United States, was asked several years ago what would be the best possible legislation action for international business. "Simple," he said after a moment's deliberation. "Shut 'em down. Put a moratorium on new laws that relate to international business and let the Congress, the Diet, the various Parliaments, and the Bundestag tamper with international business issues only once every five years. Give business a foundation it could build on, not one that's ripped apart by election-crazed politicians every year or two."

Even such an observer would likely prefer that the U.S. Congress take a few remedial steps before taking such an adjournment. U.S. tax laws may, for the present, offer rates that are attractive relative to those of many industrial nations, but behind those attractive rates lurk numerous handicaps to the global firm. After Price Waterhouse conducted a review of tax laws around the globe, Richard Hammer, director of international tax for the firm, announced in early 1989 that the U.S. tax code seems to be the only one "with a bias against operating abroad." When Arthur Young conducted a similar study it concluded likewise that the U.S. laws penalize U.S. firms abroad.

Reports highlighting the poor record of the U.S. government in promoting exports and boosting the all important international efforts of small and midsized firms appear with alarming frequency in Washington. A study by Cornell University and Xport, the trading arm of the Port Authority of New York and New Jersey, released in March 1989 reviewed the export support programs of nine industrial foreign countries and emphasized, "One inescapable conclusion is that efforts of these nine governments go far beyond the U.S. governmental response to date." Xport director, Herbert Ouida, commented, "It's very clear that our exporters are not getting the support that our competitors receive from their governments."

Perhaps such conclusions are not surprising to those who have witnessed America's international legislators at work. "What do you expect?" asked a Washington veteran of many legislative battles when the studies noted above were brought to his attention. "A Congressman from the heartlands whose political universe revolves around getting the new dam or highway built before the next election isn't going to have much helpful insight when it comes to resolving international business problems." Another lobbyist who has seen the Congress both as a legislative staffer and from the private sector observes: "Before you can expect Congress to really grasp global business issues, you have a monumental task of education and sensitizing. You'd have to start with enrolling them all in a freshman class in world geography."

Congress could do far worse for the global posture of its country than to address, as it has begun to do, the disturbing problems of illiteracy that threaten to consign entire segments of our population to a global junkheap. In some regions of America, entire generations can be found who believe that there is no need to locate the Pacific Ocean on a map, that learning a foreign language is a useless endeavor, and that foreign culture is what they see on a sitcom TV program based in Los Angeles. Westinghouse CEO, John Marous, bemoaned the fact when *Fortune* magazine solicited his views on America's global battle in 1989, "It won't be long before more than 30 percent of our population will be illiterate, and certainly that cannot allow us to be competitive worldwide."

"Critical Massing" of Technology

An aspect that should be of critical concern to government policymakers and aspiring global managers alike lies in their perspectives on technology development. To say that technology advancement is important to the global enterprise is like saying oxygen is important to human organisms. Chapter 9 has already reviewed the role of technology and research and development generally as vital leverage points for global success and survival of specific enterprises. What is missing from many international perspectives, however, is an understanding of the broader role of technology in global business trends.

A phenomenon that plays an increasing role in shaping global industries is that of "technology massing," or development of a technology that acts as a core to attract multiple related technologies. When American companies effectively surrendered the video cassette recorder technology to offshore companies, they gave up more than simply the market for VCRs or, as some were heard to describe the machines at the time, "just another television gimmick." As large as that market was, and still is, the base of VCR technology and production also gave birth to family after family of further high-tech refinements and new products involving many permutations of video, audio, and/or transmission/reception technology. When American companies turned their backs on VCRs in the early 1970s, they dealt an entire generation of American businesses out of any significant participation in a global industry worth scores of billions today, as well as a number of related product sectors, such as applications in defense systems and medical imaging. As William Hassinger of the Federal Communications Commission noted in 1988, "As the Japanese have found out, you can use consumer electronics as a sort of economic engine to pull a train that has a lot of other things on it."

The advent of high definition television (HDTV), confidently predicted by technology gurus on every continent, represents a new generation, a new critical mass of technology with far-reaching implications for the global enterprises that are able to stake a claim to it. The battle isn't simply over who will replace the world's 750 million television sets—a market in itself estimated to be as high as $100 billion by 2005. The high volume of microprocessors and other computer related components in HDTV will mean that any significant producer will automatically become a major player in the computer industry. When the American Electronics Association studied this linkage, it concluded that although American producers hold 70 percent of the global personal computer market today, that share could be maintained only if U.S. companies secure at least 50 percent of the coming HDTV market. If the U.S. HDTV share is 10 percent or less, the U.S. personal computer share is projected to plummet to 35 percent. In the words of Richard J. Elkins, Jr., CEO of computer supplier Prometrix, "If the Japanese and Europeans become major powers in HDTV at our expense, it'll be their major entree in becoming dominant in the computer business."

U.S. policymakers recognize enough of the high stakes in HDTV to allocate a slim $30 million in research funding through the Defense Advanced Research Project Agency. Prominently appearing among applicants for the U.S. funds are such foreign kings of consumer electronics as Sony Corporation, Philips, and Thomson S.A. Even if such foreign firms are kept out of federally funded programs, pessimists abound. Steven Jobs, Apple cofounder and today CEO of Next Inc., noted in early 1989: "All this stuff about how the United States is going to participate [in HDTV] is a joke. We've lost it already."

Global Reacting or Global Winning

The global manager and global enterprise understand that one thing is permanent in their world: impermanence. There are, however, many ways to deal with that reality. Many would-be global players tend to let impermanence rule them, monopolizing themselves with reacting to it, always viewing global competition in the defensive mode. Those who are global winners know that change is a basic rule of global life, and deal with it from a position of confident knowledge and strength. They use change to their advantage. They may *cause* change for strategic purposes.

The basic mentalities these perspectives represent are in wide evidence today. We are barraged with exhortations about the European juggernaut, the Fortress Europe, the vast new European economic machine that will draw strength from pending unification and conquer the world. Those who have an Eastern focus, on the other hand, insist that the next century will be the century of Asia, when all economic shots will be called by Japan, and what they would label its "client states" in other Asian regions.

As a result, in America today—and as briefly reflected in Chapter 7's discussion of CEO globalness—many individuals and enterprises are basing their international strategy on a European or a Japanese world. They are reacting to perceptions developed in the popular media, they are thinking only defensively, and they are letting such popular sentiment govern their international conduct.

By contrast, other firms always think twice about any sentiment concerning international affairs that may be labelled popular. They are *actors*. They are leaders.

The example of European unification is enlightening in this respect. Strong global firms have sufficient knowledge and international perspicacity to understand that a vague and disjointed entity under the heading of Europe will not in itself create leadership in global industries and that EC market unification efforts can never solve many problems that will continue to extract high competitive tolls for enterprises based there. Demographic burdens in Europe are huge and grow worse by the day. By the year 2030, for example, Germany's retirees are expected to outnumber its active workers; even by the year 2000 its ratio of workers to retirees is expected to be at least 36 percent, compared to 24 percent in the United States. Germany's population drops by 3,000 every week.

Those who are able to look through to the European reality understand that a unified Europe will be a confederation consisting of one island country that has, under current leadership, embraced free enterprise, and other countries operating with large doses of socialism that result in staggering social costs. The labor laws in continental Europe that have a stranglehold on many businesses have a direct and debilitating effect on many European global efforts. Global companies will not be created *per se* by EC unification. They will be created by the same diligence, skills, and application of long-term strategy required of global winners anywhere on the planet.

Indeed, many existing global firms are excited, not nervous over the possibilities raised by EC unification. Consumer product experts in the United States wax enthusiastically over the advent of genuine commercial television in Europe. Coca-Cola executive vice president John Georgas notes: "Europe is like the United States in the 1950s, when TV was just developing. For products like Coke that depend on TV, we're entering an explosive era with great growth potential."

Such perspectives are instinctive in global winners. They are not intimidated by bold talk of possible European or Asian juggernauts. They look to the subtleties that are the real forces in defining their global context. Like the student of evolution, they understand that the most compelling aspects of change, and promoters of change, are usually the small details, the less obvious, even overlooked elements of the environment, the subtleties which when eventually combined are the forces that alter the world.

These global managers, who do not spend their lives solely reacting, are gradually understanding that cheap labor is never as abundant or as permanent as once believed. To the frustration of those who for years have insisted that global battles must be waged primarily in labor-abundant developing nations, these managers know that labor-intensive operations must shift to capital-intensive operations.

They are likewise grasping that, in final analysis, knowledge may be the key to competition in many global industries. They know enough to be skeptical of those who seek to reduce trade and investment patterns to mathematical formulas. They accept that governments will grow more sensitive to the deleterious effects of protectionism but also accept that most governments will lack the confidence to totally reject its use. They know that the United States will not become the pawnshop economy some have predicted, but neither will it regain its former premier economic position. They also know that, notwithstanding the significant role of such external factors, all such aspects are overshadowed by the greatest challenge of all, the challenge of creating and sustaining the global enterprise.

Invention of the Global Enterprise

Bold new enterprises and bold new managers are required for global success. Those who face that challenge should not be intimidated, but exhilarated. The task may be of planetary proportions, but so too are the opportunity and reward.

As already described in these pages, in order to even qualify for the global race, most managers and professionals must rethink their world. They must accept the complex but compelling global reality, the inescapable fact that, in the words of Sony's Akio Morita, "the economic system is more and more like one single interacting organism."

As that organism expands into every quarter of life, we must learn to cast off old notions that international economic life consists of the exchange of goods or the simple movement of merchandise from one port to another. Reflected throughout these pages has been the much more complex reality in which capital, people, technology, goods, services, ideas and other elements of value are in constant and interdependent motion, with little regard to national borders. To say modern international business consists of trade in the traditional sense is like saying the planet consists of water and stone.

The biggest and most troubling question of all in America's global context may be how many existing managers are up to the formidable task of making this global organism work to their advantage. Few people are more qualified to address that point than Richard M. Ferry, president of Korn/Ferry International, one of the world's largest executive recruitment firms. "We're going to see the greatest level of executive turnover in history over the next 10 years," Ferry predicted in 1989, "because American businessmen are not prepared to run global businesses in the 21st century."

Only after today's global realities have been accepted and integrated into managing, planning, and strategy formulation, can the global winner begin to take shape. For long-term success, the global perspective must be integrated throughout an organization. Several years ago an American visitor to a Taiwanese factory producing transistor radios was able to walk along the production line and chat with workers. Two workers in particular stood out in the visitor's memory. One young man explained the nature of his job and his product line position in dull tones, "I get paid to solder this piece to that piece." An older man had a messy cleanup job in one of the metal working shops. Describing his job, however, he boasted enthusiastically, "I am helping to build radios for the people of the world." This episode depicts in simplest form the difference in scope between the global mentality and that of many contemporary members of the business community. The global mentality abides neither narrow-mindedness nor the many international myths which have been discussed throughout this volume.

The enterprises that successfully build on the global mentality conform to no strict pattern. The right global path is always a function of a company's own unique attributes. Those who look for a simple global template, whether as part of the Japanese obsession discussed in Chapter 6; one of the supposed global product organizations discussed in Chapter 10; or any other quick fix method are likely to meet failure of a global scale.

The complex process of inventing the global enterprise has been reflected throughout these pages. While a global template may be non-existent, these pages have revealed a number of common denominators. In simplest terms, these consist of the effective use of the global leverage points discussed herein. It takes perhaps a global perspective in itself to appreciate the vast challenges of constant adaption and vigilant strategic assessment implicit in that process.

To say that the global enterprise must be invented is no over-statement. Adapting to the global economy is never a matter of business as usual. For many, it is not even a matter of applying old skills to new jobs. Rethinking the world is not a matter of renewal. It is a matter of starting over.

The global winner that emerges from this process is inevitably a fluid organization. But fluidity does not mean constant restructuring, which has confused and misled many international efforts. Rather it means an organization that operates upon a firm core of strategy and self-identity, an organization that reflects the concept, cogently expressed by business consultant John W. Gardner, that "the only stability is stability in motion."

The global enterprise can endure neither absolute centralization nor absolute decentralization, but requires the internal strength to be able to manage diversity through interdependence. Only thus will it be able to deal with ever-changing, ever increasing competition; as most industries mature on a global basis, market share expansion increasingly will have to be taken from competitors. Not only does competition change. Values change, production venues change, leadership qualities change, markets change, materials change, designs change, investment climates change, and equity ownership changes. *The global economy is a protean machine fueled by billions of perishable facts and events.* The global enterprise must be able to absorb and react to those facts and events with razor-sharp precision.

The need to appreciate technology massing, as discussed above, and the need to geographically diversify technology development, are far from the only requirements for innovation in the global enterprise. New meaning for the word innovation is being found by many who are on the path to becoming global winners. The global enterprise must *innovate new ways to innovate*, ways that go far beyond the laboratory. The CEO may need to innovate a revolutionary role for his or her office. Innovation, like other management aspects in the global enterprise, must be multidimensional in nature.

Earning the Global Future

It would be a grave mistake to have read this volume as a eulogy for any specific company, government, society, or commercial system. As many authors and publishers have proven, it is easy enough to speak of doom and gloom in an industry, in America, in the West, even across the planet at large. There is always a ready audience for such pronouncements.

The message of the global economy, however, is not of doom and gloom. It is of vigorous new opportunities. Those who are ready to embrace a global future will be well rewarded. For many individuals who accept that future for their own, the global economy will be the linchpin to personal success. For individual enterprises it may be the key not to only success, but to basic survival.

Many enterprises will fall victim to rapidly changing environments across the planet in the years ahead, but one class of firm will survive and thrive. That class will consist of those who have integrated themselves across borders, exchanged old assumptions for new skills, and learned to balance their everchanging assets and advantages without regard to the continents and oceans that may separate them. These will be the enterprises to whom the future belongs. These will be the global enterprises.

INDEX

278 Index

Small world myth, 12–13
Sogo shosha trading companies, 121
Sony Corporation
  and Capital Records, 188–89, 193
  genesis, 191–92
  leveraging the electronic market, 192–94
  research link and, 225
Statistical month, 76
Stibel, Gary, 215
Stihl, 208
Strategic marketing/response, 214
Supplier relationships, 223–24

T

Tabulating Machine Company, 148
Takeshita, Nobura, 261
Telling, Edward, 145
Texas Instruments (TI), 234
Thoreau, Henry David, 104
Thrifty Rent-a-Car, 180
Times, The, 7
Tokyo Tsushin Kogyo Co., 191–92
Tourist managers, 173–75
Trade
  American myths, 54–56
  cost-advantage myth, 67–69
  and high technology, 53
  and small corporations, 64–65
  super-glue to car washes, 65–66
Trade account, 4
  heavy emphasis on, 72–73
  and high tech, 57
  raw-unfactored data, 75–77
  rife with error, 74–75
Trade deficits, 4
  bumper-sticker professors, 79–80
  capital goods imports and, 81–82
  deficit anxiety, 77–78
  equating deficits with failure, 82–83

Trade deficits—*Cont.*
  simple export solution, 80
Tribus, Myron, 209

U

Uniden, 200–201
Uniform financial guidelines, 262–63
United Nations Center for Transnational
  Corporations, 5–6
United Parcel Service, 258
United Technologies, 162
Upjohn Co., 225
USA Today, 259
U.S. Department of Commerce, 71–72, 189
U.S. government and export controls, 141
  Export Trading Company Act and, 142–44
U.S. International Trade Commission (ITC), 96
U.S. machine tool industry export controls and, 141
U.S. National Foreign Council, 3
U.S. Postal Service, 259
U.S. Steel, 3
U.S. tax code, 266

V–Z

Vanilla marketing, 215
VCR bust, 60–61
Volkswagen AG, 207–8
Voluntary restraint agreement (VRA), 96
Wall Street Journal, 3, 37, 72
  future CEO profile, 241
Warner-Lambert, 178
Washington International Center, 166
Water factor, 167–69
Wederspahn, Gary, 181
Wilson, Joseph C., 213
Winnebago Industries, 217
Xerox Corporation, 162, 212
  GAME program, 224
Young, John, 60